T0330152

CONFRONTING DYSTOPIA

CONFRONTING DYSTOPIA

The New Technological Revolution and the Future of Work

EDITED BY EVA PAUS

ILR PRESS
AN IMPRINT OF
CORNELL UNIVERSITY PRESS
ITHACA AND LONDON

First published 2018 by Cornell University Press

Printed in the United States of America

Library of Congress Cataloging-in-Publication Data

Names: Paus, Eva, editor. | Container of (work): Ford, Martin (Martin R.). Rise of the robots.
Title: Confronting dystopia : the new technological revolution and the future of work / edited by Eva Paus.
Description: Ithaca : ILR Press, an imprint of Cornell University Press, 2018. | "Many of the contributions to this book were presented in an earlier version at the conference, "The future of jobs: the dual challenges of globalization and robotization," that took place at Mount Holyoke College in February 2016"—Acknowledgments. | Includes bibliographical references and index.
Identifiers: LCCN 2017054549 (print) | LCCN 2017057124 (ebook) | ISBN 9781501719875 (epub/mobi) | ISBN 9781501719868 (pdf) | ISBN 9781501719844 | ISBN 9781501719844 (cloth ; alk. paper) | ISBN 9781501719851 (pbk. ; alk. paper)
Subjects: LCSH: Employees—Effect of technological innovations on—Congresses. | Industrial relations—Effect of technological innovations on—Congresses. | Work environment—Technological innovations—Congresses. | Technological unemployment—Congresses.
Classification: LCC HD6331 (ebook) | LCC HD6331 .C687 2018 (print) | DDC 331.25—dc23
LC record available at https://lccn.loc.gov/2017054549

Contents

ACKNOWLEDGMENTS

Many of the contributions to this book were presented in earlier versions at the conference "The Future of Jobs: The Dual Challenges of Globalization and Robotization," which took place at Mount Holyoke College, Massachusetts, in February 2016. The conference was hosted by the Dorothy R. and Norman E. McCulloch Center for Global Initiatives and financially supported by Dotty and Sandy McCulloch and the Purrington Fund. I am most grateful to the contributors for their collaboration and their willingness to revise and enrich their conference papers.

I thank my friends and colleagues for the spirited discussions during the team-taught course that led up to the conference: Lisa Ballesteros, Lee Bowie, Calvin Chen, Vinnie Ferraro, Shahruhk Khan, Kirsten Nordstrom, and Audrey St. John.

Special thanks go to Jean Costello and Katherine Harper for their superb assistance in copyediting the book and to Jennifer Medina for her valuable assistance throughout the whole process. I am deeply indebted to the outside reviewers for their thoughtful, detailed, and constructive suggestions, and to Frances Benson for her encouragement and guidance.

CONFRONTING DYSTOPIA

1

The Future Isn't What It Used to Be

Eva Paus

> We stand on the brink of a technological revolution that will
> fundamentally alter the way we live, work, and relate to one another.
> In its scale, scope, and complexity, the transformation will be unlike
> anything humankind has experienced before.
>
> —Klaus Schwab (2016)

Not a week passes without headlines predicting that the rise of robot-ization and digitization will have a profoundly unsettling impact on the economy and the world of work: "How Artificial Intelligence and Robots Will Radically Transform the Economy" (Maney 2016); "Six Jobs Are Eliminated for Every Robot Introduced into the Work Force" (Glaser 2017); "No One Is Prepared to Stop the Robot Onslaught. So What Will We Do When It Arrives?" (Levine 2017).

Prophecies about the devastating impact of new technologies on jobs and working conditions are not new, going back to at least the early nine-teenth century, when the Luddites smashed the steam-powered looms that were threatening their jobs. Yet time and again, such prognoses were proven wrong. Now a growing number of voices contend that we are on the eve of a new wave of innovation and change, and that this time is different (Standing 2017; Freeman 2016b; Schwab 2016; Ford 2015; Brynjolfsson and McAfee 2014; Frey and Osborne 2013). The first industrial revolution was based on steam, water, and mechanical production equipment; the second came with electricity and mass production; the third built on electronics, information technology (IT), and automated production; and the new one, the fourth industrial revolution, will be driven by cyber-physical systems that are evolving exponentially (Schwab 2016).

The predictions are that the conjuncture of advances in artificial intelligence, digital connectivity, processing speed, big data, software, and robotics will have a profound impact on the availability of jobs and working conditions over the coming decades, and may lead to dramatic changes in people's lives. In Klaus Schwab's words above, the new industrial revolution will generate a transformation unlike anything we have seen before.

This book takes a comprehensive look at the implications of the new technological revolution for future jobs, working conditions, and livelihoods. It brings together diverse perspectives to explore economic and political ramifications for the Global North and the Global South. Three central questions lie at the heart of the issues raised: (1) Will the need for labor inexorably shrink in the coming decades, generating the technological unemployment that Keynes (1930) predicted nearly one hundred years ago? (2) What will be the impact on human well-being and inequality, within and between countries? (3) What are key elements of the new institutional and social arrangements needed to sustain livelihoods on a broader basis?

With different entry points and foci, the contributors offer alternative answers to these questions. Nonetheless, a common thread that runs through their analyses and policy recommendations is that emerging dystopias of unravelling social contracts, insecure livelihoods, insufficient employment, and increasing divergence between the Global North and the Global South are not fated, but can and need to be countered with proactive strategies. Together, the authors' policy suggestions translate into a bold agenda that seeks to redress the rise in inequality and precarious living situations and to leverage the potential of the new technological revolution to improve people's lives. To implement such an agenda or parts of it, societies need to forge new social contracts with institutional arrangements that revise unfettered globalization and distribute the benefits of the technological changes broadly.

In this book, we situate the impact of the new technological revolution deliberately in the context of the globalization process since the 1980s.

Technological advances in shipping and IT enabled the fragmentation of production chains on a global scale, leading to widespread outsourcing and offshoring, first in the manufacturing sector and more recently in services. The adoption of neoliberal economic policies resulted in large reductions of trade barriers and market liberalization more broadly. And the systemic collapse in Eastern and Central Europe, together with China's opening to world markets, meant that the global labor force doubled (Freeman 2006). Together, these changes have led to an intensification of competition among producers (and workers) around the world and a weakening of labor, as capital has become increasingly mobile across national borders.

We emphasize three key characteristics of today's global reality that shape the impact of the new technological revolution. First, globalization has had a different impact on productive capabilities, jobs, and social provisions within and between the Global North and the Global South. Thus, the ramifications of the new technological revolution will likely vary across regions and countries of the world. Second, globalization and technological change have led to rising inequality within and among countries, generating growing concerns at individual and national levels. The fact that economists' books about inequality have become bestsellers (Piketty 2014; Milanovic 2011, 2016) shows how deeply the issue resonates. The fact that inequality and economic uncertainties figure prominently in political movements and campaigns in countries around the globe demonstrates more directly people's growing frustration and quest for redress. While the speed and extent of its impact are subject to debate, the new technological revolution will exacerbate the current inequality trend unless countered by deliberate policies. But the current concerns about inequality and the rise in political discontent and polarization are a response primarily to trends that have unfolded over the past few decades and not to anticipated future developments. That means that new answers are urgently needed now, before the new technological revolution has made its impact fully felt. Third, countries around the world are facing serious challenges to future human well-being, most urgently global warming and—less visibly—a vast global care deficit. Constructive responses to these challenges are in societies' long-term self-interest, irrespective of any impacts of the new technological revolution. That such responses also offer significant opportunities for the creation of new decent jobs is of particular interest for the issues discussed here.

The chapters in this book are organized in three interrelated sections. The first two focus primarily on the Global North and the third on the Global South. The four chapters in the first section, "Trends: Job Destruction and Job Creation," explore the extent of job destruction and the possibilities for job creation under the new technological revolution. The three chapters in the second section, "Risks and Repercussions: Alternative Futures," analyze the change in labor market conditions in the North under globalization and the new digitized economy, as well as political responses to growing inequality and economic insecurity. The three chapters in the final section, "The Global South: Challenges and Opportunities," investigate different aspects of the impact of robotization, digitization, and globalization on the Global South.

In spite of all context-specific differences, common features cut across countries and regions in the Global North and Global South: most importantly, the link between having employment and enjoying a decent living is becoming ever more elusive. In many countries in the North, this link has already been weakening for years, with wages stagnating and jobs becoming more precarious. In the United States, for example, average wage growth has been decoupled from productivity growth since the mid-1970s (Economic Policy Institute 2016a). Labor's share in national income has declined, and temporary employment has increased. In 2014, workers' share in temporary employment was, on average, 11 percent in OECD countries; in some, it was considerably higher, e.g., 20 percent in Spain (O'Connor 2015).

In most countries in the Global South, on the other hand, the link between economic growth and the growth of decent jobs in the manufacturing sector never developed extensively in the first place. In contrast to China and other Asian latecomers in the development process, most countries in sub-Saharan Africa and Latin America never generated large numbers of jobs in labor-intensive manufacturing. Instead, the widespread adoption of free-market policies in the 1980s resulted in premature deindustrialization and an expansion of the informal sector. The commodity price boom of the 2000s, fueled by China's high growth, accelerated the re-primarization of exports. The diffusion of robotization-cum-digitization will likely make it harder for middle-income countries to create a link between economic growth and the creation of decent jobs on a large scale (Paus 2017). The big question for low-income countries is whether they can leverage low wages to jump-start an industrialization process via labor-intensive manufactured exports before robots transform those sectors as well.

In this global context of multiple decouplings, societies have to find new institutional arrangements that provide for basic human well-being, even if people are not employed. These may include more security for the new jobs in the "platform economy," a basic income in one form or another, provision of universal social services, or more inclusive ownership of key assets.

Ultimately, the impact of the new technological revolution is a political question, not an economic one. A constructive answer to the challenges posed will require forging a social contract in support of a new institutional architecture. That is a long-term and arduous process. Avoiding dystopias will require redistribution on a significant scale, whether of hours worked or the benefits of technological change. Governments, the business sector, unions, and civil society groups have to discuss which aspects of jobs and livelihoods are most challenging given a country's economic and social conditions, and which institutional responses are necessary in the short and the long run.

An important step toward starting the dialogue is a greater awareness that the future isn't what it used to be. This book aims to advance our understanding of the complex of the effects of the new technologies and of their universal and country-specific nature.

Trends: Job Destruction and Job Creation

"Creative destruction" is the term Joseph Schumpeter (2008 [1942], 83)) introduced to describe the "process of industrial mutation that incessantly revolutionizes the economic structure *from within,* incessantly destroying the old one, incessantly creating a new one." This process of creative destruction invariably destroys existing jobs in some areas, modifies jobs, and creates new jobs in other areas. History suggests that, at least in the Global North, major technological changes have had a positive impact on job creation, when we take a sufficiently long view.

But looking ahead from the present, predictions about the destructive and creative impact of a new technological revolution are inherently fraught with uncertainty and, not surprisingly, contested. Any prognosis depends on an assessment of the likelihood that the new technologies will affect a wide array of economic activities and the development of demand for more, often new, goods and services, which could create new jobs.

In his widely acclaimed book *The Rise and Fall of American Growth* (2016), Robert Gordon contends that the century from 1870 to 1970 was a unique period of transformation, with the conjuncture of the impact and diffusion of electrification, cars, indoor plumbing, air transportation, antibiotics, and other innovations. Gordon argues that innovation has been slower since 1970 and that the higher productivity growth during 1994–2004 was a one-time boost due to the introduction of the internet. He is highly skeptical of a broad-based impact of the new technologies that would be a game changer for productivity. Robots, he argues, often complement jobs rather than substitute for them; the benefits of big data have been limited mainly to marketing so far; and the realization of driverless cars, for example, still faces many technical and regulatory challenges.

By contrast, Ford (2015), Brynjolfsson and McAfee (2014), Frey and Osborne (2013), and others argue that the new technological revolution will be transformative. Computers and digital devices are doing for mental power what steam did for muscle power. Nonroutine tasks have become computerizable at remarkable speed and thus opened up, for the first time, a slew of manual and cognitive tasks to displacement. Advances in artificial intelligence, with increasing machine-learning enabled by the exponential growth of big data, may generate the possibility for previously unseen large displacements of human labor. It is the combination of these factors that makes the new technological paradigm a general-purpose technology with unprecedented potential for the destruction of jobs and tasks. That is why this time is different.

One of the reasons why technology pessimists such as Gordon are skeptical of the widespread impact of a new technological revolution is that it has not made an impact on aggregate productivity growth, which—in the United States and other countries of the Global North—has been rather anemic for the past few years. This argument echoes a concern Robert Solow (1987, 36) expressed thirty years ago when he wrote, "You can see the computer anywhere but in the productivity statistics."

The technology optimists counter that many of the benefits of IT-based innovation to date are not captured by output data,[1] and that it may take a generation or two for a general-purpose technology to become diffused throughout the economy. History shows that the diffusion of major technological changes takes time and is contingent on context. David (1990), for example, offers a fascinating account of the lengthy and complex process of the diffusion of electricity and the dynamo.

Prognoses of job destruction resulting from the new technological revolution differ considerably depending on the methodology used. Using 2010 data, Frey and Osborne (2013) suggest that 47 percent of the US labor force works in occupations that have a more than 70 percent chance of being automated. Arntz et al. (2016), on the other hand, focus on tasks within occupations rather than occupations and conclude that only 9 percent of US workers have a high probability of losing their jobs to automation. The two methodologies generate similar differences in estimates for other industrialized countries.

These projections indicate the potential for job destruction based on technological factors. But whether jobs will actually be displaced depends on cost and other factors. With respect to 3D printing, for example, Citi (2016, 87) concluded, "Today's 3D printers have yet to achieve the speed, capacity, and most importantly the price to rival traditional manufacturing processes such as injection molding and milling." How quickly job destruction will materialize depends also on the policies that shape the transformation process.

Studies of actual job destruction in the United States on account of automation and robotization find a relatively small impact to date. Analyzing changes in manufacturing employment in the United States during the period 1980–2007, Autor et al. (2015, 624) conclude, "Whereas import competition leads to sharp declines in local manufacturing employment and corresponding growth in local unemployment and nonemployment, exposure to routine task specialization has largely neutral overall employment effects." Acemoglu and Restrepo (2017), on the other hand, estimate that in the period 1990–2007 the aggregate job loss in the United States due to robots was between 360,000 and 670,000. At the upper end, that means a loss of forty thousand jobs per year. In the scheme of things, that is not a very big number, and substantially smaller than the job losses due to outsourcing to China. That leads Mishel and Bivens (2017, 1) to argue that the limited job growth and stagnant wages in the US have other underlying causes, such as "intentional policy decisions regarding globalization, labor standards, and unemployment levels."

With respect to the creation of new jobs in the future, the contributors to the first section of this book highlight the need for new public policies and major institutional changes. Two of them advocate different ways to share the fruits of technological change, whether through some form of basic income or other ways of redistribution. The other two, on the other hand, focus on the opportunities for the creation of new jobs by tackling major global challenges.

In "The Rise of the Robots: Impact on Unemployment and Inequality," Martin Ford argues that we are at an inflection point where the combined effect of advances in artificial intelligence, machine-learning, and software automation will lead to rapid technological change with widespread impact on jobs and living standards. Unlike technological changes in the past, machines are now not only replacing routine manual and cognitive tasks, but also starting to take on nonroutine cognitive tasks. The combined result will be a significant displacement of wage workers with limited skills and education (both in manufacturing and services) and also of workers in tasks that require more education. Ford predicts that inequality will continue to increase and flags the danger of slow growth or stagnation due to insufficient demand. After all, robots do not create final demand. He advocates leveraging the power of the new technologies for the benefit of society and establishing a basic income.

Irmgard Nübler offers a more nuanced view. In "New Technologies, Innovation, and the Future of Jobs," she suggests that the impact of technologies on jobs is a nondeterministic process that will differ across countries, and that countries that proactively shape this process can create good new jobs. Because the composition of tasks varies within a given occupation as well as across occupations and industrial sectors, Nübler argues that the job impact of these new technologies will vary with the skill composition of the manufacturing sector and the structure of workers' educational attainment in different countries. Furthermore, compensating effects may counter the destruction of jobs, including the growth of the skilled-craft sector. The expansion of markets for existing goods and services and the creation of new products and services will generate more jobs. But such compensatory effects, she submits, are contingent upon the distribution of the benefits from technological change. For Nübler, the impact of robotization and digitization on jobs is, in the end, a political, not a technological, issue. The future of jobs will be different depending on countries' ability to create the conditions that generate such redistribution.

Many new jobs can be created if governments implement policies that tackle some of the big problems we are facing, nationally and globally. Two contributors analyze the possibilities for such win-win scenarios: one focuses on combating global warming, the other on addressing the care deficit.

In "Expanding Job Opportunities through Global Green Growth," Robert Pollin shows that we can reduce CO_2 emissions and create new jobs. At a global level, these emissions have to decline by 40 percent in twenty years to stabilize the global mean temperature at two degrees Celsius above preindustrial levels. He argues that countries can achieve such a reduction if they redirect 1.5 to 2 percent of gross domestic product (GDP) away from maintaining a fossil fuel–dominated energy infrastructure and toward greater energy efficiency and renewable energy sources.

Using country-specific input-output tables, Pollin calculates that such investments will lead to positive net job creation due to the labor intensity of spending on clean energy, the installation of solar panels, and the higher labor content of domestic spending. The main areas of job creation would be in bioenergy production, construction (retrofitting and electrical grid updates), and the manufacture of solar panels. Pollin finds significant positive net job effects for large fossil fuel–producing countries (Brazil, China, India, Indonesia, South Africa, the United States). The effect is smaller for large fossil fuel–importing countries (Germany, South Korea, Spain), but it is still positive. For both types of countries, he argues, a global green growth strategy can be part of a broader full-employment program.

Mignon Duffy's chapter, "Building Sustainable Jobs and Supporting Human Potential in the Care Sector," focuses on another win-win opportunity to create jobs while addressing a major global challenge, in this case, the global care deficit. The labor of providing for the needs of children, the elderly, the sick, and the disabled cannot be outsourced and automated easily and is in high demand everywhere. Fourteen of the top twenty occupations least likely to be automated are in the care sector

(UNDP 2015). Duffy suggests that care work *is* the future of work. There is a huge care deficit in both the Global North and the Global South. Migration from the latter to the former has alleviated the problem in the North, Duffy argues, but exacerbated the problem in the South.

While there are highly paid professional jobs in the care sector (e.g., doctors), many others are at the low end of the wage spectrum. And much of care work is actually unpaid. Duffy contends that it is the gendered nature of care work, the assumption that women are naturally good at nurturing, that accounts for the extent to which care work is unpaid and, where it is paid, undervalued. The low wages, in turn, explain why many positions currently go unfilled. To create more decent jobs in the care sector, Duffy offers a number of policy suggestions, ranging from increased public investment in the care sector to bringing all care workers under the umbrella of national and international labor laws. One of the most important, though most difficult, changes needed is to break the links in the cycle of gendered devaluation of care.

Risks and Repercussions: Alternative Futures

The chapters in the first section focus primarily on the quantity and types of jobs that are predicted to be destroyed with the diffusion of the new technological paradigm and on promising areas for new job creation. In the second section of this book, the authors analyze the quality of jobs, changing working conditions and livelihoods, the concomitant rise in inequality, and political responses.

Over the past two to three decades, globalization and technological changes have led to a significant increase in inequality (Milanovic 2016). Since the late 1970s, the relative bargaining power of labor has been reduced significantly. Between 1980 and 2012, union density in OECD countries declined by half, from 34.1 to 17.2 percent (OECD 2017).[2] Similarly, the share of labor income in national income declined in most OECD countries (and many developing countries as well). An OECD study found that between 1980 and the late 2000s, the share of labor in national income declined by .3 percentage points annually in the G-20 countries (cited in ILO/OECD 2015, 3). Karabarbounis and Neiman (2014) show that, since the 1980s, the labor share has declined in forty-two out of the fifty-nine countries they analyzed, in the majority of industrial sectors, and in two-thirds of the US states.[3]

In the United States, workers' average pay stopped rising along with productivity thirty-five years ago. Economy-wide productivity and a typical worker's hourly compensation rose in lockstep between 1948 and 1973. But after 1973, productivity kept rising while hourly compensation remained basically flat. At the same time, the nation's CEO-to-worker compensation ratio increased more than tenfold, from 22.3 in 1973 to 275.6 in 2016 (Economic Policy Institute 2016a and b).

The new technological revolution will increase inequality even further. Many experts argue that the labor market will become more bifurcated, with well-paid, highly skilled IT workers and managers, software developers, and others on one side and both low-skilled and more high-skilled workers on the other, often in precarious working conditions.

There is ample evidence that the top 1 percent of income earners has pulled away from the 99 percent in recent years. But recent research challenges the usual view that the increase in inequality is due mainly to skill differentials. Song et al. (2015) find that nearly all the growth in inequality in the United States between 1978 and 2012 can be explained by the increased difference in pay between firms at the top and firms at the bottom (measured by firms' mean income).[4] Barth et al. (2016) come to similar conclusions. Their decomposition of the increase in inequality over the past thirty years shows that it is due to an increase in wage inequality among workers with similar skills and characteristics. Freeman (2016a) concludes that growing inequality is not so much about skills differentials, but rather other employment and wage-setting issues, including the growth of new arrangements of "temporary help agency workers, on-call workers, contract workers, and independent contractors."

A decline in formal labor contracts and an increase in freelancers have indeed been key changes in the labor market. Katz and Krueger (2016, 2) find that workers engaged in these alternative work arrangements accounted for 10.7 percent of the US workforce in early 2005 and 15.8 percent in late 2015. Workers in the gig economy (working through an online intermediary such as TaskRabbit and Uber) accounted for 0.5 percent of the workforce in late 2015. Manyika et al. (2016) estimate that 20–30 percent of workers in Europe and the United States engage in some form of independent work, some by choice, others out of necessity.

The chapters in this section of the book analyze how the digital economy is transforming the global labor market and how the growth in economic insecurity shapes political dispositions and responses. One contributor analyzes the landscape of new labor arrangements under "platform capitalism"; two others investigate the connections between job automation, demands for redistribution, and the reality of redistribution; and the third examines the link between growing inequality, sentiments of disenfranchisement and anxiety, and the rise of right-wing politics in liberal democracies.

In "Taskers in the Precariat: Confronting an Emerging Dystopia," Guy Standing argues that the speed of change has increased due to the confluence of technological disruption of traditional jobs, labor regulations undermining professions, increased global competition, and the emergence of "tasking" platforms. As a result, we have seen the growth of the "precariat" class, with unstable labor, a rise in the share of unpaid work relative to paid labor, and a move away from fixed workplaces and fixed work times. Digital tasking platforms have become online labor markets where people offer short-term and micro tasks. Standing suggests that the old terms "employee" and "self-employed" are not appropriate anymore, and he offers up a new one: "taskers." He distinguishes three categories of taskers in "platform capitalism": the concierge economy (where taskers perform services commissioned through digital platforms, e.g., cleaning), cloud labor (where people perform online tasks, e.g., accounting), and on-call employment (where people have employment contracts, but are called upon only as needed and paid accordingly).

Under platform capitalism, platforms make profits through the ownership and control of technological infrastructures and property rights and the exploitation of taskers and unpaid work. Tasking platforms are a new putting out system that is eroding old forms of service provision (as, for example, Uber and the traditional taxi business). Standing stresses the transformative impact of the growth of the gig economy, both directly, through the generation of tasking labor for tens of millions of people, and indirectly, by undermining the traditional providers of these services. His policy recommendations include regulation of labor brokers, redistribution through a universal basic income, social protection to redress growing inequities, and a code of ethics and good practice for participants in tasking platforms.

In "Automated but Compensated?: Technological Change and Redistribution in Advanced Democracies," David Rueda and Stefan Thewissen investigate whether workers whose jobs are more susceptible to automation are more likely to favor redistribution. Using data from the European Social Survey for all Western countries for the period 2002–2012, they find that there is indeed a robust positive relation between the degree to which an occupation is routinized and the demand for redistribution. This preference increases with income level (as a person has more to lose from automation), and also when a person works in a sector that is more exposed to technological change. However, Rueda and Thewissen encounter that individual preferences for greater redistribution did not translate into actual greater redistribution at the country level. There is no empirical correlation between exposure to technological change and higher real levels of redistribution that would mitigate the risks of automation. The authors suggest that this so-called "redistribution paradox" does not bode well for demands for greater social insurance in the future.

Vinnie Ferraro offers an answer to this paradox using a broader framework to analyze the political consequences of globalization and automation that have caused growing inequality and workplace insecurities. In "The Crisis of the Liberal International Order: Technological Change and the Rise of the Right," he stresses that the embrace of neoliberalism in the 1980s led to more open economies and more deregulated labor and capital markets. In this context of greater wealth and income concentration, elites have defined the "public good of creating wealth in terms of their private interest." As jobs became more precarious, average real wages stagnated, and the impact of technological changes started to spread, feelings of insecurity and anxiety have risen significantly. As people lose their sense of meaning and place in the world, they lose faith in government and established institutions. Elites exploit this by defining enemies that are "tangible" but remote from the actual causes of alienation and uncertainty, and by mobilizing fear and anger rather than offering constructive responses. Ferraro distinguishes two threads in the new politics that challenge neoliberal politics and explain the rise of new right-wing parties and movements: a deep distrust of globalization and a profound aversion to multiculturalism. Interests become defined in national, ethnic, and racial terms, and the Right's political responses invoke terrorism, immigration, and globalization. Ferraro draws parallels between post-2008 right-wing rhetoric and that of the 1920s and '30s. Although he offers policy suggestions for positive change, he clearly fears for the future of liberal democracies.

The Global South: Challenges and Opportunities

In the third section of the book, the focus shifts from the Global North to the Global South. Countries in this region share many common characteristics. Compared to industrialized countries, average incomes in the Global South are much lower. In 2015, the average GDP per capita was $1,644 for low-income and $10,820 for middle-income countries (current international purchasing power parity), compared to $44,696 for high-income countries (World Bank 2016). Poverty rates are often considerably higher than in countries of the Global North, educational achievements and indicators of social well-being much lower. And productive capabilities, particularly those related to innovation, are—by definition—substantially less advanced.

Transformation of the production structure is at the heart of economic development. An industrialization process that generates technological spillovers, develops increasing returns activities, engenders higher productivity growth, and creates decent-paying jobs has historically been the driving force of economic development in most of today's high-income countries. Few developing countries have successfully achieved such structural transformation over the past fifty years. A phase of state-led development initiated an industrialization process in many developing countries from the 1950s to the late 1970s. But the move to a market-led strategy, the so-called Washington Consensus, led to a deindustrialization process and slower growth in most of Latin America and sub-Saharan Africa.[5] The exceptions are countries, mostly in East Asia, that continued to pursue more strategic government interventions and supported the development of domestic productive capabilities with intentionality. The upshot of the development experience for many developing countries is captured well by the title of Lant Pritchett's 1997 article "Divergence, Big Time."

Globalization has offered new opportunities for developing countries, through increased market access and potential technology spillovers from inflows of direct foreign investment. But in the absence of sufficient domestic productive capabilities, few countries were able to leverage globalization for growth-inducing transformations of their productive structure. The most remarkable success story is China, which grew at nearly double-digit rates for about three decades. Convergence, Big Time. The commodity price boom of the 2000s was a boost for the primary commodity exporters among developing countries, but it also accelerated a re-primarization process in these economies.

Against this backdrop, it is likely that the new technological revolution will exacerbate the trend of premature deindustrialization and informal sector growth that has unfolded under globalization in developing countries (Rodrik 2015). The World Bank's 2016 *World Development Report* focuses on the impact of digital technology on developing countries. Based on the Frey and Osborne (2013) methodology, the report suggests that two-thirds of all jobs in the developing world are susceptible to automation. Estimates based on tasks would be smaller. In either case, the numbers reflect only technological possibilities; whether and how fast job displacements would materialize depends on cost factors and country-specific contexts and policy decisions, just as in the Global North. In a study of the labor market impact of the new technological revolution, Citi GPS (2016, 19) concludes that "while the potential for labour market disruption associated with the expanding scope of automation is likely to affect the developing world later than advanced economies, it may be potentially more disruptive in countries with little consumer demand and limited social safety nets."

The chapters in this section of the book highlight the heterogeneity among developing countries and different concerns about the new technological revolution. One focuses on China, which is at one end of the development spectrum and has huge ambitions to become one of the global leaders in the new technological revolution. At the other end are countries in sub-Saharan Africa, where digital capabilities are very limited. Another chapter analyzes the conditions under which these countries might exploit their low-wage comparative advantage and jump-start an industrialization process through labor-intensive manufactured exports before robotization possibly enters these sectors as well. In view of the insufficient generation of decent job creation in the past and the high uncertainty about the ability to create enough well-paying jobs in the future, the third chapter focuses on the importance of expanding universal social services in middle-income countries (and others) as a way to improve people's livelihoods.

In "Advanced Manufacturing and China's Future for Jobs," Dieter Ernst stresses that China, an upper-middle-income country, is very different from other developing countries. It has not experienced premature deindustrialization—manufacturing employment actually increased until 2013—and its productive capabilities are considerably more advanced than in other middle-income countries. As China has moved closer to the technological frontier and wages have risen, its government has doubled down on advancing innovation. In 2015, it rolled out two strategic initiatives: the China Manufacturing 2025 Plan (MIC 2025) and the Internet Plus Plan, the goal of which is to support and speed up firm-level innovation capabilities, with an increased use of robots and network-based upgrading across the entire value chain and related services.

Ernst identifies several big challenges for the successful implementation of MIC 2025, modelled on Germany's "Industry 4.0" (flexible automation and the internet of things). First, much of China's manufacturing sector is still moving from Industry 2.0 (assembly work) to Industry 3.0 (more industrial automation, electronics, IT). Second, the authorities have not taken into account the potentially negative employment impact of the new technological revolution, in a context where labor force participation rates have been falling and the unofficial unemployment rate has been as high as 11 percent over the last decade, more than twice the official statistic. Third, the country may not have enough workers with the skill sets needed to achieve the goals of MIC 2025. And finally, even if China succeeds in moving to the technological frontier in some areas, it is not clear that enough decent jobs will be created to generate the demand for the new output, given the high level of inequality.

As wages in China have risen over the past few years, multinationals have begun to relocate labor-intensive production to countries with lower wages. Vandana Chandra hopes that some countries in sub-Saharan Africa (SSA) will be among the beneficiaries of this reorganization of global production chains. In "Light Manufacturing Can Create Good Jobs in Sub-Saharan Africa," she argues that the challenge in this region is that there is too little digital technology rather than too much. SSA is at the low end of the digital divide, which means that these countries have not reaped the productivity benefits from digitization. Many have limited access to the internet, a limited pool of skilled labor to leverage it, and limited scale for using it profitably.

Most countries in SSA have a large informal sector, a rapidly growing population, and a poorly educated work force. Until the middle of this century, half of the global growth in population generally and working-age population specifically will come from SSA. It is estimated that Africa needs to create 1.1 billion jobs by 2060 to provide employment for everybody of working age. That is a staggering challenge. Chandra suggests that it is critical for SSA countries to pursue long-term goals such as improved education, improved digital infrastructure, and productivity growth in agriculture. But in the short run, she contends, the greatest promise for job creation lies in the development of low-wage, low-skilled manufacturing jobs in export-oriented light manufacturing. She advocates active government policies to identify and support, at a country-specific level, the sectors that have the greatest potential and to adopt an open-arms approach to foreign direct investment.

Large informal sectors are not particular to SSA countries. Many other developing economies in Asia and Latin America also have them, demonstrating that they have not been able to incorporate labor into the production process with decent-paying jobs. As a result, write Juliana Martínez Franzoni and Diego Sánchez-Ancochea, it is more important than ever for middle-income developing countries to focus on expanding "social incorporation": that is, promoting people's well-being independently of the job nexus.

In "Why and How to Build Universal Social Policy in the South," Martínez Franzoni and Sánchez-Ancochea argue that the provision of a basic income is one answer to the need for social incorporation. But they suggest that this income should complement public social services, not substitute for them. The positive effects of universal social services include a greater redistribution of income, more support among different segments of the population, less stigmatization of the poor, greater social cohesion, and more productive economies. The authors propose that we need to explore the politics and political economy of achieving universal social services and to understand the necessary technical design as well. They introduce the concept of "policy architectures"—the policy instruments involved that decide who has access to which services, when, and how—as a useful analytical device to delineate, at a country-specific level, the sequence of policy implementation with the move toward greater unification of policy architectures, rather than further fragmentation.

Emerging Dystopia? What Is to Be Done?

Will the new technological revolution lead inexorably to a decline in the demand for labor in the coming years? Predictions about the future are always uncertain, especially when it is predicted to be so different from the past. But there is a high likelihood that advances in robotization, digitization, and artificial intelligence will displace a large number of jobs, that economic insecurity will continue to rise, and that inequality will become more accentuated, within and among countries.

As the precariat increases and "taskers" become ever more numerous, the political reactions to growing inequality are likely to intensify. Even though we cannot know how quickly technological advances will be diffused, the changing nature of working conditions has already contributed to increasing anxieties and uncertainties, and sentiments are growing that the current rules of the game do not work well for too many. The challenges are magnified for many countries in the Global South, as the economic well-being of so many people is lower to start with, and the technological wherewithal to compete and thrive under this new technological paradigm is considerably more limited.

If the new technologies lead to a disproportionate decline in jobs relative to the working-age population, where will jobs be created? What work will remain, and how will it be distributed? What is the role of the government if private demand fails to lead to full employment?

Strategic policy efforts are needed to address the emerging dystopias and shape a future that will enhance human well-being on a broad scale. The analyses in this book, and elsewhere, offer a number of broad answers. I group the proposals into five interrelated areas: revision of the rules governing globalization, improvement of working conditions for employees and taskers, increase in demand for new products and services, redistribution of existing work, and expansion of social incorporation in the Global

North and the Global South. They address the impact of globalization as well as those of automation and the new technological revolution. Some recommendations are more short-term, others more long-term. Some may be more feasible within the current structure of power distribution; others are substantially more radical, and their relative importance will vary with country specifics.

The need for constructive government actions is a common thread across all proposals. As Freeman (2016a) concludes, for the United States, "The invisible hand needs help if the U.S. is to avoid evolving a new dual economy with a small number of giant multinationals with great knowledge capital but few employees at its core and an increasingly informal labor market at the periphery."

Revision of the Rules Governing Globalization

The current wave of discontent with globalization reflects the sentiment that the past thirty years have left many individuals, groups, and countries behind. At a 2017 conference of the Berggruen Institute, Pascal Lamy, the former head of the World Trade Organization, said, "Let's call globalization by its real name—capitalism, the market above all else" (cited in Gardels 2017). In *The Globalization Paradox*, Dani Rodrik (2011) highlights the problems with "the market above all else." He argues that we are facing a political trilemma where we cannot have national determination, economic globalization, and democracy at the same time. Hyperglobalization impinges on democratic policy choice in a number of important areas.

The policy area I want to highlight here is the limitation on policy space for developing countries under the rules of the World Trade Organization and, more deeply, under the many bilateral trade and investment agreements that a number of countries in the Global South have signed. The rules regulating globalization are not written in stone, but were decided by national governments. As such, they can be modified to respond to the need for greater policy space for development and other legitimate concerns. Policy space for developing countries must be expanded; governments have to be able to adopt the policies needed to develop the domestic productive capabilities that lead to a growth-inducing transformation of their economies and put them on a path to convergence. That is what the experiences of South Korea, China, and other latecomers have shown us.

Improving Working Conditions for Employees and Taskers

Working conditions have deteriorated, with many employees experiencing a decrease in firm-based benefits and others earning minimum wage, the real value of which, in the United States, has declined significantly over the past fifty years.[6] There is a growing movement to increase the minimum wage for US workers to $15 per hour by 2024. Currently, 42 percent of workers earn less than that (Tung et al. 2015).

Another set of policy recommendations aims to increase legal protection for employees and taskers. Mignon Duffy (this volume) highlights that the most vulnerable care workers (e.g., nannies, home care aides) are excluded from basic labor protection. She points to first improvements with the passage of the Domestic Workers' Bill of Rights in Massachusetts and the inclusion of domestic workers under the Fair Labor Standards Act, both in 2014. Guy Standing (this volume) calls for regulation of labor brokers, a tax on earnings from labor brokering, and a collective bargaining system that includes bargaining between complementary or substitute occupational groups, not just employers and employees.

A third area of policy suggestions addresses the significant transition costs for workers who lose their jobs due to the new technological revolution or specific policy decisions. One response, discussed below, is a universal basic income. Other recommendations are more sector-specific. Robert Pollin (this volume), for example, proposes the establishment of a superfund for workers who lose their jobs as a result of necessary transitions to renewable energy sources.

Increasing Demand for New Products and Services

In the past, major technological changes have destroyed tasks and jobs in some areas, but then created new ones in other areas as activities developed that complemented the technological developments and demand increased for existing and new products. Increases in demand are dependent on consumers with the requisite purchasing power. Like many others,

Ford (this volume) fears that the inequality of income will limit the growth of demand. And Nübler (this volume) argues that a significant increase in demand is contingent on a distribution of the benefits arising from technological change. If working hours are reduced, as described below, Nübler suggests that demand for leisure activities could increase, which would create more jobs.

Governments can and must increase demand (and thus create jobs) as well. They can do so directly through government spending and indirectly through regulations and incentives that induce private-sector demand. Duffy, for example, proposes public investment in the care sector (e.g., sanitation infrastructure and universal access to care). Pollin advocates a green growth strategy, where 1.5 percent of GDP spending is redirected from the fossil fuel industry to clean energy. Markets cannot find the green growth direction on their own, because "there is no ready-made route that will make the multiple possible directions and disparate innovations profitable" (Mazzucato and Perez 2014, 13).

Redistribution of Existing Work

In 2015, 193 governments signed on to the Sustainable Development Goals to end poverty, fight climate change, and increase equality. The eighth of these goals focuses on decent work and economic growth and includes a subgoal to "achieve full and productive employment and decent work for all women and men, including for young people and persons with disabilities" by 2030. Full employment is a lofty goal, in light of the large size of the informal sector in most developing countries, the need for 1.1 billion jobs in SSA by 2060, and high youth unemployment rates in many countries in the Global North.

The new technological revolution adds an entirely new dimension. On the one hand, it holds out huge promise for humanity, eliminating drudge work and freeing people to pursue more creative lives. Thompson (2015) even muses about the potential for a life without work, for a transition from a labor force to one of leisure. Nearly a century ago, Keynes (1930) predicted that technological achievements would free his grandchildren from needing to work for as many hours to satisfy their basic needs. With the struggle for subsistence solved, the challenge would be to readjust habits and find new purpose and meaning in life that is not tied to work.

The Fair Labor Standards of 1938 established an eight-hour workday and five-day workweek for US workers. We need a Fair Labor Standards Act for the twenty-first century that reflects the need to work fewer hours and the rise in temporary work arrangements. The big question is how we would distribute the work that exists and how it would be paid. The answer is primarily political, not technical.

Greater Social Incorporation

The phase of capitalism where, in the Global North, jobs provided decent incomes for many workers and benefits were tied to jobs is coming to an end. In most countries in the Global South, the link between a job and decent income and benefits was always limited to a small segment of the work force, if it existed at all, and the possibilities that developing countries will generate enough decent jobs in the future seem limited. Against this backdrop, calls have increased for greater social incorporation, or ways to promote people's well-being independently of the job nexus, in both the Global South (Martínez Franzoni and Sánchez-Ancochea, this volume) and the Global North (Ford, Standing, this volume).

A universal basic income (UBI) for everybody, regardless of link to the labor market, is a policy proposal that has been gaining increasing traction. UBI is not a new idea. Proponents include Friedrich Hayek, Milton Friedman, John Kenneth Galbraith, and Martin Luther King Jr., among others. Today, the idea is championed by libertarians (Zwolinki 2014) and union leaders (Stern 2016), by academics (Standing 2017) and politicians (Benoît Hamon, candidate in the French Socialist Party primaries in 2017).

To be sure, there are many issues of debate. Should a UBI complement universal social services, or should it substitute for some or all of them? Should it be unconditional or conditional? What is the amount that strikes the right balance between the guarantee of a minimum standard of living and an incentive to look for work? And how could a UBI be financed?

One of the longest-lasting examples of a UBI is the Alaska Permanent Fund (established in 1976 under a Republican governor), which distributes dividends to every Alaskan. The amount has varied from a low of $386.15 in 1983 to a high of $2,072 in 2015. A few experiments, started in 2017 at the local and state level, aim to gather empirical evidence that may inform answers to the questions above. In Finland, researchers are comparing the behavior of two thousand randomly selected unemployed people who are receiving a monthly stipend of €560 for two years (while continuing to receive the in-kind benefits to which they are entitled) to the behavior of two thousand unemployed men and women who do not get the stipend. In Ütrecht, the Netherlands, 250 people are receiving a monthly sum of €960 for two years. In Switzerland, a UBI was the subject of a referendum in June 2016. The proposed monthly level of 2,500 Swiss francs was substantially higher than the stipends in the regional experiments above. Swiss voters rejected the plan.

Regarding funding a UBI, Freeman (2016b) argues for greater worker ownership of shares and say in decisions about how new technologies should be implemented, while Standing (this volume) proposes a democratically controlled sovereign wealth fund, established with taxes on exploitation or ownership of assets. Whatever the mechanism of redistribution, Breman and van der Linden (2014, 934) argue that "the common denominator is to hold capital accountable for the condition of labor whether it is employed or not."

Other proposals for raising funds do not necessarily focus on a UBI, but aim to address the challenges we are discussing. Bill Gates (cited in Waters 2017) proposes a tax on robots to fund retraining for workers who lose their jobs. And Hoy and Sumner (2016) advocate taxes on national resources and a reallocation of public funding to eliminate the lowest levels of poverty.[7]

The Political Economy of Change

In *The Great Transformation* (1944), Karl Polanyi described the development of the market society from the mid-nineteenth to the mid-twentieth century. The first phase, he argued, was a disruptive phase of unregulated (disembedded) markets. It was followed by a second phase where new rules embedded markets in society. Welfare provisions rose, unions and labor regulation became stronger, and governments were expected to play a significant role in the economy, directly and indirectly. Now we are in another great transformation: under neoliberalism and hyperglobalization, markets have again become more disembedded, and the new technological revolution will lead to major disruptions in the world of work.

The contributors to this book suggest strategies and policies for a new phase of market embeddedness to redress current problems and avoid major social and economic upheaval. But for the most part, they do not focus on the question of whether governments actually would or could adopt these policies. This is not a book about the political economy of change. But we would be remiss if we did not highlight the importance of analyzing the political economy of implementing any of the proposals discussed here.

What are the bases for building coalitions of shared interest in support of any of these policies? The answers differ, of course, depending on the issue, specific policy, and country. One thing we know for certain is that a number of proposals require a redistribution of income or wealth, be it through taxes or new regulations. This raises the all-important question of whether elites will be willing to subordinate their short-term interests to the goal of long-term stability and well-being, their own and that of the people of the countries in which they live.

History is short on examples we could point to. Industrial revolutions have led to major social disruptions and upheaval in the past. Will this time be different? The rise of the Right, discussed by Ferraro (this volume), does not bode well for the willingness of elites to address the core problems we confront. In his speech at Harvard's 2017 commencement, Mark Zuckerberg, founder and CEO of Facebook, talked about the need for a new social contract that might include some form of basic income, portable health insurance, and affordable childcare, and he suggested that people like himself should pay for it. If others follow suit, then there is hope for constructive and peaceful actions to shape the impact of the new technological revolution with foresight.

Part I

TRENDS

Job Destruction and Job Creation

2

THE RISE OF THE ROBOTS

Impact on Unemployment and Inequality

Martin Ford

The fear that machines might someday displace workers and produce long-term structural unemployment has a long history, stretching back, at a minimum, to the Luddite revolts that took place in England just over two hundred years ago. In the years since, the alarm has been raised again and again.

One of the most notable instances occurred in March of 1964, when a prominent group of intellectuals sent a formal document known as the "Triple Revolution Report" to President Lyndon Johnson. The report warned that industrial automation was poised to throw millions of people out of work and create economic and social upheaval. In an accompanying letter, the authors wrote that unless the government took action, "the nation [would] be thrown into unprecedented economic and social

The author used the FRED (Federal Reserve Economic Data) database from the Federal Reserve Bank of St. Louis to assemble some of the data used in this paper. See the reference list for information on the specific series used.

disorder."[1] The feared disruption, of course, did not occur, and the report has now been largely forgotten.

Given this long record of false alarms, contemporary economists are generally dismissive of arguments that technological progress might lead to unemployment as well as falling wages and soaring income inequality. History shows that the economy has consistently adjusted to advancing technology by creating new employment opportunities and that these new jobs often require more skills and pay higher wages.

The post–World War II period in the United States offers an especially powerful demonstration of the historical synergy between technological progress and increasing overall prosperity. During this "golden age" of the American industrial economy, wages for nearly all workers increased as productivity soared. The result was the emergence of a massive US middle class. Workers, in turn, increased their spending in line with their rising incomes, creating strong demand for the products and services being produced by the economy. This virtuous cycle encompassing production and consumption drove America's economic growth and prosperity and gradually became the model for other industrialized countries throughout the world.

The mechanization of the US agricultural sector offers one of the most extreme historical examples of technologically induced job losses. In the late 1800s, about three-quarters of workers in the United States were employed in agriculture. Today, the number is between 1 and 2 percent. Advancing agricultural technology irreversibly destroyed millions of these jobs. This did, in fact, result in significant short- and medium-term unemployment as displaced farm workers migrated to cities in search of factory work. However, the unemployed workers were eventually accommodated by the rising manufacturing and service sectors and, over the long run, average wages as well as overall prosperity increased dramatically.

The conventional wisdom suggests that we should expect a similar transition to unfold in the face of today's rapid advances in robotics and artificial intelligence. However, there are important reasons to be concerned that this time might turn out to be very different. Because information technology accelerates (roughly doubling every two years, according to the well-known Moore's Law) rather than increasing in a linear fashion, we can anticipate that the coming years and decades will see far more progress than we might expect based on an analysis of history. In the future, the impact of automation will no longer be limited to lower-wage workers with limited skills and educations. Technologies such as artificial intelligence, machine learning, and software automation will increasingly enable computers to do jobs that require significant training and education. College graduates who take knowledge-based jobs will find themselves threatened not only by low-wage offshore competitors, but also by machines and software algorithms that can perform sophisticated analysis and decision making.

Continuing progress in manufacturing automation and the introduction of advanced commercial robots and self-service technologies will likewise continue to diminish opportunities for lower-skilled and less-educated workers. Technological progress is relentless, and artificial intelligence seems likely to eventually approach the point where it will match or exceed the average worker's ability to perform most routine, predictable work tasks. At that point, nearly all rational businesses will be faced with a powerful incentive to substitute machines for workers.

In the past, disruptive labor-saving technologies have typically been specialized, and they have made their effect felt on a sector-by-sector basis. Workers have adapted by moving from routine jobs in one area to routine jobs in some new emerging industry. For example, in the United States, workers transitioned from farms to factories and then ultimately to service jobs, which now provide the vast majority of employment. Today's artificial intelligence (AI) and robotics technology, by contrast, is nothing like the mechanical innovations that transformed agriculture. Information technology has far more broad-based implications: it is a general-purpose technology that has invaded, and will increasingly disrupt, every sector of the economy. For the first time in history, computers and machines are beginning to take on intellectual tasks that were once the exclusive province of the human brain. Information technology will continue to accelerate, and is certain to be tightly integrated into any industries that arise in the future. The upshot is that it seems very unlikely that there will be new labor-intensive employment sectors capable of absorbing the millions of workers displaced from existing industries as technology advances.[2]

Evidence of information technology's impact on employment can already be found in the industries that have emerged over the past decade or two. Companies such as Google and Facebook have achieved enormous influence and market valuations, with workforces a fraction of the size of those found in more traditional industries. In 2012, for example, Google generated about US$14 billion in earnings while employing just thirty-eight thousand people. Compare that with General Motors, which peaked at roughly 840,000 employees in 1979, while earning only US$11 billion (measured in 2012 dollars)—about 20 percent less than Google.

Economic Trends That Suggest Technology Is Already Having an Impact

Soaring inequality in the United States, in terms of both income and wealth, has recently become a widely discussed and debated topic. Over the seventeen-year period between 1993 and 2010, more than half of the growth in US national income was captured by the top 1 percent of households. ("Politics" 2012). Emmanuel Saez, an economist at the University of California, Berkeley, found (2013) that during the economic recovery between 2009 and 2012, a full 95 percent of US income gains likewise went to the top 1 percent. Wealth inequality is even more extreme. The top 5 percent of US households own nearly two-thirds of private assets, and the combined net worth of the four hundred wealthiest Americans is now greater than that of the 150 million people at the bottom of the income distribution.

A number of theories have been put forward to explain the relentless increase in inequality. These include a rightward drift in politics and policy that began with the administration of President Ronald Reagan and, in particular, the almost complete elimination of organized labor in the US private sector. Globalization, especially the migration of factory jobs to China, is another often-cited driver of inequality. The increasing dominance of the US financial sector, the extraordinary rise in compensation paid to corporate executives and superstar entertainers, and assortative mating—in which individuals with similar educational backgrounds and incomes tend to marry—have all been singled out as important contributing factors.

While it is very likely that all these factors have contributed to the relentless, decades-long drive toward increased inequality in the United States, and to a lesser degree in many other countries, a number of important economic trends—especially when considered together—point to the importance of advancing technology. In addition, it is critical to keep in mind that, because information technology continues to be driven by exponential progress, there is good reason to expect that it will rise above other factors and become the dominant force shaping the future economy.

Stagnant Wages and Consistently Increasing Productivity

Between the end of World War II and 1973, wages for typical workers in the United States rose in nearly perfect lockstep with increasing productivity. In 1973, however, wages for private-sector production and nonsupervisory workers (a category that includes over 60 percent of the total US workforce and about 80 percent of private-sector workers) reached a historical peak of US$767 (measured in 2013 dollars)—and then went into a decades-long decline. By 2013, a comparable worker earned only about US$664, or about 13 percent less than in 1973 ("Hours" 2013). Over the same four decades, productivity (or real output per hour) rose by nearly 110 percent.

Figure 2.1 shows how compensation (wages plus the value of benefits) for US workers and productivity growth in percentage terms compare over different periods going back to the years following World War II. The chart makes it clear that productivity has grown significantly faster

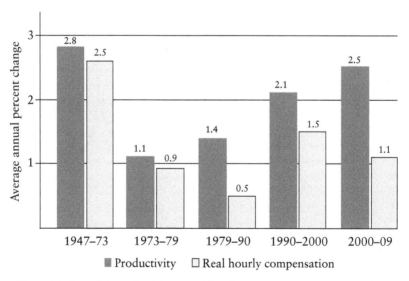

Figure 2.1 Growth in productivity vs. real hourly compensation in the US nonfarm business sector. US Bureau of Labor Statistics 2011.

than compensation in every decade since 1979. The difference is especially notable from 2000 to 2009: productivity growth during this period is more than double the corresponding increase in compensation. Indeed, since the trend reversed in the 1970s, the gap between productivity and compensation appears to be consistently increasing over time. This widening gap illustrates the extent to which the fruits of technological progress throughout the economy are being captured almost entirely by business owners, investors, and others at the top of the income distribution, rather than by average workers.

Declining Labor Share of National Income

The share of national income going to labor vs. capital has historically been quite stable. In the United States in the two decades following World War II, labor's share of income varied in a relatively narrow range, averaging somewhere around 64 to 66 percent. Beginning in the early 1970s, the US labor share began to decline; in the years following 2000, the decline has become far more precipitous. (See figure 2.2).

This decline of labor's share of national income relative to capital is not limited to the United States. In a 2013 analysis, economists Loukas Karabarbounis and Brent Neiman of the University of Chicago found that

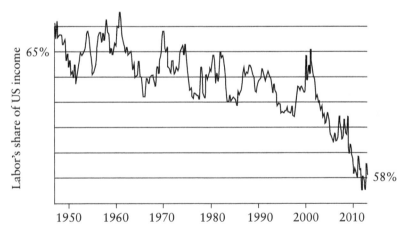

Figure 2.2 The decline in labor's share of US income. US Bureau of Labor Statistics and Federal Reserve Bank of St. Louis (FRED), using data from Jacobson and Occhino 2012.

forty-two out of the fifty-nine countries they analyzed showed a significant decline in labor's share. Japan, Canada, France, Italy, Germany, and China all had more substantial declines than the United States, measured over a ten-year period. In China, it fell at about three times the US rate. Karabarbounis and Neiman (2013, 1) conclude that "efficiency gains in capital producing sectors, often attributed to advances in information technology and the computer age, induced firms to shift away from labor and toward capital to such a large extent that the labor share of income declined."

Job Market Polarization

David Autor, an economist at the Massachusetts Institute of Technology, has done extensive analysis of the "hollowing out" or polarization of the job market. Polarization happens when solid middle-skill jobs that provide middle-class incomes disappear and are replaced with large numbers of low-wage, low-skill jobs (typically in the service sector, in areas such as fast food and retail), as well as high-skill jobs that generally require advanced education and training. In research published in 2010, Autor identified four midrange occupational categories that have been dramatically affected: sales, office-administrative, production-craft-repair, and operators-fabricators-laborers. Between 1979 and 2009, the percentage of the US workforce employed in these four areas fell from 57.3 percent to 45.7 percent; the rate of decline became more rapid between 2007 and 2009. As with the fall in labor's share of national income, polarization is not an exclusively American trend. It is occurring in a variety of industrialized countries. Between 1993 and 2006, sixteen European Union countries experienced a significant decline in the fraction of their workforce employed in midrange occupations. Autor (2010, 2) suggests that the primary reason for polarization is "the automation of routine work and, to a smaller extent, the international integration of labor markets through trade and, more recently, offshoring."

Declining Labor Force Participation and an Explosion in Disability

The US labor force participation rate—a measure of the percentage of adults aged eighteen to sixty-four who are currently employed or actively seeking a job—peaked at about 67 percent in 2000 and has been in decline ever since. By 2013, the rate had fallen below 64 percent. The participation rate for people aged twenty-five to fifty-four, which includes most who are beyond the age where they are likely to be in school full time and yet not old enough to retire, also declined from a high of 84.5 percent to 81 percent as of 2013 (Federal).

There has also been an explosion in applications for the US Social Security disability program, which is intended for workers who suffer serious workplace injuries. Between 2000 and 2011, the number of disability applications more than doubled, from roughly 1.2 million per year to nearly three million (Van Zandweghe 2012). This suggests the possibility that many discouraged workers are relying on the disability program as a kind of unemployment insurance system.

Less Job Creation and Longer Jobless Recoveries

In nearly every decade since the 1960s, the US economy has created fewer new jobs, in percentage terms, than in the preceding ten-year period. The 1990s nearly matched the 1980s, with about 20 percent growth in employment, but this was heavily driven by a surge of new jobs that appeared during the technology boom in the second half of the decade. Table 2.1 shows the percentage of new jobs generated in each decade.

In addition, when recessions occur it is taking the economy longer and longer to return to the previous level of employment. Table 2.2 shows the length of recovery for recent recessions, measured in months from the start of the recession. The Great Recession of 2007–2009 unleashed a jobless recovery of historic proportions. It took about six years for employment to return to its pre-crisis level.

Table 2.1 US job creation by decade

Decade	Percentage increase in employment
1960s	31
1970s	28
1980s	20
1990s	20
2000s	0

Source: US Bureau of Labor Statistics and Federal Reserve Bank of St. Louis (FRED).

Table 2.2 Months for US employment to recover (from start of recession)

Recession	Months to recover
1974–1975	15
1981–1982	27
1990–1991	30
2001	46
2007–2009	80

Source: US Bureau of Labor Statistics and Federal Reserve Bank of St. Louis (FRED).

Technology Offers the Best Explanation for These Trends

Each of these trends has been the subject of analysis and research by economists, and a number of competing theories have been put forward to explain them. Many factors (including, for example, globalization, demographics, and political shifts) have doubtless played a significant role and may provide at least partial explanations for one or more of these trends. However, when all of the trends are considered together, a strong case can be made that technology is the most important underlying factor. Note, for example, that both a decline in labor's share and job market polarization have been found in a number of countries with vastly different political orientations. Germany and Canada continue to have influential organized labor movements, while unions have been almost entirely eliminated from the US private sector. China, a country that benefits greatly from globalization, has seen a rapid collapse in the share of national income labor. Clearly, some global force is exerting a powerful influence. Technology is arguably the only factor that can reasonably explain all of these trends in all the countries in which they have been observed.

Occupations Affected by Automation, Now and in the Near Future

Examples of the rapid progress being made in robotics and AI are widespread, and more appear on nearly a daily basis. Industrial Perception, Inc., a small company (now owned by Alphabet/Google) based in Silicon Valley, California, has built a robot capable of visually perceiving and moving boxes of various shapes and sizes. In a remarkable demonstration of the kind of cross-fertilization that is common in the information technology sector, the robot uses an advanced three-dimensional machine vision system that was originally developed for the Microsoft Kinect—a US$150 add-on for the company's video game system. Industrial Perception expects its robot to eventually be able to continually move, load, or unload boxes at a rate of one every second, far exceeding the capability of a human worker (Markoff 2012). It goes without saying that this robot will never get tired, never suffer a back injury, and certainly never file a worker's compensation claim. This is just one example of how robotic technology is rapidly encroaching on jobs that, until now, have been relatively safe from automation. As the technology becomes more affordable, reliable, and ubiquitous, it seems poised to have a disruptive impact on jobs in the materials handling arena.

Low-wage jobs in industries such as fast food and retail will likewise be increasingly susceptible to automation as well as vastly improved self-service technologies, often powered by mobile phone apps. Retail jobs will also continue to be threatened by the continuing onslaught from Amazon and other online retailers. Amazon itself relies increasingly on labor-saving technology, and in 2012 purchased Kiva Systems, a company that manufactures robots used in warehouse automation.

It seems inevitable that many jobs in the fast-food industry will ultimately be threatened by automation. Venture-backed startup companies are already focusing on robotic production of hamburgers and pizza. The strong political movement in favor of a higher minimum wage in the United States may, to some extent, accelerate automation in the industry.

The advent of fully automated cars and trucks has the potential to directly threaten millions of jobs for professional drivers, possibly within the next decade or two. In a number of US states, driving a vehicle of some type is the most common occupational category, especially for non-college-educated men. Most analysts expect automated cars to evolve into shared resources (at least within urban areas). In other words, self-driving cars will operate like Uber or Lyft—but without the drivers. Indeed, both Uber and Lyft are actively investing in research and development of self-driving vehicle technology. If we eventually move toward a world in which most people do not own cars, millions more jobs and small businesses in areas such as auto repair and insurance could also eventually be vulnerable as the automotive sector transitions from a widely distributed owner-operator model to centralized fleet ownership.

Highly skilled and college-educated workers are by no means exempt from the impact of these technologies. The "big data" phenomenon is resulting in new management approaches where vast amounts of information are analyzed for correlations that can be used to drive business decisions. The approach will often require fewer analysts and middle managers, as decisions are made algorithmically. Narrative Science, Inc., a Chicago-area company with approximately thirty employees, has developed a system capable of autonomously writing news articles and internal corporate reports. The system is first configured to analyze a data stream and then can continuously output reports and articles that contain intelligent analysis and are written in natural language. A number of top news sites use the company's service, including *Forbes* magazine. One of the company's cofounders thinks that within fifteen years, "more than 90 percent" of news articles will be written by computer algorithms (Levy 2012).

IBM's Watson computer, introduced in 2011, was another vivid illustration of the advances being made in systems that will influence knowledge-based work. Watson, which combines deep analysis with a remarkable facility with natural language, was able to prevail against the best human contestants in the television game show *Jeopardy!*—an unprecedented feat for a computer. Other skilled professions being affected include attorneys and paralegals (by software able to autonomously analyze documents and decide if they are relevant to legal cases), doctors specializing in radiology and pathology (by automated systems that can analyze medical images and perform tests on tissue samples), and pharmacists (by massive pharmacy robots already in many large hospitals that completely automate the medication-dispensing process).

The most startling advances in artificial intelligence are occurring in the field of "deep learning," a type of machine learning that is based on neural networks that loosely model the way biological brains work. Neural networks have been in use for basic pattern recognition tasks for decades; however, recent years have seen remarkable progress in building far more complex ("deep") networks with many layers of simulated neurons. Deep learning systems are already outperforming humans at recognizing visual images and have succeeded in at least basic real-time spoken-language translation. In 2016, Google DeepMind software succeeded in defeating one of the world's best players of the ancient game of Go. Unlike chess, Go, which is very popular in Asian countries, cannot be approached with a "brute force" algorithm geared toward computing nearly every possible move. Instead, it must be approached using more humanlike thought. Remarkably, Google's system succeeded in part by training itself to play the game—and then rapidly achieved the ability to defeat virtually any human being.

This demonstrated propensity by artificial intelligence and machine learning to take on more intellectual tasks, and to climb the skills ladder and affect the jobs held by highly educated workers, is one of the most important, and disruptive, trends likely to unfold in the coming years and decades. The conventional solution to the automation of low-skill jobs has always been more education or retraining, so that the affected workers can move up to higher-skill work. As technology accelerates, this solution is likely to become ever less effective. In order to remain relevant, it will no longer be sufficient for workers to simply acquire new skills and move into a new type of routine, predictable work. Rather, they will have to find opportunities that involve genuinely nonroutine or creative tasks. Some workers will, of course, successfully make that transition, but there is a real question as to whether there will be enough of these jobs, as well as whether many workers will be capable of adapting.

The concern that robots and automation may eventually threaten huge numbers of jobs is supported by formal academic research. In 2013, Carl Benedikt Frey and Michael A. Osborne of the University of Oxford published research that includes a formal analysis of over seven hundred occupations tracked by the US Department of Labor. Frey and Osborne (2013, 38) concluded that about 47 percent of total US employment— more than sixty million jobs—will be highly susceptible to automation within roughly the next two decades.

Technology-Driven Inequality and Its Impact on Consumer Spending and Trade

Over the course of the two decades between 1992 and 2012, the percentage of total US consumer spending attributed to households in the top 5 percent of the income distribution rose from 27 to 38 percent. Over the same period, the percentage of consumption associated with the bottom 80 percent of American consumers fell from 46.6 to 39 percent (Schwartz 2014). American economic growth is becoming more and more dependent on a small number of elite consumers with relatively high incomes.

In the decades leading up to the 2007 financial crisis, American consumers continued to spend more overall even as income became dramatically more concentrated at the top. Between 1972 and 2007, average spending as a share of disposable income increased from about 85 percent to over 93 percent. For most of that period, consumption was both the largest and fastest-growing component of US Gross Domestic Product (GDP) (Cynamon and Fazzari 2014).

This increase in overall consumption is quite surprising, because it is well-known to economists that higher-income households spend less of their total income (and save or invest much more) than do middle-class or poor households. We would logically have anticipated seeing weaker overall spending as an increasing share of national income was captured by a few households at the top of the income distribution, since these elite consumers would be inclined to spend a smaller fraction of their incomes.

In January 2014, economists Barry Cynamon of the Federal Reserve Bank of Saint Louis and Steven Fazzari of Washington University in St. Louis published a paper that attempted to explain this mystery of rising income inequality combined with increased overall consumer spending. They came to the conclusion that the long-term increase in American consumption was made possible by a dramatically increased debt load taken on by the lower 95 percent of American households. Between 1989 and 2007 the ratio of debt to income for the bottom 95 percent roughly doubled from around 80 percent to nearly 160 percent. For the top 5 percent of households, the same debt/income ratio saw little or no increase at all, staying at around 60 percent. The greatest increase in debt levels occurred while the US housing bubble was rapidly inflating in the years immediately leading up to the financial crisis. Cynamon and Fazzari (2014, 18) suggest that the debt burden taken on by the bottom 95 percent of US households ultimately proved unsustainable, and that "financial fragility created by unprecedented borrowing triggered the Great Recession when the inability to borrow more forced a drop in consumption."

Cynamon and Fazzari also found a dramatic difference in the top 5 percent vs. the bottom 95 percent during the recession recovery that began in 2009. By 2012, spending by the top 5 percent had increased by about 17 percent. The bottom 95 percent had seen no increase at all; spending remained at approximately 2008 levels. In other words, the recovery in overall consumer spending was powered entirely by consumers in the top 5 percent of households by income.

The recovery from the Great Recession has generally been characterized by soaring corporate earnings coupled with far less impressive increases in revenue. This demonstrates that the profits are coming from cost-cutting rather than market expansion.

Consumption in the United States is typically around 70 percent of GDP. An important future risk is that, as consumer spending becomes more and more concentrated among a small number of high-income households, it will become more and more difficult to sustain economic growth. Many of the households in the top 5 percent depend on knowledge-based or professional work for their relatively high incomes. As we saw earlier, many of these occupations are certain to be vulnerable to automation as advances in artificial intelligence and machine learning continue. Likewise, these advances could make it increasingly difficult for new college graduates to someday climb to the high income levels that will allow them to make outsized contributions to consumer spending. The result could turn out to be even more dramatic concentration in the number of households with sufficient purchasing power to sustain overall consumer spending as well as economic growth.

It is important to keep in mind that all final demand for products and services throughout any economy comes ultimately from household consumer spending and, to a lesser extent, spending by governments. While businesses, of course, also buy products and services, this does not constitute final demand. If a business is unable to sell its own output, it will stop purchasing inputs and, eventually, will close its doors. When machines or software replace workers (or, alternatively, deskill jobs so that wages are driven down to the minimum), that means less consumption. Machines do not create final demand. For example, a robot in a factory will use energy and require maintenance and spare parts, but these are inputs to the production process. If the factory's output cannot be sold, the robot will be shut down. The bottom line is that all demand across the economy is ultimately dependent on purchases made by households—and the vast majority of households, in turn, are dependent on jobs for nearly their entire income.

Consumer Spending and Economic Growth

If rapid acceleration in robotics and artificial intelligence technologies eventually creates widespread unemployment or causes wages for a large fraction of households to fall, there is likely to be a substantial impact on consumer spending, and therefore on economic growth. If the technological impact comes in the form of software automation focused on relatively highly paid knowledge workers, who are responsible for a growing share of consumer spending, the resulting reduction in consumption could be especially significant.

In the coming decades, dramatic technological progress can be expected in all the advanced economies that are currently responsible for a large fraction of the consumer demand that is a critical driver of global trade. Robotics and automation will likewise have a substantial impact on the economy of China and other emerging countries. All this creates the potential for a situation where there are too few viable consumers to provide sufficient demand across the global economy. Indeed, many economies are already caught in a trap in which central banks (such as the US Federal Reserve) have been forced to maintain interest rates near zero levels. If technological progress in the coming years results in unemployment and even higher inequality, it will become even more difficult for central banks to raise interest rates and avoid deflation. The ultimate result could be little or no economic growth and possibly even financial crises if households again become overly dependent on debt as a means to maintain spending in the absence of rising incomes.

Impact on Developing Nations and the Global South

The impact of advancing technology will by no means be limited to advanced nations. In China, for example, robots are already having a dramatic impact on the labor-intensive factories that provide employment for many millions of workers. Indeed, China is now by far the largest global market for industrial robots. Even so, the country's robot density—or the number of robots per one hundred workers—is among the lowest of all major manufacturing economies. In other words, the transition to automation remains at a very early stage: there is far more to come.

For those poorer countries that have not yet enjoyed the progress seen in China, the story may be especially grim. As I wrote in my 2015 book *Rise of the Robots,*

> The challenges faced by China are even more daunting for poorer countries, which are much further behind in the race against technology. As even the most labor-intensive areas of manufacturing begin to incorporate more automation, the historical path to prosperity may be poised to largely evaporate for these nations. According to one study, about 22 million factory jobs disappeared worldwide between 1995 and 2002. Over the same seven-year period, manufacturing output increased 30 percent. It is not at all clear how the poorest countries in Asia and Africa will manage to dramatically improve their prospects in a world that no longer needs untold millions of low-wage factory workers (Ford 2015).

The path to broad-based prosperity for developing countries has always been to build labor-intensive factories that provide jobs for large numbers of unskilled workers. There is evidence that this path is already beginning to erode. In 2015, Harvard economist Dani Rodrik published a paper documenting what he dubbed "premature deindustrialization." In other words, developing countries are losing their manufacturing jobs before they are able to climb the prosperity ladder that was navigated by advanced countries such as the United States in an era when technology was far less advanced. Mexico is one of the countries that Rodrik identifies as struggling to make the leap to prosperity in the robotic age (Rodrik 2015).

What Is the Solution?

Over the course of the coming decades, nations in both the developed and developing worlds will face the challenge of adapting to the impact of rapidly advancing robotics and artificial intelligence technology. The goal should be to leverage the power of these technologies for the benefit of both society and the economy, while finding a way to mitigate the likely impact on employment opportunities, economic security, inequality, and consumer confidence. Historically, there has been only one conventional policy response to the advent of automation: to subject workers to ever more training and education in the hope that they can outrun the capability of the machines. As we have seen, artificial intelligence is proving adept at climbing the skills ladder, and jobs and tasks performed by highly educated workers such as journalists, lawyers, and radiologists are already being affected. As the rate of technological progress accelerates, it is easy to imagine a future in which workers are unable to keep up with the rate of change.

If education and retraining ultimately prove insufficient, we will eventually need to consider a more radical solution. We will have to find a way to restructure our economic system, and that will likely involve decoupling income from traditional jobs. Some form of guaranteed income or universal basic income (UBI) is the most viable way to do this. The essential idea is that a nation would provide every adult with at least at least a minimal guaranteed income that would provide essential economic security as well as the means to actively participate in the economy as a consumer and thus help drive overall economic growth.

Implementing a guaranteed income is certain to present a staggering political challenge, especially in the United States. Therefore, eventual success will require a pragmatic approach. In my two books, *Rise of the Robots* (2015) and *The Lights in the Tunnel* (2009), I suggested two ways that an absolutely "universal" and "unconditional" guaranteed income scheme might be modified to make it more effective, affordable, and, perhaps, politically palatable.

First, basic incentives could be incorporated into the income scheme. Most important would be an incentive to pursue further education. People who succeed in completing higher levels ought to receive somewhat higher basic incomes. In the absence of this, non–academically inclined students might be presented with a perverse incentive to simply drop out of school, knowing that they would, in any case, be eligible for the basic income. Education is a vitally important public good, and a well-educated population provides many benefits to society. Any basic income scheme should be designed to ensure that citizens continue to experience direct personal gain from remaining in school and pursuing the highest level of education that is compatible with their ability. Such incentives might also be extended to other areas, such as meaningful contributions to communities or to humanistic or artistic endeavors. Indeed, a basic income with incentives built in might eventually offer at least a partial solution to the age-old complaint that the market economy does not place adequate value on many of the endeavors that are most critical to the positive development of both individuals and society as a whole.

Secondly, one of most important tenets of a strictly defined UBI is that the income is not means-tested. Everyone receives it unconditionally. This ensures that there is no disincentive to work or engage in entrepreneurial activity that will result in a higher overall income level. This is crucial to avoiding a "poverty trap" scenario, where those who receive the income are discouraged from improving their lot because of the risk that they will lose eligibility for their existing benefits. In theory, an unconditional income for everyone should also help to galvanize political support for the program. This approach is, however, much costlier than a guaranteed minimum income that is phased out as other income increases. I think there is middle ground that could reduce the overall cost of a basic income while making it more politically feasible: The income could be means-tested against "passive" income (pensions, social security, rents and royalties, investment income) but not against "active" income (wages, income from an actively managed small business, etc.). This would preserve the incentive to work or start a business while reducing the cost of the program. It would also improve the political optics by limiting the eligibility of those who already enjoy adequate guaranteed incomes from other sources.

It should be noted that a basic income scheme can, of course, be combined with other initiatives. One promising avenue might be policies geared toward encouraging "work sharing," in which jobs are shared in some way among more than one worker. This approach might be fairly simple to implement in blue-collar hourly positions (perhaps by simply mandating a reduction from the standard forty-hour week). It would likely be much more difficult to extend a work-sharing policy to skilled white-collar and professional occupations. The idea that a decreasing work burden could be shared goes back at least to John Maynard Keynes's 1930 essay "Economic Possibilities for our Grandchildren," in which he envisioned a fifteen-hour workweek as an attempt to "spread the bread thin on the butter—to make what work there is still to be done to be as widely shared as possible" (Keynes 1930). Perhaps Keynes's vision will ultimately be realized, but current trends suggest that it is very unlikely that the market economy, left to its own devices, will produce sufficient incomes for part-time workers. Instead, it may come about through income supplementation via a UBI combined with explicit work-sharing policies.

It seems likely that practicality, and a willingness to address legitimate concerns about the creation of a disincentive to work, will be required if a basic income is ever to become politically viable. At this point in time, an obvious first step would be to initiate some pilot programs or small-scale experiments in order to test various basic income schemes. These experiments would provide data that might be used to craft an eventual program that could be scaled out at the national level.

We should begin this process as soon as possible. The history of universal health care in the United States offers a cautionary tale regarding the extreme sluggishness of the political process. It took the nation approximately eighty years from the time that Franklin Roosevelt proposed a national health insurance program until the implementation of the Affordable Care Act (Obamacare), something approaching universal health coverage. It's very unlikely that we will have anything close to that length of time as we attempt to navigate the coming transition. The progress of information technology continues to accelerate and the impact on the job market could well materialize long before we are prepared for it.

3

New Technologies, Innovation, and the Future of Jobs

Irmgard Nübler

New technologies are major drivers of growth and development with the power to fundamentally transform the world of work. The recent wave of technological changes is once more garnering widespread attention among policymakers, researchers, business leaders, and workers. The "New Machine Age," the diffusion of increasingly mobile, autonomous, and learning robotics, as well as innovative use of Information and Communication Technologies (ICT) and platform-based services, are expected by some researchers to be highly disruptive—deep in impact, wide in scope, large in scale, and accelerating rapidly in pace. Many economists are skeptical about the future of jobs, expecting past trends of job destruction, polarization, and rising income inequality to continue. Others disagree, as they are confident that economic, social, and political forces will lead to adjustment processes that create new and better jobs. This optimism is supported by historical experience, and though it has been challenged, it was dominant among economists for most of the nineteenth and twentieth centuries (Krugman 2013). However, the skeptics claim that this time, technological change is different: they expect a "jobless future." They therefore claim that new institutions need to ensure basic income and social protection for all.

While the future is uncertain and we cannot know the revolutionary knowledge, inventions, and innovations that may emerge, this chapter provides a framework to analyze the nexus of technological change, innovation, and jobs. It explores the forces that have been shaping this process, historical regularities describing the impact of new technologies on jobs, and whether we can expect these forces and regularities to also shape the future of jobs.

Technological change is a complex, nonlinear, and costly process. It is not homogenous, and it is here defined broadly to take into account the forms of innovation that affect the quantity and nature of jobs in different ways. It is reflected in the discoveries of new scientific principles and inventions; in the implementation of new or significantly improved products and new industries (product innovations); and in new production techniques, organizational routines, and business models (process innovations); as well as in the wide diffusion of these innovations in the economy.

This chapter will first analyze the market forces that have shaped the search for new technologies and innovations and, in this context, created processes of job destruction and creation and increased the quality of many jobs. The quest for increasing competitiveness in industries producing standardized goods and services has created long-term trends in process innovations such as automation and fragmentation of production, which increase productivity and reduce costs, but destroy jobs. In the context of highly competitive global markets, this trend will continue, increasingly so in services, research and development, logistics, and the professions. This is the focus of the more pessimistic perspective in the debate on the future of jobs. These new process technologies transform the nature of jobs and increase the complexity of those in which workers collaborate with machines and coordinate fragmented tasks. A new wave of technological changes, reflected in the diffusion of mobile robots, "smart" machines, 3D printing, the Internet of Things, and the globalization of services and data-related activities, will also transform and increase jobs' complexity this time around.

The history of technological change demonstrates that phases of process innovations and job destruction are typically followed by phases of market expansion and product innovations that create new jobs. These effects are triggered by an expansion and change in demand for new consumer and capital goods. These compensation effects will also be mobilized in the future, if the benefits arising from technological change will be broadly distributed within societies to enhance demand for existing and new products.

As will be discussed in more detail below, the future of jobs is not deterministic: it needs to be shaped. Markets cannot achieve the transformative changes that are required to create new jobs at a massive scale. Such transitions are social and political choices, and those countries that proactively shape their social, technological, and economic transformation processes will create good jobs. Education and training policies aligned with targeted industrial and structural transformation policies play a role, as do mission-oriented technology, science, and innovation policies and fiscal and labor market policies. Such a strategy requires institutions to support the forging of a new social consensus on the futures of technological change, innovations, and jobs.

Market Forces Shaping the Dynamics of Job Destruction and Creation

Historical experience shows that markets are important drivers of technological change and innovation. In industries that produce standardized goods and services (mass production) and compete in price, costs, and quality, the search for new technological knowledge, inventions, and innovation is driven by market competition and the quest for higher productivity. These pressures have driven automation and fragmentation of production systems since the Industrial Revolution. They have enhanced productivity by saving labor and thereby destroying jobs. However, at the same time, markets create adjustment mechanisms that have the potential to create new jobs and to compensate for these job losses.

Job Destruction: The Quest for Increased Competitiveness

Automation destroys jobs by replacing workers with machines, while fragmentation of production processes destroys jobs by relocating tasks.

The history of technological change shows that both automation and fragmentation of production processes have destroyed tasks, jobs, and occupations, though each time with some occupations being affected more than others.

Automation of Tasks and the Future of Jobs   A major feature of the industrial production mode introduced by the industrial revolution is the standardization of products and production processes. Standardization allowed for the routinization of work procedures and the automation of tasks. Machines substitute for workers in performing tasks, thereby lowering costs, reducing human error, and enhancing product quality. As a general principle, since the industrial revolution, each wave of technological change has automated jobs, initially routine manual jobs, then nonroutine manual jobs, then, increasingly, cognitive routine and nonroutine tasks. While the fixed industrial robots of the past largely replaced jobs, the newly developed mobile robots tend to complement human tasks. Because they replace mainly nonroutine manual and interactive tasks and complement nonautomated tasks, they destroy work, but not jobs.

Most recently, the combination of new sensor technologies with data-processing machinery and the creation of powerful optimizing algorithms has provided the opportunity for automation of nonroutine cognitive tasks such as recognizing patterns in texts and behavior. Also, learning robots are emerging rapidly. They learn through algorithms that self-improve at tasks involving analysis and prediction, and they do so at an increasing pace as higher computer capacity enables machines to run loops of trial and error at greater speed (Thomas, Kass, and Davarzani 2014). These smart, learning machines collaborate and interact with humans, thereby augmenting the latter's cognitive and collaborative capabilities.

The quest for higher productivity and competitiveness will continue to drive automation of nonroutine cognitive tasks through the development of artificial intelligence tools. This new phase of innovation is expected to replace jobs increasingly in services, R&D, logistics, and the professions. "Smart" production systems in industry and commercial agriculture are intended to fully automate and control the production process. This new technology is expected to replace jobs, especially in coordination, planning, and logistics, as sensors collect real-time data and feed it into a network of computers that analyze it and coordinate activities along the process ("Automation" 2016). Learning computers with self-improving algorithms will increasingly automate the tasks performed by professionals. Smart computers can provide diagnostics of similar or higher quality as those of an average radiologist. They can analyze texts and even draft articles for newspapers. These learning machines are expected to reduce demand for professions such as doctors, lawyers, linguists, journalists, and pilots, and also to transform the nature of tasks in these professions. Such collaborative worker-machine interactions require a higher level of autonomy, shifting focus from rule-following to value-finding.

This expected impact on labor markets has triggered a new debate in economics on the magnitude of jobs destruction, and a variety of estimation attempts have been made. Frey and Osborne (2013) explore the potential automatability of occupations (that is, the technical ease). They estimate that 47 percent of total US employment will be in a high-risk category "over the next decade or two." The comparable estimate for the UK is 35 percent, and studies for Germany and France produced similar results. Critics, however, argue that future automation is unlikely to destroy complete occupations. Because jobs vary within occupations, while some of the former may disappear, others will only change (Autor and Handel 2013). Studies analyzing jobs rather than occupations find significantly lower risks for job losses. Arntz, Gregory, and Zierahn (2016) find that automation will replace some tasks, which will fundamentally change the nature of jobs workers will perform, but the job itself is not at risk. They conclude that, on average, about 9 percent of jobs in Organisation for Economic Co-operation and Development (OECD) nations are at a high risk of being automated, with estimates ranging from 12 percent in Austria, Germany, and Spain to around 6 percent or less in Finland and Estonia.

Moreover, Balconi, Pozzali, and Viale (2007) identify technical limits to automation of intellectual and cognitive tasks. Michael Polanyi (1958) argues that the performance of a person in executing a particular task is based on procedural knowledge, and that this knowledge is tacit, in the sense that it cannot be articulated and codified, as it resides in the subconscious level. In the past, automation was possible when the tacit procedures were expressed in physical performance. Engineers and software developers could observe the sequence of actions a person performed while executing a task and develop algorithms for machines to simulate these sequences. Intellectual activities, however, are not expressed in observable, physical human actions, but are hidden in the brain. The performance of critical thinking, creativity, flexibility, judgment, common sense, and intuition cannot be observed, and therefore cannot be simulated with existing technologies. Since automation increases the importance of such tasks in many occupations, the rate of future automation may be limited by technical factors.

Fragmentation: Specialization and Relocation of Tasks   Another long-term pattern of technological change that can be observed historically is the fragmentation of the production process and the specialization in a limited set of tasks. Throughout history, this trend has been supported by technological and institutional change that has reduced transport, information, communication, and transaction costs. Relocation and the division of tasks generate specialization and agglomeration benefits that enhance productivity but destroy jobs.

At the early stages of industrialization, factories divided the work process into narrow sets of tasks. While a craftsperson producing customized goods and services had performed a broad range of different tasks in the workshop, the new mode of production in factories was based on division of labor. In a next step, firms specialized in particular tasks within local value chains. Several factories, each with its own specialization, processed inputs such as raw materials and parts and produced finished goods. Most recently, fragmentation of the production system expanded to the global level through outsourcing and offshoring, thereby exploiting the comparative advantages of different locations. The recent wave of globalization was supported, in particular, by declining transaction costs due to international institutions enforcing contracts and securing property rights, or ensuring data security, and by rapidly falling information and communication costs due to digitalization.

The trend of fragmentation is expected to continue in highly competitive global markets, although the next wave of outsourcing is likely to take place primarily in the service sector. While the early phase of globalization during the 1980s and '90s was dominated by manufacturing and reflected a tremendous increase in the trade of components and intermediate manufactures, new evidence suggests an increasing share of services in international trade. Examples of emerging services in global value chains are remote maintenance and repair services provided for digitized production systems such as Industry 4.0. Engineers at any place in the world with access to the internet will be able to undertake diagnostics when such digital systems break down, solve problems in the software domain, and inform technicians to repair hardware or computers and robots to replace broken physical parts. In addition, the division of tasks is expected to change, with R&D, finance, design, and marketing services shifting increasingly to developing countries with an educated and qualified young workforce, but wages one-third of those in developed countries.

Moreover, the potential for further fragmentation within the manufacturing sector is limited. Lall, Albaladejo, and Zhang (2004) point out that technologies differ in divisibility, and that the technical possibilities of separating production segments and placing them at different locations are limited in many sectors. While the transport vehicle industry, the electrical and electronics sectors, and the apparel sector demonstrated high divisibility and developed regional and global value chains, sectors using capital-intensive processing technologies—for example, basic metals (smelting and casting) or chemicals—show low potential for fragmentation of production systems.

In addition, insourcing of manufacturing jobs is a new trend in many developed countries. New machines are developed that have the potential to automate tasks that had, until that point, been outsourced and performed by workers in low-wage countries. This is, to some extent, the result of policies implemented in many developed countries to bring jobs back home. R&D and innovation policies support the development of machines that can reverse factor intensities, allowing advanced countries to regain comparative advantages and generate jobs in manufacturing while destroying jobs in low-wage countries and disrupting value chains. For example, recent inventions at MIT seem to provide the technological inputs required for developing robots that can perform sewing tasks such as stitching together garments, which had previously remained a job for "nimble fingers" and been outsourced to low-wage countries ("Made" 2015).

At the same time, newly emerging information and communication technologies reducing the costs of international data transfer and global governance enforcing international rules, standards, and agreements to secure data and cyberspace are expected to boost outsourcing of services to countries with a highly educated labor force but relatively low wages. Brown and Lauder (2013) expect "digital Taylorism" of business and professional service tasks within firms. Similar to Taylorism in manufacturing, these service tasks will be divided, modularized, and outsourced. Futurologists anticipate that the work of professions will be decomposed and jobs broken down into their component parts. While some of the tasks will still require expert advisers acting in traditional ways, many others will be standardized and relocated. Cloud sourcing and computer sourcing represent such new forms of service specialization. The former allows firms to access global labor markets in search of specialists and experts, and to exploit wage differences. In addition, firms increasingly use cloud computing to outsource IT tasks to specialized providers of IT services, which allows them to focus on their core tasks (Intuit 2008).

Increasing Complexity of Jobs

Technological change not only destroys jobs, but also induces fundamental changes in the nature and quality of jobs and occupations. While there are various ways of describing its quality, the International Labour Organization (ILO) (1990) defines a job as "a set of tasks and duties, performed, or meant to be performed, by one person, including for an employer or in self-employment." This definition allows the description of a job by the scope, nature, and diversity of tasks and properties that determine its complexity. Similar and related jobs can be grouped into occupations, which the ILO (1990) defines as a "set of jobs whose main tasks and duties are characterized by a high degree of similarity."

We describe jobs by their level of complexity, which is defined by the range, diversity, and nature of tasks to be performed. Complex jobs require workers to perform a wide range of distinct and complementary tasks at the intellectual, cognitive, interactive, and manual level. Most importantly, competent performance of a job requires the worker to develop "smart" routines in performing each of the tasks, as well as "meta" procedures that effectively coordinate, sequence, and integrate them. As explained above, procedural knowledge is tacit, in the sense that it cannot be articulated.

As described above, whenever the performance of such procedures is expressed in physical activities, it can be observed and simulated. The performance of many intellectual and cognitive tasks, however, especially the meta procedures, is not expressed in physical human actions and therefore cannot be observed. Consequently, the rules and procedures underpinning performance of intellectual tasks cannot be inferred from human actions, which makes it impossible for software developers to simulate them by algorithms and machines. As new technologies require workers to perform more intellectual, cognitive, and meta procedures, each period of automation and fragmentation increases the complexity of existing jobs at the machine-human interface and occupations in coordination, communication, and logistics, respectively. Complexity arises from the fact that tasks can neither be automated nor fragmented.

Industries: Increasing Complexity at High-Level Occupations   The history of technological change shows a long-term trend of increasing complexity in jobs. The development of new machines, automation, and fragmentation of production processes has been associated with an increase in jobs that require more and higher-level skills. Automation enhances job complexity, particularly at the machine/human interface. This has been identified as the "paradox of automation," where machinery increasingly demanded "highly-skilled, well-trained, well-practiced people to make systems resilient, acting as the last line of defence against the failures that will inevitably occur" (Baxter et al. 2012).

This trend will continue, with mobile robots, smart machines, and artificial intelligence to enhance the collaborative worker-machine interaction. Workers will use mobile robots and smart machines to augment rather than replace jobs. Managers working with smart machines that support day-to-day management activities and even take over routine decisions require more soft skills such as good judgment, creativity, and problem-solving—skills acquired mainly through experience. They will have to frame the questions the computers have to answer, address exceptional circumstances highlighted by increasingly intelligent algorithms, determine the targets and risk levels to be reflected, and learn to cope with ambiguity. Also, the nature of jobs in research, development, and design will become more experimental as digital modelling and simulation make experiments less expensive, and work processes will increasingly be structured around "design-build-test" cycles (Thomas, Kass, and Davarzani 2014; Dewhurst and Willmott 2014).

The complexity of jobs in managing, coordinating, and communicating within global production networks will increase as well. Globalization through outsourcing of business services such as crowd and computer sourcing, research collaboration, and new global business models emerging in the Industrial Internet of Things (IIoT), will enhance the complexity of coordination procedures. Managers, workers, and administrative staff will have to be able to collaborate across countries and cultures and perform complex communication tasks across language and cultural domains.

Skilled Crafts Sector: Increasing Complexity in Medium-Level Occupations The skilled crafts represent another occupational group where new technologies and innovations enhance the complexity of jobs. The crafts mode was the dominant organization of production prior to the industrial revolution, the core of which is often seen as the transition from the crafts mode to the mass production mode. Historical experience shows that this was indeed the case in those countries that destroyed the traditional institutions of the crafts sector, such as guilds and their apprenticeship systems. However, a number of industrialized countries, such as Germany, Austria, Switzerland, and Denmark, reformed rather than abolished the traditional institutions, and the industrial sector evolved along with a skilled crafts sector. A major characteristic of skilled craft occupations is their embeddedness in a system that provides training in all relevant skills and competences of the occupation. Skilled craftspeople typically belong to the middle level of the occupational and job hierarchy.

The skilled craft sector may itself be divided into three different sectors. The first of these, the artisanal production sector, produces goods for local markets that meet demand for individual tastes and needs. The makers of these products—food, beverages, garments, blown glass, jewelry—compete with the industries. The second, the industry-related crafts sector, provides customized products and tailor-made solutions based on a client's particular needs and specifications. Occupations in construction and in installation of industrial machines and equipment provide customized goods and services to industries. The third, craft occupations, provide customized and tailor-made goods and services to consumers that cannot be standardized, as, for example, in the repair, health, and beauty sectors.

Jobs in the skilled craft occupations are complex, as workers need to perform a broad range of diverse tasks. These include routine and nonroutine manual and cognitive tasks such as interacting with clients, competences such as performing in a reliable and committed manner, and good judgment. These actions cannot be automated and fragmented. Builders of musical instruments, for example, require an ample set of knowledge about materials and tools, a good ear for sounds, an adequate sense of touch, the competence to solve problems, and interactive skills to deal with clients. A carpenter producing a piece of furniture according to the specifications of a particular customer must have well-integrated and sophisticated procedures in order to deal with clients, understand their expectations, design innovative products, select materials, calculate costs and prices, and solve problems arising while performing the tasks (Nübler 2016).

Innovation in the craft sector is reflected not in automation, but in the use of new technologies such as computers and the internet and advanced tools and instruments to upgrade work processes and product quality. These tools establish a competitive advantage, as craftspeople tend to compete more in "craftsmanship" than in prices and costs.

Sennett (2008) argues that "craftsmanship" is based on "the skills to do things well" and the "desire of doing a job well for its own sake," and that these competences and mindsets are major sources of innovation and change. Innovation is driven by the aspiration and competence to perform tasks at high levels, to find individual solutions, and to meet demand for customized products. Sennett asserts that the competent craftsman searches for new solutions even when repairing. In the craft sector, the impetus for innovation comes largely from a strong link between firms and their customers when tailor-made problem solutions need to be found (Astor, Bucksteeg, and Pfeiffer 2006; Womack, Jones, and Roos 1990).

New technologies will continue to enhance the complexity of jobs in both industries and the crafts sector. In industries, they will replace tasks in the medium-level occupations but enhance the complexity of jobs in the higher-level occupations. This will contribute to the polarization of jobs observed in many countries. By contrast, in the crafts sector, new technologies enhance the complexity of jobs at the middle occupational levels. This suggests that their impact on occupational structures will be different for countries with a strong skilled crafts sector and those without such sectors. Job polarization may not be an issue in the former economies.

Evidence from the United States and Canada shows that new craft activities are already mushrooming in the "new artisan economy" (Intuit 2008; Katz 2014; "Rise" 2014; Slothower 2015). Skilled workers start their own businesses by recombining their technical skills and knowledge with advanced technologies and their passion for a particular trade or occupation. There are fashion consultants, landscape designers, and producers of cheese, beer, and chocolate—local products with a new taste for local customers. The *Financial Times* reports that, despite the drop in consumption of beer in Europe by 8.5 percent since the recession, the number of European breweries has soared over the past five years by 73 percent. Almost 100 percent of the new entrants are microbreweries producing specialty or "craft" beers.

The new crafts economy has the potential to create good jobs for the middle class. Katz (2014) even suggests reforming the US education system and expanding liberal-arts education in order to equip young people with broad competences to enable them to enter the craft sector. New materials and new technologies such as 3D printing and mobile robots are expected to open up vast opportunities for the sector to innovate and to generate good jobs at the middle occupational levels. It allows craftspeople to produce tailor-made forms as demanded by clients, as well as forms that cannot be created through traditional methods such as carving, cutting, or molding. Moreover, this technology can produce objects with zero lead time, on demand, and in response to customer orders when and where it is needed.

Job Creation: Product Innovation and Market Expansion

While productivity-enhancing process innovations destroy jobs, their effects on productivity, working time, and demand for capital and software also have the potential to trigger new economic activities and create jobs. There are indeed various mechanisms that can channel such changes (Vivarelli 2007).

Income and Market Expansion Effects   Technology-induced productivity growth, if translated into higher wages and reduced prices, will enhance demand for domestic products and expand output. Furthermore, lower costs will enhance competitiveness, while higher profit stimulates investment that will lead to further productivity gains through innovation and scale economies. These income and market expansion effects have the potential to compensate for employment losses due to process innovations (Vivarelli 2007; Acemoglu and Restrepo 2016).

Expansion of Capital Goods and the Technology-Producing Sector   The same process innovations that displace workers in the user industries create demand for workers in the producer industries. The new robots and smart machines need to be developed, designed, built, maintained, and repaired. The fragmentation of production systems, the Internet of Things, Industry 4.0, digital Taylorism, driverless cars, and the like will increase demand for the construction of new infrastructure, transport equipment, and IT equipment, as well as increasingly complex software and new institutions. The rising demand in the capital goods industry has created new jobs for scientists, engineers, technicians, software developers, IT experts, and managers. In other words, as process technologies become more capital-intensive, knowledge-intensive, and complex, demand for skilled workers increases, which establishes a complementary relationship between capital and human capital. New occupations will emerge, in particular at the intersection of professions, software, and machines, such as big data architects and analysts, cloud services specialists, software developers, and digital marketing professionals—occupations that hardly existed just a few years ago (Frey 2014). Susskind and Susskind (2015) predict that a range of new legal roles will be created at the intersection of software and law, such as legal knowledge engineer, legal technologist, project manager, risk manager, and process analyst.

Declining Working Hours and Demand for Leisure Activities   Declining working hours have been a major effect of the implementation of labor saving process technologies. This has led to increasing demand for leisure-related activities—sports, health, recreation, tourism, music, TVs, computer games, restaurants, fairs, museums, and the do-it-yourself movement—a wide range of product innovations, entire new leisure industries and services, and the creation of new jobs. Evidence also shows that the leisure industries have become increasingly technology-intensive, and hence, its jobs have become increasingly complex (Posner 2011). The potential of future demand for leisure activities to increase depends on the translation of productivity into reduced working time rather than unemployment. Moreover, the distribution of productivity gains arising from new production technologies to consumers is critical to ensure rising purchasing power and demand.

Technology Spillover and New Business Models New scientific knowledge opens "exploitable opportunities" not only for process technologies, but also for the development of new products. Research and development as well as creative entrepreneurs designing and developing fundamentally new goods and services have the potential to create new jobs. The IIoT and Big Data have created a new manufacturing-cum-service business model in which firms combine manufacturing with data creation, which is leading to product innovations. For example, Michelin has developed tires with sensors to collect information on road conditions, temperature, and speed; this gives the company the opportunity to provide services to truck fleet managers to reduce fuel consumption and costs. At the same time, software enterprises such as Google have combined new technologies to expand into manufacturing by developing a driverless car (Daugherty et al. 2015).

Will this time be different? These compensation effects were generated by the intended and unintended consequences of process technologies. They enhanced demand for existing products and triggered demand for new goods and services, which created new industries and jobs in increasingly sophisticated occupations. These effects, however, were not created "automatically" by market forces. They came about because increasing productivity was shared in the form of higher income and reduced working time, leading to increased demand. Moreover, enterprises learned to compete in capital goods industries and the newly developing consumer industries. This time will not be different if countries can generate new social and economic demand and productive capacities to enter new industries and create good jobs.

Empirical Evidence: Country-Specific Impact on Jobs

Empirical evidence from cross-country studies and the analysis of the craft sector in Germany demonstrate significant differences in the impact of new technologies on jobs. The reason for this is that the nature and rate of innovation and its diffusion within the economy are shaped by local conditions, which "determin[e] what kinds of inventions . . . product characteristics and factor-saving biases . . . will be profitable to develop and exploit" (Rosenberg 1993, 111). Moreover, the innovation behavior of firms differs across industries and some sectors provide more opportunities to automate or outsource tasks than others (Dosi 1982; Malerba and Orsenigo 1996; Marsili and Verspagen 2012). Empirical evidence also shows that innovation behavior and job-creating compensation effects are shaped by the dynamic capabilities embodied in the knowledge base of societies (Vivarelli 2007; Calvino and Virgillito 2016).

Cross-Country Studies: Robotization, Globalization, and Job Losses

Two recent studies provide evidence on the impact of robotization (automation) and global value chains (fragmentation) on jobs and occupational structures in different countries. Both studies refer to the time frame between the mid-1990s and the end of the 2000s, a period of rapid digital automation and globalization.

The cross-country study by Graetz and Michaels (2015) analyzes the impact of robotization on productivity, wages, and job structure in seventeen developed countries and fourteen different industries between 1993 and 2007. It finds significant differences in the density of industrial robots (measured by the number of robots per million hours worked) across industries, with the highest density observed in the automobile and electronics industries. These differences were larger across industries than countries, which highlights the relevance of the industrial structure in explaining a country's rate of robotization. The study finds, moreover, that all countries experienced increases in productivity and wages; however, it seems that not all were able to translate this into demand and market expansion to the same extent.

A further analysis of the relationship between industrial robotization and manufacturing employment shows that the former has no statistical relationship with the change of the latter. Data show that, despite experiencing high growth in robot density between 1993 and 2007, Germany, Denmark, Italy, and the Republic of Korea (South Korea) lost significantly fewer jobs in manufacturing (measured by manufacturing employment as a share of total employment) than did the United States and UK, two countries with much lower growth in robot density in the same time period. This suggests that countries such as Germany experienced high growth in robotization largely due to their comparatively large car and electronics industry, but that the job losses were compensated for with higher competitiveness, market expansion, and growth of the capital goods industry. As a result, the net loss in manufacturing employment was low.

A study by Timmer, Los, and de Vries (2014) estimates the impact of participation in global value chains (GVC) on employment between 1995 and 2008. They measure the change in GVC-related jobs as a share of all workers in the economy for twenty-one countries (the European nations, the United States, Japan, Canada, Australia, and the Republic of Korea). GVC-related jobs are directly and indirectly involved in the production of manufacturing goods. With the exception of Germany, where the share of GVC-related employment remained stable, all of these countries saw a decline in GVC-related workers. What stands out are the massive decline and job losses in the United States, the United Kingdom, and Japan. As a result, in 2008, 26 percent of German workers were involved in the global production of manufactures, by far the highest share across all advanced countries. This share was lowest in the United States and UK, with 11.1 and 12.6 percent, respectively.

Most interestingly, the data provided by this study show that countries differ in their patterns of change. One striking difference is in the change in occupational structures. (See figure 3.1.) Most countries show a decrease in low-skilled jobs and an increase in skills-intensive jobs. The difference lies in the change of middle-skilled occupations. In most European countries—e.g., France, Germany, Spain, and Italy—the number of GVC-related jobs in the middle-skills occupations increased, while this number decreased in United States, United Kingdom, Japan, Republic of Korea,

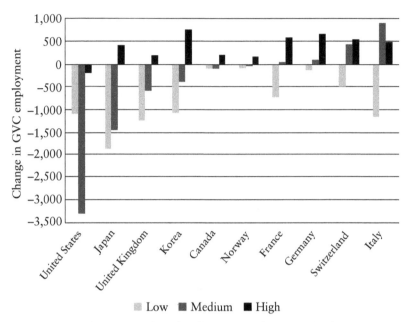

Figure 3.1 Change in number of workers employed in GVC-related activities producing manufacturing goods, in thousands, by skill type, 1995–2008. Author's calculation based on Timmer et al. 2015 (World Input-Output Database).

and Canada. For example, in European countries, the number of workers involved in the production of manufactures in GVC declined by 1.8 million between 1995–2008. This net job loss was the result of an increase in the number of high-skilled jobs of almost four million, while medium-skilled jobs barely grew and more than six million low-skilled jobs were lost. Timmer et al. (2013, 4) therefore conclude, first, that globalization in these countries resulted in an increasing specialization in skills-intensive tasks, but did not contribute to the polarization of the occupational structure. Second, they conclude that European countries had the "ability to realise employment growth in activities that are productive and relatively well-paid in a highly competitive international environment."

The change in occupational structure in the UK, Japan, and Korea was similar to the one in European countries in that they experienced a decrease in low-skilled and an increase in high-skilled occupations. Because the decline in middle-skilled occupations has always been slower than that for low-skilled jobs, this pattern of change may also be characterized as nonpolarizing. This leaves the United States with a very distinct and unique pattern of change, because employment in GVC-related manufacturing decreased in all three jobs categories—low-, medium-, and high-skilled jobs—with the medium-skilled occupations losing the most. Globalization therefore had a dramatic effect on job loss and job polarization in the USA. The decrease in medium-skilled jobs was almost three times as high as the decrease in low-skilled jobs. This pattern of change in production systems contributed to the country's high productivity growth between 1995 and 2004; however, GVC-related jobs were lost at a massive scale, particularly in the middle-skilled occupational categories. These findings from the US labor market confirm the analysis of Autor, Levy, and Murnane (2003), who identified a strong job polarization effect in the United States since the 1980s.

The German Experience: Middle Occupations in the Crafts Sector

The German experience may be at least partially explained by the strong crafts sector in its economy. Empirical evidence shows that this sector was able to maintain its competitive advantages vis-à-vis industries and, even more importantly, a new skilled crafts sector emerged as a complement to industries, thereby creating many good jobs in the middle occupations during periods of technological change. The share of skilled crafts in employment displays a remarkable continuity between 1968 and 2012: 15 percent in 1968, 14 percent in 1977, 16 percent in 1995, and 12.5 percent in 2012. Most interestingly, technological change has affected the different occupational groups within the crafts sector in different ways. Between 1967 and 2012, the high end of the craft sector (that is, firms providing services and specific solutions to industries) experienced a significant increase in employment. The growth of this sector was driven by the demand of industries for customized machinery and specialized services. This high-level craftsmanship drove industries to adopt new technologies and innovate, an important factor in German industries' maintaining a high level of competitiveness in global markets.

Moreover, occupations in the health and beauty sectors remained stable. However, the structure shifted from lower-level to more complex and sophisticated jobs. New occupations, such as dental technicians and opticians, represent the fastest growing segments within the skilled crafts, and these rely on advanced machinery and computer algorithms, including 3D printing, to create tailor-made products such as dental implants. Finally, clothing and textiles and food and craft sectors, which compete with the industrial production mode, experienced a prolonged period of contraction due to inexpensive mass production.

The craft sector will also play an important role in the future by generating good jobs at the middle occupational level. German labor market data show that the middle-skilled jobs in these occupations (e.g., plumber, refrigeration technician, heating technician, electro machine builder) are in high demand and a severe shortage of many others is predicted by 2020 (Zika and Maier 2015).

Social Capabilities for Innovations and Job Creation

How can we explain these differences across countries in the pattern of innovative behavior and industrial change? Why are some countries more successful in innovating, enhancing competitiveness, and transforming economies for new jobs? Economic conditions are highlighted as one important determinant of the nature and scope of innovations. Countries differ in factor endowment, productive capacity, industrial structure, and comparative advantages, which determine cost structures and, therefore, which technologies and products are profitable. The fundamental issue, however, is what enables a country to take advantage of new technological opportunities and create a dynamic process of product innovation and productive transformation that generates more and better jobs.

Societies differ in their capabilities to generate a dynamic process of innovations, diversification into new goods and services, and patterns of productive transformation that generate good jobs. Hence, while markets drive the search for technological change and inventions, they are not operating in a vacuum: they are embedded in societies. Market outcomes are therefore also shaped by social capabilities. The relevance of social capabilities to technological and economic development has been widely recognized by economic historians (Abramovitz 1986; List 1841) and evolutionary economists (Chang 2010; Cimoli, Dosi, and Stiglitz 2009; Lall 1992). In other words, the impact of technological change on the future of jobs is not deterministic, but is influenced by the capabilities that a society has accumulated through past experience, and by those it will develop in the future.

The Concept of Social Capabilities

The ILO has developed a knowledge-based theory to explain where capabilities reside, how they are created, and how they shape structural and technological change (Nübler 2014). Social capabilities play two important roles in a country's techno-economic development process. First, they determine the technologies, products, and industries that a country can easily develop. These capabilities reside in the knowledge base of societies, and they are embodied in the particular mix of cultural, formal, and technical knowledge of the labor force. They are shaped largely by socially shared knowledge systems: the formal knowledge provided by the education system, the vocational and technical knowledge acquired by the labor force in the production and training system, and the cultural knowledge and belief systems acquired in social networks such as families and communities (Nübler 2014). The distinct sets of formal and informal knowledge elements embodied in a society determines the nature of product innovations a country can feasibly implement.

Second, social capabilities also determine a society's competence to manage the processes of change, search for new solutions, mobilize creativity, entrepreneurship, and craftsmanship, and sustain this process. Institutions are the carriers of such collective competences. How well they perform these tasks depends on the rules and procedures they provide. Societies need to develop "smart" institutions in order to create innovation processes that create more and better jobs. For example, Acemoglu and Robinson (2012) have shown that inclusive institutions benefiting large parts of society have also been central drivers of technological change. Schumpeter (1911) highlighted the important role of social institutions in explaining differences across societies in "entrepreneurial spirit" and their ability to drive processes of creative destruction. The development of craftsmanship in the labor force depends on "smart" apprenticeship institutions that enforce high-quality training in broad competences of an occupation and high status in society (Nübler 2016).

Knowledge structures and institutions are the memories of society, and the development of capabilities is therefore fundamentally a learning process at the collective level. Societies learn in two fundamental ways: first, by enriching, broadening, and diversifying the knowledge base and transforming their shared knowledge and belief systems and second, by transforming institutions and the rules that guide individual and organizational behavior. Societal learning may be evolutionary, resulting in incremental enrichment of knowledge sets and capabilities and the development of similar products. Learning, however, can also be revolutionary when societies fundamentally change their belief and knowledge systems and institutional rules that may enable economies to leapfrog into fundamentally new goods and services (Nübler 2016).

The critical issue is how such societal learning processes are triggered and what forces drive learning. History shows that emerging technologies and the new opportunities they open up have triggered and supported the evolution of new ideas, philosophies, ideologies, expectations, and attitudes. For example, economic historians claim that industrial development in Western countries was triggered and sustained by the emergence of a new belief system (McCloskey 2010; Mokyr 2002). The new ideas of the Enlightenment were developed in a broad debate by prominent thinkers such as John Locke, Voltaire, Jean-Jacques Rousseau, David Hume, Immanuel Kant, Denis Diderot, and Benjamin Franklin, all of whom saw themselves as "educators of societies." The new ideas fundamentally changed how people thought about business, exchange, innovation and profit, human liberty and dignity, and the role of education and training. It drove the creation and wide diffusion of new scientific and technological knowledge. As countries industrialized, education systems were transformed to disseminate these new knowledge and belief systems and provide new competences in new occupations, enabling R&D to generate new scientific knowledge and new industries to develop (Nübler 2016). Another example is the belief system that supported the development of the so-called consumer society and the Golden Age phase of the 1950–'60s. Fromm (1976) explains how modern society has become materialistic, preferring "having" to "being." He mentions the great promise of unlimited happiness, freedom, material abundance, and domination of nature, and the social status that was increasingly linked to "having." These new ideas transformed belief systems in Western societies and their consumption patterns and lifestyles.

On the other hand, societal learning processes are endogenously induced by the unintended consequences of technological change (Nübler, 2016). Unemployment, rising inequality, economic bubbles, financial crises, technological anxiety, and deteriorating working conditions have disruptive impacts on societal textures and social cohesion, while negative effects on the natural environment such as climate change or rising sea levels threaten people's health and livelihoods. These unintended consequences of technological change triggered learning processes, in particular when societies were no longer willing to tolerate the impact of these changes. Learning is expressed in new institutions to prevent, mitigate, and even reverse these negative consequences; they create new social and political demand for different types of goods and services and different directions and rates of R&D, invention, and innovation.

Karl Polanyi (1944) described the Great Transformation toward market economies as a process of social and economic change. Polanyi argues that the development of a new economic system has always been accompanied by a change in the organization of society itself. The evolutions of market economies were only possible because market societies evolved. While the self-regulating markets brought boundless and unregulated changes to societies, human society would have been annihilated if it had not created protective countermoves. These resulted in new institutions such as trade unions and factory laws. A "deep-seated movement sprang into being to resist the pernicious effects of a market-controlled economy" (Polanyi 1944, 76).

So, the question of whether technological change will be different this time and lead to a jobless future needs to be phrased differently: Will societies be able to trigger a learning process that expands capabilities to innovate and creates new demand structures so that new and better jobs will be created in the emerging activities and sectors? The challenge is to revise the knowledge base of society for a dynamic process of job-creating productive transformation.

Educational Attainment Structures, Economic Structures, and Jobs

Education plays a central role in generating capabilities for developing new and more sophisticated industries that create good jobs in manufacturing.

The ILO has explored the link among education, industrial structures, and technological advancement, and has identified the Educational Attainment Structure (EAS) as an important carrier of capabilities that shape structural transformation (Nübler 2016). The EAS measures the share of the labor force that has graduated from primary, lower secondary, upper secondary, and postsecondary education.

Figure 3.2 demonstrates significant differences in EAS across countries and regions, but also how similar they are between neighboring countries or countries belonging to the same language group. This typology of EAS finds the distinction between the "strong middle EAS" and the "missing middle EAS" particularly relevant. The strong middle EAS has a bell-shaped curve with lower or secondary education having the highest share. It is found in Germanic-language countries such as Germany, Austria, and Switzerland, the transition countries, and the Scandinavian countries, as well as in Korea and Hong Kong. By contrast, the missing middle EAS is characterized by a low share of upper secondary education and a significantly higher share of postsecondary education (more than 20 percent). Missing middle EASes in different forms are found in the United Kingdom and Japan, as well as in the United States, Canada, New Zealand, and Latinate-language countries such as France, Spain, Portugal, and Italy.

These various EASes provide different capabilities and options for structural and technological transformation. In particular, evidence shows that countries with a strong middle EAS have also developed and maintained strong manufacturing sectors, while the missing middle EAS countries tend to have lower shares in manufacturing. (See figure 3.3.)

The Industrial Advance Index (IAI) is a composite index taking into account the share of manufacturing in GDP and in exports (UNIDO 2005; Nübler 2013). The median IAI for all missing and strong middle EAS countries is 0.53 (average 0.52). Figure 3.3 shows that most countries with a missing middle EAS have IAI values below 0.53, while most of those with a strong middle EAS demonstrate IAI values above 0.53. The median within the group of strong middle EAS countries is 0.58, while it is only 0.52 in the missing middle EAS countries. The technological advance index (TAI)—the share of medium- and high-technology products within the manufacturing sector—shows no systematic differences between the strong and missing middle countries. The overall median is 0.57. It is 0.56 in the strong middle EAS countries and 0.58 in the missing middle EAS countries.

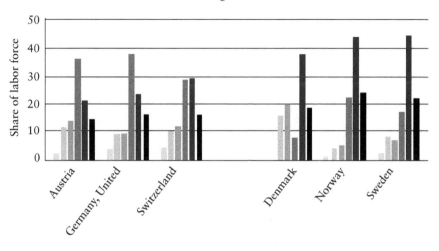

Strong middle

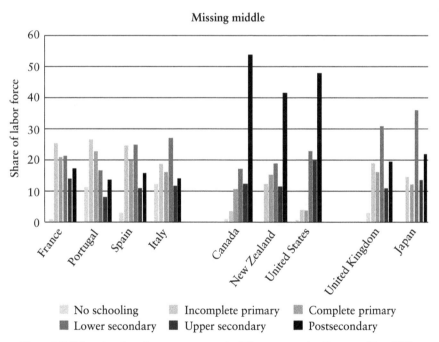

Missing middle

Figure 3.2 Educational attainment structures in different countries. Barro and Lee 2013; author's calculations.

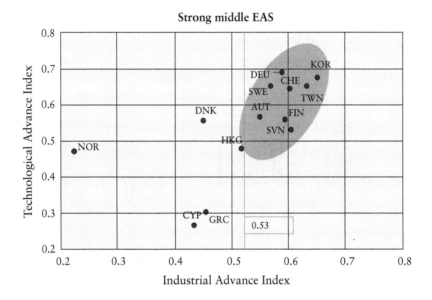

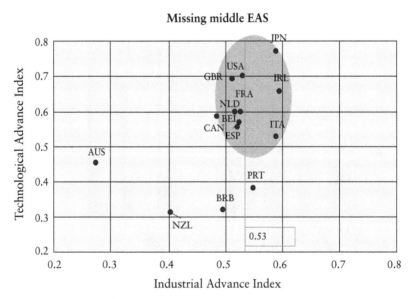

Figure 3.3 Technological and industrial structures, by missing-middle and strong-middle EAS. UNIDO 2005; Nübler 2016.

In other words, these findings suggest that developed countries with a strong middle EAS differ from countries with a missing middle EAS in their capabilities to sustain and develop new manufacturing industries. Moreover, strong middle EAS countries tend to have a slight advantage in capabilities to drive medium and high technology. In this context, it is interesting to note that, in developing countries, strong middle and missing middle EAS countries differ substantially in both capabilities. Strong middle countries show both higher IAI and TAI when compared to missing middle EAS countries.

Historical analysis shows that the evolution of the education attainment structure is path-dependent. Such path-dependencies are enforced by social belief systems, and therefore the values societies attach to different types of education and training. For example, a publication by the Brookings Institution argues that, in the United States, "there is an insistence that every student attends a four-year college . . . and few parents want their children to train for manufacturing jobs" (Karsten and West 2015). This statement reflects the US society's long-standing beliefs that the path to upward mobility is through general education. Moreover, these attitudes give low status to jobs in manual and middle-level occupations. Hence, while industrial policies in the United States invigorate jobs in manufacturing, an estimated two million vacant manufacturing jobs cannot be filled in industries. The US Bureau of Labor Statistics (2017) reports that currently more than five million vacancies cannot be filled—largely skilled-trades positions such as plumbers, chefs, butchers, bakers, mechanics, and electricians, as well as executive secretaries, teachers, sales representatives, managers, nurses, and technicians.

Transforming Societies for a "Golden Age of Job Creation"

The evolutionary approach analyzes the long-term dynamics of technological change and of the job-creating and job destroying process (Dosi 1982; Perez 1983; Perez 2002; Schumpeter 1911). Perez (1983) introduces the framework of shifting techno-economic paradigms that suggest that technological changes come in long waves and cycles, and that phases of productivity-enhancing innovations and job destruction are followed by phases of product innovations that create fundamental new goods, services, and jobs. This second phase, which Perez (2002) calls the Golden

Age, has each time led to interconnected innovations—"technical and organizational and managerial innovations . . . opening up an unusually wide range of investment and profit opportunities" (Freeman and Perez 1998, 47–48). This is the phase where enterprises create value by developing new products and markets, where new industries replace old ones as drivers of growth, and where highly dynamic processes generate new jobs at a massive scale.

Most important, the transition into the second phase cannot be achieved by markets: it has always been a socio-political choice. The reason is that creating a Golden Age phase requires a fundamental transformation of economies and this can only be achieved by transforming societies, which is essentially a process of collective learning. Perez shows that each time a country has made the transition from the first to the second phase, the end of the first was marked by high productivity gains, rising inequality, financial bubbles, and job destruction. These are the intended and unintended consequences of revolutionary technological changes that trigger a process of societal learning, the development of new institutions, and new regulatory frameworks that generate new social and political demand.

Based on her framework of historical recurrences, Perez (2013) argues that countries are currently at the turning point that needs social and political choice, a new social consensus of societies about the direction of technological change, and new institutions that support the transition to new consumption and production patterns. Such fundamental changes require new belief systems that change people's thinking about work and motivation to work, the meaning and value of leisure, and distribution of productivity gains. Declining working hours create jobs by redistributing work as well as by increasing leisure time. This challenges societies to develop a new understanding of leisure, and to value leisure activities that contribute to well-being and help societies to meet their aspirations. While Keynes, in his 1930 article "Economic Possibilities for Our Grandchildren," famously predicted a future where the workweek would shrink greatly, liberating time for pursuit of "the arts of life as well as the activities of purpose," working hours have dropped only modestly in recent years (OECD 2017, 373). We can go even further and argue with Polanyi (1944) that market economies are but one model of organizing production, work, and distribution, and that, therefore, the so-called standard forms of employment represent just one specific model that will change with changing technologies and societies. For example, digital technologies create new opportunities to organize work in a more flexible manner, allowing workers to become self-employed and develop new activities and income opportunities. This enhances people's choices; however, new institutions and regulations are needed to provide social security and ensure workers' rights.

So, the question of whether this time will be different is about societal learning and social transformation—whether intended and unintended consequences created by the first phase of the current techno-economic paradigm of robots, digitization, and globalization will lead to a new social consensus, new social demand, and new social capabilities for the massive creation of new tasks, activities, and work to meet people's aspirations. The emerging debates, movements, and institutions suggest that societies have entered such a learning process. The debates over climate change and the recent international agreement achieved in Paris, high and rising inequality, and the role of the state in creating mission-oriented innovation policies and promoting structural transformation in economies have gained strong momentum. They challenge existing belief and knowledge systems and national and global institutions to support societies in achieving a new social consensus.

Analysis shows that market forces will continue to drive the search for new technologies and inventions; however, the nature, scope, and rate of innovations, and their diffusion within the economy, are expected to differ significantly between countries. The future of jobs is therefore not deterministic, but determined by country-specific conditions. While economic conditions are important, social capabilities play a central role in driving the direction and dynamics of technological change, strengthening market expansion and compensation effects, and managing the transition into the transformative and job-creating innovation phase of the current techno-economic paradigm.

A fundamental message is that markets cannot generate such processes. Such transitions are based on socio-political choices. In other words, the future of work needs to be shaped, which requires deliberate choices and policies. Those countries that proactively shape this process will create good jobs.

Education and training policies are challenged with creating a knowledge base in the labor force that enables the economy to develop and implement new technologies and to achieve multiple objectives. Governments whose aim is to promote jobs in existing and new industries, particularly at the middle occupational levels, are challenged with developing or maintaining a strong share of upper secondary graduates in the labor force, combined with high-quality and broad occupational training. Such a knowledge base has the potential to drive the growth of the industrial and craft sectors and of good jobs at the middle occupational levels. Such shifts require a fundamental change in society's attitudes, and the value and status given to vocational and technical training and occupations. Changing these shared mindsets is so important because they shape people's educational, training, and occupational choices.

Productive transformation policies to support the growth of targeted industries with high potential to generate good jobs require a consistent policy package. Investment, trade, and macroeconomic policies need to be closely aligned with education, training, and labor market policies. Sustained growth in productivity and good jobs requires diversification of the economy, the expansion of high-tech activities, and a dynamic growth in domestic and foreign demand.

Moreover, policies are challenged with guiding and influencing the direction of new technologies, the nature of innovation, and its diffusion in order to achieve social and political goals. Mission-oriented science, technology, and innovation policies focus on promoting the development of transformative technologies and innovations, as these will open up wide opportunities to develop new industries, create high productivity gains, and generate many good jobs.

While process technologies enhance productivity and destroy jobs, policies to redistribute productivity gains and work strengthen the compensation effects and the creation of new jobs. Fiscal and wage policies to share high productivity gains with workers increase purchasing power and demand for existing and new products. This effect is strengthened by policies intended to distribute work more equally within the labor force, which increases demand for leisure activities. Redistribution of productivity gains to creative entrepreneurs supports investment in start-ups and job creation, in particular for middle-skilled workers. Fiscal policies will thus contribute to a reversal of job polarization and to a reduction in inequality.

Managing the process of technological, social, and economic transformation to shape the future of jobs requires a comprehensive strategy. This involves the forging of a new social consensus on the objectives and direction of innovations and the future aspired to by societies. Social dialogue between all groups in a society is key in generating such a process of societal learning and forging a new social contract. Governments are challenged with developing institutions to facilitate and drive social dialogue and consensus-finding procedures.

4

EXPANDING JOB OPPORTUNITIES THROUGH GLOBAL GREEN GROWTH

Robert Pollin

What will be the opportunities, moving forward, for people throughout the world being able to work at decent jobs—jobs that pay living wages, with reasonable conditions, and with effective ladders for advancement? To be sure, as Martin Ford's paper in this volume explains, robotization has led to employment losses for millions of people in recent decades and it is likely that this pattern of labor-displacing technical change will accelerate in the future. But this does not mean that overall employment opportunities will necessarily contract. We are facing a range of massive economic challenges in the global economy in areas including health care, education, infrastructure, and housing. Addressing these challenges is capable of making these sectors major new engines of global job creation.

Most of this paper is adapted from my 2015 book *Greening the Global Economy* (Cambridge, MA: MIT Press), in particular, chapter 6.

The imperative of building a global green energy economy is the most important of these challenges. In the aftermath of the November 2015 UN-sponsored Paris Climate Change Summit, there is now an official global consensus that climate change poses a fundamental threat to human and ecological well-being. This represents a major step forward toward the imperative of advancing viable climate stabilization programs on a global basis. More specifically, it is widely recognized that annual global carbon dioxide (CO_2) emissions must fall by at least 40 percent within twenty years and by 80 percent within thirty-five years to stabilize the global mean temperature at 2° Celsius above preindustrial levels. Making these dramatic emissions reductions will entail sharply diminishing the global economy's reliance on burning fossil fuels to produce energy and to replace fossil fuel energy sources with massive new investments in energy efficiency and clean, renewable energy sources.

At the same time, there remains a widely held belief that controlling climate change and expanding job opportunities are necessarily conflicting goals that, therefore, impose severe and unavoidable trade-offs in all regions of the world. This position is wrong. In a series of recently published research studies, my coauthors and I have developed a unified program that can realistically achieve dramatic reductions in global carbon dioxide emissions, while at the same time generating widespread and broadly-shared economic benefits.[1] In particular, this program is capable, by 2035, of driving down global CO_2 emissions by roughly 40 percent relative to current levels. But, as I will show, this climate stabilization program is equally capable of expanding employment opportunities in all regions of the globe, relative to an economic trajectory that maintains our current dependence on a fossil fuel–dominated energy infrastructure.

It is especially critical that developing countries be able to raise living standards for working people and the poor as the global clean energy transformation proceeds. Reducing opportunities for higher living standards in the name of climate stabilization is simply not viable. Most importantly, there is no reasonable standard of fairness that can justify working people and the poor sacrificing opportunities for rising living standards to achieve climate stabilization. In addition, any climate stabilization program that would entail reducing mass living standards will face formidable political resistance. This, in turn, will create unacceptable delays in advancing an effective climate stabilization program. My aim is to show how the clean energy transformation, employment expansion, and poverty reduction can advance in mutually supportive ways, throughout the world.

By itself, the project of building a global green energy economy will not generate enough new jobs to offset all sources of job losses through robotization. But it is capable of countering such job losses to a significant degree, while concurrently advancing a viable solution to climate change, the single most critical issue facing global well-being now and into the future. A global green growth program is also the most effective possible framework for advancing full employment policies for countries at all levels of development. In turn, as I discuss further below, a commitment to full employment—i.e., to creating through public policy an abundance of jobs with at least decent wages, benefits, and working conditions—is both a critical and a feasible policy goal, even after we allow for the challenges.

The 1.5 Percent Solution and Jobs

The basics of my green growth proposal are simple. The global economy can achieve a 40 percent absolute reduction in CO_2 emissions by 2035 if most countries—especially those with either large GDPs or populations—devote between 1.5 and 2 percent per year of GDP to investments in energy efficiency and clean, low-emissions renewable energy sources. The consumption of oil, coal, and natural gas will also need to fall by about 35 percent over this same twenty-year period, i.e., at an average 2.2 percent rate per year. In its essentials, just to emphasize again, this is the *entire* global clean energy program I am proposing.

The major investments in energy efficiency and clean renewable energy necessary to stabilize the climate—again, amounting to between 1.5 and 2 percent of global GDP per year—will also drive job expansion in all regions of the world, for countries at all levels of development. If this is true, what then is the basis for the widely held view that protecting the environment and expanding job opportunities are necessarily in conflict, creating severe and unavoidable trade-offs?

Aside from posturing by fossil fuel industry spokespeople or pure ideologues, two serious issues contribute to the confusion. The first is that all modern economies, regardless of their current level of development, need an abundance of affordable energy in order to grow at healthy rates and thereby expand job opportunities. Limiting the supply or raising the price of oil, coal, and natural gas would, by definition, make fossil fuel energy more scarce and costly. Employment opportunities would then have to fall, according to this logic.

However, as I have documented in my book *Greening the Global Economy* and elsewhere, the full energy mix resulting from twenty years of investments will include roughly 30 percent from clean renewables. This is after efficiency standards will have dramatically increased. The evidence I present in this book shows there is no reason to expect that the costs to consumers of obtaining the services they seek by consuming energy would have to rise under this scenario. This is, first of all, because investments in energy efficiency will generate major savings on expenditures to achieve a given level of energy services. In addition, most clean renewable energy prices will be at rough parity with or lower than those from fossil fuels and nuclear power.

The second issue is that building a clean energy economy will be bad for *fossil fuel industry* jobs specifically. In the United States, for example, this position was advanced aggressively regarding the proposed Keystone pipeline expansion project. It is a given that expanding the existing Keystone pipeline system that runs from the Canadian border through the Midwest to Louisiana would have created jobs—probably between two and four thousand in construction and up to thirty thousand for suppliers to the project during the construction phase. Permanent jobs in management and maintenance would have been fewer than one hundred.[2] Regardless of what the exact number might have been, by blocking the project on environmental grounds, the Obama administration prevented these jobs from being created.

This second argument is true, as far as it goes. There is absolutely no way to reduce global fossil fuel production by 40 percent within twenty years without also cutting employment in the fossil fuel industry by roughly proportional amounts. That can only mean far fewer jobs for coal miners, oil rig operators, and natural gas delivery-truck drivers. But what this perspective leaves out is that, overall, building a clean energy economy will be a positive source of *net job creation* in all regions of the globe, even after the job losses generated by fossil fuel industry retrenchments are taken into account.

This conclusion is supported by work my coauthors and I have done on job creation through spending within both the clean energy and fossil fuel sectors in various countries. We have studied this question for a diverse set of nine major economies: Brazil, China, India, Indonesia, Germany, South Africa, South Korea, Spain, and the United States. (We are continuing this work for other countries as well.) We have found that building a clean energy economy will be a positive source of job creation in all of these countries, despite substantial differences in labor markets and energy infrastructures.

Tables 4.1, 4.2, 4.3, and 4.4 present the main findings of our work. Tables 4.1 and 4.2 show the number of jobs that will be generated in each country through spending $1 million on either building a new clean energy economy or maintaining the country's existing fossil fuel–based energy infrastructure. Tables 4.3 and 4.4 give the same estimates for spending 1.5 percent of current-level GDP. That is, the data in Tables 4.3 and 4.4 simply date the figures from Tables 4.1 and 4.2 and scale the level of spending to 1.5 percent of each country's GDP as opposed to spending a flat $1 million on clean energy in each country.

Table 4.1 Jobs generated through spending $1 million on clean energy versus fossil fuel production (large-scale fossil fuel–producing countries)

	Clean energy jobs per $1 million	Fossil fuel jobs per $1 million	Job increase through clean energy spending relative to fossil fuels (%)
Brazil	37.1	21.2	+75
China	133.1	74.4	+79
India	261.9	129.1	+103
Indonesia	99.1	22.0	+350
South Africa	70.6	33.1	+113
United States	8.7	3.7	+135

Source: See Pollin et al. 2015c, chapter 6 and appendix 2, for estimating methodology.

Table 4.2 Jobs generated through spending $1 million on clean energy versus fossil fuel production (large-scale fossil fuel–importing countries)

	Clean energy jobs per $1 million
Germany	9.7
South Korea	14.6
Spain	13.4

Source: See Pollin et al. 2015c, chapter 6 and appendix 2, for estimating methodology.

Table 4.3 Jobs generated through spending 1.5% of GDP on clean energy versus fossil fuels (large-scale fossil fuel–producing countries)

	Total clean energy jobs created through investing 1.5% of GDP	Net clean energy jobs created after subtracting fossil fuel job losses	Clean energy job creation as share of total labor force	
			Total job creation (%)	Net job creation (%)
Brazil	925,000	395,000	0.9	0.4
China	11,400,000	6,400,000	1.5	0.6
India	12,000,000	5,700,000	2.6	1.4
Indonesia	954,000	752,000	0.8	0.6
South Africa	252,000	126,000	1.4	0.7
United States	1,500,000	650,000	1.0	0.5

Source: See Pollin et al. 2015c, chapter 6 and appendix 2, for estimating methodology.

Table 4.4 Jobs generated through spending 1.5% of GDP on clean energy versus fossil fuels (large-scale fossil fuel–importing countries)

	Total clean energy jobs created through investing 1.5% of GDP	Clean energy job creation as share of total labor force (%)
Germany	330,000	0.8
Spain	320,000	1.4
South Korea	175,000	0.6

Source: See Pollin et al. 2015c, chapter 6 and appendix 2, for estimating methodology.

How Clean Energy Investments Create Jobs

Where the Data Come From

My estimates draw directly from national surveys of public and private economic enterprises within each country. These data are organized systematically within national "input-output" statistical tables for each country's economy. Here is one specific example of our methodology. If a business invests an additional $1 million on energy-efficiency retrofits to an existing building, we are able to measure, using the input-output tables, how much of that sum the business will spend on paying wages and benefits to workers and on needed supplies (such as windows, insulation, and lumber), how much will be left over to keep as profits, and how many new workers will be hired by the window, insulation, and lumber companies as a result. We also examine this same set of questions for investment projects in renewable energy as well as spending on operations within the fossil fuel energy sectors.[3]

Dividing Countries between Fossil Fuel Producers and Importers

I have divided our full set of nine countries into two groups in the four tables. The first group includes countries that are, at present, large-scale producers of oil, coal, natural gas, or some combination of all three. The second group includes countries that are heavily dependent on imports for their fossil fuel supplies. This distinction is crucial for assessing the impact on job opportunities within each country through advancing a clean energy transition. That is, for countries in the first group, we have to allow that the shift away from fossil fuels to clean renewables and energy efficiency will also entail a significant decline in employment opportunities in their fossil fuel industries. For this set of countries—Brazil, China, India, Indonesia, South Africa, and the United States—I am assuming for our discussion that an increase of 1.5 percent of GDP in clean energy investments is equally matched by a 1.5 percent of GDP decline in spending on fossil fuel production. Thus, net job creation occurs in these countries through their clean energy investment project only when spending a given amount of money on clean energy investments creates more jobs within the country than spending the same amount of money on fossil fuel production.

To use the United States as an example, if clean energy investments and fossil fuel production both generate ten jobs per $1 million in spending, then shifting $1 million out of fossil fuel production and into clean energy investments will produce no net gains in jobs at all. In fact, as we see in Tables 4.1 and 4.2, spending $1 million on clean energy investments generates, on average, 8.7 jobs, while fossil fuel production generates 3.7 jobs. Shifting energy-sector spending from fossil fuels to clean energy therefore produces an average of five new jobs per $1 million in spending within the US economy. Table 4.1 reports the figures for the United States and the other fossil fuel–producing economies. Table 4.3 then shows the net gains in job creation for these countries from shifting 1.5 percent of GDP into clean energy production and out of fossil fuel production.

In our second, smaller group of fossil fuel–importing countries—Germany, South Korea, and Spain—the jobs generated by investing 1.5 percent of GDP in clean energy are not counteracted by an equivalent shift out of domestic spending on fossil fuel production, but rather only a decline in fossil fuel imports. In Table 4.2, I therefore show for these three countries the figures for job creation through clean energy investments, without also reporting figures on jobs created by fossil fuel production. In Table 4.4, I then show job creation in each of these economies through channeling 1.5 percent of GDP into clean energy investments.[4]

Beyond these specific job creation issues, it is important to recognize, more generally, that the heavy fossil fuel–importing countries will enjoy greater proportional benefits through their clean energy investment programs: first, these countries produce clean energy–related jobs without facing counteracting fossil fuel sector job losses; and second, equally critically, they reduce their dependency on imported energy sources.

Job Creation Estimates by Country

As we see in Tables 4.1 and 4.2, the number of jobs created through spending within the energy industry varies widely by country. Among the six fossil fuel–producing countries, we see that investing $1 million in clean energy investments generates about nine jobs in the United States, thirty-seven in Brazil, seventy-one in South Africa, 133 in China, and 262 in India. For the three fossil fuel–importing countries, clean energy investments generate about ten jobs in Germany, thirteen in Spain, and fifteen in South Korea.

These differences are driven mainly by the wide range of average wage levels. As of 2010, average manufacturing wages were about $1.50 per hour in India, $11 in Brazil, and $44 in Germany. Such differences need to be kept in mind. But our main interest is with the relative job creation figures *within each of the countries*. This is especially the case for the fossil fuel–producing countries, in which we need to counterbalance job gains from clean energy investments against job losses through declining spending within domestic fossil fuel industries.

We see in Table 4.1 that in all six fossil fuel–producing countries, investing in clean energy generates more jobs per $1 million in spending than channeling that same amount of money into the fossil fuel industry. In most cases, the net increase in job creation is substantial. The largest difference is in Indonesia, where clean energy investments generate ninety-nine jobs per $1 million, while spending on fossil fuels produces only twenty-two—a difference of 350 percent. In Brazil, China, South Africa, and the United States, clean energy investments generate between 75 and 135 percent more jobs than spending on fossil fuels. With Germany, South Korea, and Spain, again, we do not need to match the job increases per $1 million in clean energy investments against job losses through withdrawing $1 million from fossil fuel spending.

Focusing now on the fossil fuel–producing countries, why is it that, in all six cases, clean energy infrastructures generate more—often significantly more—jobs per $1 million in spending than does the existing fossil fuel infrastructure? The reason has nothing to do with climate stabilization per se. There are two separate factors at play. The first is the higher level of *labor intensity* that results from spending on clean energy: more money is spent on hiring people and less on machines, supplies, and energy consumption. This is not surprising if we imagine channeling investment funds to, for example, hiring construction workers to retrofit buildings or install solar panels as opposed to drilling for oil. We would see a lot more people on the retrofitting job site than at the oil drilling rig relative to the size of the project. The second factor is the *domestic content* of spending—how much money stays within the domestic economy as opposed to buying imports. When an economy retrofits its existing building stock, improves its public transportation system, or invests to install solar panels, a much higher share of overall spending and job creation remains within the country than when it is purchasing imported oil.

Scaling the Job Effects to 1.5 Percent of GDP

In Tables 4.3 and 4.4, showing the employment effects of channeling 1.5 percent of GDP into clean energy investments, we again first see that the differences in the job creation figures between countries are large. Among the fossil fuel–producing countries, investing 1.5 percent of GDP on clean energy investments will produce around 250,000 jobs in South Africa, 1.5 million in the United States, between 925,000 and 950,000 in Brazil and Indonesia, and between 11.4 and twelve million in China and India. For our three fossil fuel–importing countries, clean energy investments at 1.5 percent of GDP generate 175,000 jobs in South Korea and between 320,000 and 330,000 in Germany and Spain. These large differences are driven both by relative wage rates and by large differences in each country's GDP.

But here again, our main interest is with the total levels of jobs *within each country* as well as the net job creation after we subtract jobs lost to the contraction of the fossil fuel industry in our six fossil fuel–producing countries. Of course, in these countries, it is not necessarily the case that fossil fuel spending will contract by the same amount that the clean energy economy expands. But this assumption provides a simple illustration of the net job gains that will occur through a clean energy investment project in fossil fuel–producing countries, even when the expansion of each country's energy efficiency and renewable energy investments are matched dollar-for-dollar by fossil fuel industry retrenchments.[5]

Tables 4.3 and 4.4 also show, for each country, the level of job creation as a share of each country's overall labor force. These figures are not large, with respect to both the fossil fuel producers as well as the fossil fuel importers. They range between 0.6 and 2.6 percent for total job creation and between 0.4 and 1.4 percent for net job creation, after subtracting the jobs lost through fossil fuel retrenchments, including the cuts in the oil-refining sectors in Germany, South Korea, and Spain. Of course, we would not expect these job figures to be much larger, given that we are setting the overall increase in clean energy investments (and fossil fuel retrenchments) at no more than 1.5 percent of each country's GDP.

What these figures make clear is that clean energy investment programs, scaled at 1.5 percent of GDP, will not, by themselves, deliver full employment in any given country. But clean energy investments will nevertheless be a positive new source of job opportunities. Certainly these net job increases—roughly 6.4 million in China, 5.7 million in India, 750,000 in Indonesia, 650,000 in the United States, 400,000 in Brazil, 300,000 in Germany and Spain, 175,000 in South Korea, and 125,000 in South Africa—are not trivial. Politicians in all nine countries would be very pleased to claim credit for job gains of this magnitude. Moreover, for virtually all countries, clean energy investments will mean more over-all job opportunities relative to maintaining the country's existing fossil fuel energy infrastructure. The one set of countries that could experience employment losses would be those that rely heavily on fossil fuel exports as their main engine of economic growth. But even with these countries, it does not follow that experiencing contraction in their energy exports will necessarily be detrimental to growth and employment opportuni-ties. For example, Indonesia experienced a sharp decline in its fossil fuel exports over the years 2001–2010. But this was not associated with a decline in the country's average GDP growth rate.[6] In other words, broadly speaking, building clean energy economies in all regions of the world will not require sacrifices by working people. Working people will rather benefit, in many cases substantially, from the overall growth in job opportunities.

At the same time, employment conditions will not improve for *all* workers under all circumstances in this scenario. Who is likely to fare better or worse through a clean energy investment agenda? To answer this question, we need to address three additional important issues beyond the figures we present in Tables 4.1, 4.2, 4.3, and 4.4: the impact of labor pro-ductivity growth over time on job creation, the *quality* of the jobs being generated, and the inevitable difficulties that will be faced by workers dependent on the fossil fuel industry. I take these up in turn.

Labor Productivity Growth and Job Creation

The employment effects reported in Tables 4.1, 4.2, 4.3, and 4.4 are based on the production methods currently used in each country. So, spend-ing $1 million on clean energy investments will generate, on average, 8.7 million jobs in the United States and 261.9 jobs in India, based on what we know about the current production methods being used today. But clean energy technologies will certainly improve over the twenty-year investment cycle. These improvements will typically increase aver-age labor productivity. This means that fewer workers will be needed to raise energy-efficiency levels or expand clean renewable energy production. What will be the impact of such labor productivity improvements on our overall finding that clean energy investments will be a positive source of job creation throughout the world?

In fact, gains in employment opportunities should increase over time, even after we allow for average labor productivity improvement every year. Considering past patterns of productivity growth, my coworkers and I find that, since the mid-1990s, the rate at which productivity has improved in the clean energy sectors varies considerably by country. For example, productivity gains have been relatively modest in Brazil, Indonesia, South Africa, and the United States, but rapid in India and South Korea. Of course, we cannot know from these past productivity trends what is likely to happen moving forward. Still, if anything, we should generally expect labor productivity in the clean energy sectors to accelerate, as a result of much faster rates of investment in these sectors. This should, in turn, encourage innovation and productivity improvements.

Nevertheless, regardless of how slowly or quickly labor productivity improves in various countries, the key to achieving strong gains in employment opportunities is rapid expansion of investment in energy efficiency and clean renewables. Indeed, based again on past economic trends in all countries, it is almost certain that the growth in investment spending and operational activities will outpace improvements in labor productivity. As a result, the expansion in employment opportunities should increase over time, even in countries where labor productivity grows at relatively rapid rates.

Job Quality and Skill Requirements

Increased employment opportunities will be spread widely in all countries. Moreover, the majority of jobs created by clean energy investments will be in the same areas of employment in which people already work. Constructing wind farms, for example, creates jobs for sheet metal workers, machinists, and truck drivers, among others. Increasing the energy efficiency of buildings through retrofitting relies on, among others, roofers, insulators, and building inspectors. Expanding public transportation systems employs civil engineers, electricians, and dispatchers. Increasing demand for bioenergy will mean a significant increase in employment in standard agricultural activities. At the same time, we do still need to address several issues: where the new employment opportunities are most likely to open up, the likely pay levels and other conditions on these jobs, the likely gender balance among them, and the kinds of new educational and skill requirements that might be needed.

Expanding Job Opportunities by Sector

Three economic sectors, broadly defined, will see relatively large increases in employment. The first is agriculture, where increasing job opportunities will result from the expansion of bioenergy production. Construction jobs will also increase substantially, due to both energy-efficiency building retrofits and infrastructure investments to upgrade electrical grid and public transportation systems. Manufacturing jobs will increase to meet the increased demand for solar panels, wind turbines, and other renewable energy equipment.

Of course, not all countries will expand employment equally in all of these areas. The agriculture and construction jobs will most likely grow in all countries in rough proportion to the overall expansion in clean energy investments, since agriculture and construction activities typically rely mainly on their own domestic workforce and other resources. By contrast, many countries will rely on imports to meet at least some of the increased demand for renewable energy manufacturing products. As such, the employment gains through expanding clean energy will be lower when a country purchases imports as opposed to producing these goods domestically. But even when, for example, a country is importing solar panels, a growing reliance on solar energy will still generate more jobs for workers who are transporting, installing, and maintaining the solar equipment as well as upgrading the electrical grid system for transmitting solar power.

Countries importing a large share of their manufactured clean energy products can also consider policies to expand domestic production. When domestic production increases, domestic job opportunities will expand as well. I consider this issue further in Pollin (2015) and Pollin, Garrett-Peltier, Heintz, and Chakraborty (2015).

Informal Employment

In all but the most advanced economies, employment in agriculture and construction is, at present, mostly informal. This means that there is a high proportion of very small enterprises and self-employment. Most of the time, working in informal enterprises means low pay and benefits and little to no job security.

At the same time, the new agricultural and construction jobs are not necessarily consigned to being bad jobs. The major increase in investment flowing into these sectors could create new opportunities to raise labor standards. For example, in Brazil, the expansion of its bioenergy sectors has slowly encouraged increased agricultural mechanization and rising productivity. The growth of employment resulting from Brazil's bioenergy investments has therefore been less than it would have been if traditional agriculture methods had continued to prevail and productivity had consequently remained low. But this mechanization trend also creates greater opportunities for better pay and working conditions for the large numbers of jobs that will remain in agriculture. Of course, nobody should expect that mechanization and faster productivity growth will, by themselves, deliver better jobs. But such gains in productivity will create new opportunities for workers and their representatives, along with public policy makers, to support major upgrades in labor standards.

Opportunities for Women

Throughout the world, the construction and manufacturing sectors are heavily dominated by male workers. If this situation were to continue, clean energy investments that rely heavily on construction and manufacturing would yield relatively few new employment opportunities for women. These investment areas include hydro, wind, solar, and geothermal power, as well as efficiency investments in building retrofits and electrical grid upgrades. The share of female employment generated by these clean energy investment areas ranges between 20 and 30 percent in most countries, including both advanced and developing economies. Clean energy investment projects should be used as an opportunity to highlight the need for much greater gender equity in these currently male-dominated areas.

Education and Skill Requirements

The general level of educational attainment for workers in the clean energy sectors is not, for the most part, significantly different than those for workers presently employed in the oil, coal, and natural gas sectors. Thus, as jobs in the fossil fuel sectors are reduced, there will be an increased supply of workers available to operate within the clean energy sectors with appropriate levels of general educational credentials.

At the same time, some of the newly created jobs generated by clean energy investments will also require new skills. For example, installing solar panels on roofs and wiring them so they supply electricity are distinct tasks relative to the jobs that are traditionally performed by either roofers or electricians. Similarly, refining agricultural wastes into biofuels is different than refining corn into ethanol or, for that matter, refining petroleum into gasoline. Countries advancing clean energy investment projects will need to make provisions for these and similar areas that demand new types of training and skill acquisition. But how extensive will the need be for new training and skills?

A study by the International Labour Office, *Skills for Green Jobs: A Global View,* concluded that clean energy and other green-economy occupations will, for the most part, require updating existing skills as opposed to training workers for entirely new occupations. For example, the authors observe, "The number of existing occupations that will change and update their skills content by far exceeds the number of new occupations that will emerge. . . . The greening of established occupations implies incremental changes in qualifications. New skills are needed because specific competencies are currently lacking [and] some existing skills relating to job tasks that become obsolete cease to be used" (Strietska-Ilina et al. 2011, 100).

Inevitably, there will be some difficult transition periods and bottlenecks in most countries as the growth in clean energy investments generates increasing demand for workers with new types of specific skills. Still, these will be less severe than they might be otherwise. This is because, as we have discussed, most jobs and skill requirements in the clean energy economy are not significantly different than those already required of most people currently working in other sectors. In addition, the general educational attainment levels for most jobs within the clean energy sectors will be roughly comparable to those within the fossil fuel sectors facing retrenchments. The net result is an increase in the number of workers who can move into clean energy. In addition, countries facing shortages of skilled workers in specific areas can rely on imports to cover these gaps until their own supply of qualified workers expands.

Just Transition for Fossil Fuel Sector Workers

There is no denying that workers and communities whose livelihoods depend on people consuming oil, coal, and natural gas will lose out in the clean energy transition. In order for the global clean energy project to succeed, it must provide adequate transitional support for these workers and communities.

The United Nations Environmental Programme addressed this issue in a 2008 study, *Green Jobs: Towards Decent Work in a Sustainable, Low-Carbon World*. The authors describe what they term a "fair and just transition" for workers and communities that are currently dependent on the fossil fuel industries: "The shift to a low carbon and sustainable society must be as equitable as possible. . . . From the point of view of social solidarity, and in order to mobilize the political and workplace-based support for the changes that are needed, it is imperative that policies be put in place to ensure that those who are likely to be negatively affected are protected through income support, retraining opportunities, relocation assistance and the like" (Renner, Sweeney, and Kubit 2008, 27). The arguments made in this study for a "fair and just transition" build from the ideas of the late US labor and environmental leader Tony Mazzocchi, who developed the idea of a "Superfund" for workers who lose their jobs as a result of necessary environmental transitions. Mazzocchi's use of the term refers to the US environmental program that was implemented in 1980 to clean up sites at which corporations had dumped hazardous wastes from petrochemical, oil, and nuclear energy production. As Mazzocchi wrote as early as 1993, "Paying people to make the transition from one kind of economy—from one kind of job—to another is not welfare. Those who work with toxic materials on a daily basis . . . in order to provide the world with the energy and the materials it needs deserve a helping hand to make a new start in life. . . . There is a Superfund for dirt. There ought to be one for workers."[7] The critical point in Mazzocchi's idea is that providing high-quality adjustment assistance to today's fossil fuel industry workers will represent a major contribution toward making a global climate stabilization project viable. It is a matter of simple justice, but it is also a matter of strategic politics. Without such adjustment assistance programs operating at a major scale, the workers and communities facing retrenchment from the clean energy investment project will, predictably and understandably, fight to defend their communities and livelihoods. This, in turn, will create unacceptable delays in proceeding with effective climate stabilization policies.

Still, the impact on workers and communities from retrenchments in the fossil fuel sectors will not depend only on the level of support provided through explicit adjustment assistance programs, no matter how generous their provisions. The broader set of economic opportunities available to workers will also be critical. The fact that the clean energy investment project will itself generate a major expansion in new job opportunities in all regions of the globe means that there will be new opportunities for displaced fossil fuel sector workers within the energy industry itself. There will be more jobs for, among other occupations, operations managers, mechanical engineers, construction managers, farmers and ranchers, roofers, electricians, and sheet metal workers.

But further than this, the single best form of protection for displaced workers in all countries is an economy that operates at full employment. A full-employment economy is one in which there is an abundance of decent jobs available for all people seeking work. In a full-employment economy, the challenges faced by displaced workers—regardless of the reasons for their having become displaced—are greatly diminished simply because they should be able to find another decent job without excessive difficulty. It also follows that, in a full-employment economy, the costs to taxpayers of providing reasonable levels of financial support for displaced workers would be greatly diminished. Overall, then, in the realm of overarching social, economic, and environmental policy priorities, a commitment to full employment should be understood as fully consistent with and supportive of the project of building a clean energy economy.

Considering the global green growth project as one component of a broader full-employment program also enables us to focus more clearly on the nature of the challenge to employment opportunities posed by robotization. Robotization will certainly entail substantial employment losses in many areas of economic activity. But if public policy becomes committed to the principle of full employment—an abundance of decent jobs—then a wide array of projects that require large-scale efforts by people to succeed will become newly viable. For economies at all levels of development, these include greatly expanding educational opportunities and the provision of health care as well as improving housing, infrastructure, and transportation systems. But global green growth will need to be the centerpiece of such a full-employment project, since it is the only framework through which expanding job opportunities can be made fully compatible with long-term ecological sanity.

5

Building Sustainable Jobs and Supporting Human Potential in the Care Sector

Mignon Duffy

Care Is the Future of Work

In a context in which globalization and automation have led some experts to fear the disappearance of work, the care sector of the labor market is large and expanding across the globe. While scholars and policymakers often speak of labor market sectors such as manufacturing or high-tech, the notion of a "care sector" is unfamiliar to many. Conceptually, care work is the labor of providing for the needs of children, the elderly, and those who are ill or disabled. Throughout history and around the world, mothers, wives, and daughters have performed a large proportion of caring labor as unpaid family work. But worldwide there are also cadres of paid care workers, who make up a significant sector of the labor market.

The most visible of these workers are those who are directly involved in personal care through face-to-face relationships: these "nurturant" care workers include doctors, nurses, social workers, teachers, childcare workers, and home health aides. Behind the scenes in hospitals, schools, and nursing homes, scores of "nonnurturant" care workers in food, laundry, and cleaning jobs make the work of care possible (Duffy 2005; Duffy 2007). In practical terms, then, the care sector of the labor market includes the industries of health care, primary and secondary education, childcare, mental health, and elder care. In addition to institutional care workers, domestic workers provide both personal nurturant care of family members and nonnurturant support work in private homes.

While the sector contains a wide range of jobs, with few exceptions, care requires the worker and the person being cared for to be in the same place at the same time. These are jobs that cannot be outsourced to another country in the same way that manufacturing or call center positions can be. Among nurturant care workers, relationship and responsiveness to unpredictable human needs are part of the job. These workers cannot be replaced by robots in the same way that delivery drivers or grocery cashiers can be. In fact, of the twenty occupations that the United Nations has designated least likely to be replaced by machines, fourteen are nurturant care jobs (UNDP 2015). This is not to say that automation is not at all relevant for care workers. (For just one example of the scholarly debate around automation and care, see Folbre 2006.) But the complexity of human interaction required in care work, as well as the need for physical proximity, mitigate the forces pushing toward worker replacement with artificial intelligence more than in other parts of the labor market.

In addition to being resistant to outsourcing and automation, jobs in the care sector are in high demand around the world. The UN estimates that there is a shortage of 13.6 million workers needed to care for the growing aging population around the world. Numbers of domestic workers have surged in recent decades, reaching a current estimated total of fifty-three million people worldwide. And it is estimated that the world will need over eight million additional trained teachers by 2030 to reach the goal of educating all children (UNDP 2015). Despite the enormous potential, many occupations in the care sector suffer from persistent shortages and high turnover rates. While there are professional jobs within the sector, some of the fastest-growing segments of the paid care labor force are at the low end of the wage spectrum, barely providing workers with the possibility of earning a living. Importantly, labor shortages and wage inadequacy in the care sector contribute to gaps in both the quantity and quality of care available, leaving needs unmet for health care, childcare, education, elder care, and mental health services. Focused public policies to strengthen the care sector globally would therefore address two crucial social problems simultaneously: expanding opportunities for sustainable work and addressing the care needs of some of the most vulnerable members of society.

In this chapter, I will begin by outlining the characteristics of the care sector in the Global North and in the Global South, showing the substantial gaps between care needs and care provision. After introducing the main dynamics of devaluation that undermine wages and working conditions in the care sector, I will discuss the way in which care workers' current migration patterns exacerbate care gaps around the world. Finally, I will end with a number of policy recommendations to grow the care sector in ways that provide quality care as well as sustainable livelihoods for care workers.

Changing Needs and Growing Gaps: The Care Sector in the Global North and Global South

While this volume focuses on the contemporary technological revolution driven by automation and artificial intelligence, the paid care sector in the Global North has been shaped largely by the much earlier industrial revolution. The large-scale scientific, technological, and institutional transformation of the late nineteenth and early twentieth centuries created the modern industries of health care, education, childcare, elder care, and mental health services, driving a rate of demand for a wide range of paid care workers that has outstripped their growth in numbers. By contrast, many people who live in the Global South still lack access to some of the technologies of this first revolution, and weak infrastructures and scattered systems of health care, education, and childcare leave many people without necessary services. In both cases, the gap between care needs and available care creates human deprivation, which could be ameliorated by tapping into the enormous potential for work and jobs created by that same gap.

The impact of the industrial revolution on care is perhaps most clearly visible in health care. In the United States, as in much of the Global

North, in the space of one hundred years, the modern health care industry emerged from a scattered system of domestic and family work that consisted largely of "sitting with" the sick. Significant technological innovation in the nineteenth century paved the way for the growth of the health care sector. The widespread use of automobiles created the conditions whereby patients could get to a doctor, and there were enormous advances in basic medical science, diagnostic technology, and treatment alternatives. Importantly, these material gains were accompanied by a cultural shift toward the prioritization of science and expert knowledge (Duffy 2011). In conjunction with advocacy efforts by newly organized professional organizations, these developments led to the emergence of a large number of fast-growing occupations, ranging from high-status and well-paid jobs (e.g., physicians and surgeons) to low-wage jobs with few opportunities for advancement (e.g., nursing aides and support workers in hospitals).

In part as a consequence of the transformation of health care, new needs for care characterize the Global North. In the United States, many more people with severe disabilities and chronic illnesses survive, often needing additional care at home or in institutions beyond the acute care provided in hospitals and physicians' offices. Another consequence of development across the Global North was the expansion of modern sanitation, water, and energy infrastructures to universal or near-universal coverage. Combined with the emergence of modern medicine, these developments contributed to a dramatic increase in life expectancies. Between 1900 and 2004, average US life expectancy grew from forty-seven years to seventy-eight, an astounding change that has fundamentally altered care needs (Arias 2007). Elder care and long-term care have emerged as new needs faced by almost every country in the Global North. As the population of older adults continues to expand in the coming decades, demand for health care workers and elder care workers is predicted to increase exponentially. Between 2014 and 2024, the need for home health aides in the United States alone is expected to grow by 38 percent (US Bureau of Labor Statistics 2016).

By contrast, in the Global South, large segments of the population still do not have access to modern sanitation, water, or energy infrastructures—and while, in theory, health care technologies are global, the reality of a fully developed health care system is unrealized in many poor countries.

The current total number of physicians, nurses, and midwives globally is around thirty-four million—but only 3.6 percent of these are in sub-Saharan Africa, a region that contains 12 percent of the world's population (UNDP 2015, 146). And, although average life expectancies in some of the richest countries on the planet have surpassed eighty years, in many poor countries average life expectancies remain between fifty and sixty-five (222). In many countries in Africa, for example, the immediate cause of increased demand for health care and long-term care is not an aging population, but rather the presence of disease pandemics, especially HIV-AIDS (Yeates 2010). Similar to the situation in the Global North, however, there is enormous unmet demand for health care workers. Investment in this sector would close gaps in human needs at the same time as creating large numbers of jobs.

The transformation in the way we care for children and youth in the United States and other rich countries has been perhaps less obvious than the shifts in health care, but it is no less dramatic. The economic shift from agriculture to industry changed not only the nature of work for many people, but also the nature of care. Children who once worked side by side with adults on their family farms now needed a different kind of care as many fathers left family homes to work in city factories. They also needed a different set of skills to enter the changing labor force, training increasingly offered by schools rather than at home. While in the 1800s few children in the United States attended formal school with any regularity, by 1920 schooling was compulsory in almost all states. The growth of compulsory education and its public expansion to more and more groups of children led to the rapid growth of the teaching workforce (Duffy 2011). More recently, care for the youngest children has become an increasing focus of US public discourse, as rates of maternal labor force participation have grown and research has shown the importance of these early years to brain development and future success. While there is important national variation in how much unmet need for childcare exists, in at least some countries in the Global North (such as the United States), there are still large gaps in the quantity and quality of childcare available that could be filled by expanding the sector workforce.

In many poor countries, education remains the exception rather than the rule for children, who are often still contributing to their families through labor. Across many countries in the Global South, the average total school attendance for boys is as low as four years, with averages even lower for girls (UNDP 2015, 222). The United Nations has set a goal of providing an opportunity for an education to all children by 2030, an effort that will require an enormous expansion of the teaching workforce across the globe. In many developing countries, the number of children under fifteen is 70 percent of the number of adults aged fifteen to sixty-four, creating a very different picture of care needs from the more developed countries, where this ratio is closer to 30 percent (UNDP 2015). Again, moving toward education as a goal for these large numbers of children provides yet another opportunity to meet human needs while expanding job opportunities in the care sector.

These patterns in health care and education parallel developments in mental health and other social services as well, with the result that, across the care sector, there are opportunities for strong job growth while simultaneously meeting human needs in many countries in both the Global North and the Global South. But there are some important barriers to realizing this potential. First, jobs in the care sector are vulnerable to a number of intersecting dynamics of devaluation, undermining both their attractiveness to workers and the ability of these jobs to provide real livelihoods. Second, current patterns of global migration among care workers exacerbate both care gaps and the devaluation of care around the world.

Devaluation, Inequalities, and Livelihoods in the Care Sector

In large part because women around the world have long been expected to provide it for free, care work has been associated with natural characteristics of women rather than with skilled labor. This dynamic not only contributes to the undervaluing of care work in the labor market but also limits women's ability to resist exploitative wages and working conditions. These workers are often seen as good at their jobs only if they are not "doing it for the money," but rather have altruistic motives. These gendered expectations are deeply ingrained in many care workers, as well as in the societies in which they work, and have contributed to the creation of a set of paid care occupations that, at best, are underpaid and, at worst, are profoundly exploitative (Duffy 2011).

Despite the growing importance of paid care occupations, the majority of care work around the world is still performed as unpaid family labor and done overwhelmingly by women. This is the work of taking care of children and ill and older family members, plus all of the support work that goes into that—for example, procuring food and water and maintaining a clean home. In the United States, it is estimated from time-use surveys that, on average, women spend about 4.5 hours a day engaged in unpaid care activities, about twice the time spent by men (Folbre 2012, 52). In countries that lack access to basic services, where women fetch water, gather firewood, and care for homes not well-protected from the elements, the number of hours is even higher. Women's responsibility for unpaid care is part of the explanation for their lower participation in the paid labor force: globally, this is 50 percent, compared to 77 percent of men (UNDP 2015, 11). Unlike paid labor, the hours spent in unpaid caring labor are not recognized as work and bring neither financial nor cultural rewards.

Importantly, the lack of recognition as valued labor carries over when care work is performed in the paid labor market. Researchers in the United States have found that, across the labor market, care workers are paid 5 to 6 percent less than other workers whose jobs have similar characteristics, including the level of education required. This wage penalty is over and above the wage differential between female-dominated and male-dominated jobs; that is, there is something unique about the work of care that is devalued in the labor market even more than other female-dominated occupations (England, Budig, and Folbre 2002). Comparative research has found wage penalties for care work across a range of countries (Budig and Misra 2010).

The care penalty is one important dynamic of devaluation, and it is particularly relevant for higher-wage care occupations in countries where the sector is well-developed (Budig and Misra 2010; Lightman 2016). Another important measure and consequence of the devaluation of care work is the proportion of the sector that falls into the most low-wage and low-opportunity part of the labor market. Scholars in the United States have suggested that the polarized growth of the care sector is one of the underlying causes for the increasing polarization of the US labor market as a whole (Dwyer 2013). Within the sector, jobs have developed into a fairly rigid hierarchal structure that is stratified by pay, opportunity, gender, race, and migration status (Duffy 2011). It is not clear how much this dynamic applies to countries outside of the United States, but research has shown that wage penalties for care work are higher in countries with higher levels of income inequality (Budig and Misra 2010), and polarization and increasing inequality are not phenomena limited to the US context. Both the devaluation of compensation for care work and the pushing of significant groups of care workers to the margins of the labor market undermine the potential of the care sector to provide jobs and livelihoods to large numbers of workers.

One subset of workers within the care sector merits a particular mention with reference to livelihoods and working conditions. Some of the fastest-growing care occupations around the world are those that involve work in private homes as general domestic help, home care aides, and elder care and childcare providers. In most countries, these jobs are exempted from basic labor protections—that is, they are literally not considered work—leaving these workers extremely vulnerable to exploitation and abuse. Employers have the power to force women to work for up to eighteen hours a day for low or even no wages, limiting their access to food, health care, freedom of movement, and social interactions. Domestic workers also report high rates of physical and sexual abuse (UNDP 2015, 45). The lack of recognition of the status of these—almost exclusively—women as workers, combined with the isolation and invisibility of their work, places them uniquely at risk.

Largely as a consequence of these gendered dynamics of devaluation, men have not entered care work in large numbers, even as more traditionally male-dominated occupations such as manufacturing have declined—and even as women in the Global North have made significant inroads into previously male-dominated occupations. In the United States, between 85 and 95 percent of registered nurses, licensed practical nurses, and nursing aides and orderlies are female (Duffy 2011, 84). Care of preschool-age children is an over 90-percent female occupation. Teachers are still overwhelmingly women, as are social workers and domestic workers (Duffy 2011; UNDP 2015). A controversial 2010 article in *The Atlantic* argued that men's inability to adapt to the new growing sectors of the economy, dominated by nurturant care occupations, is part of the explanation for the crisis the author provocatively called "The End of Men" (Rosin 2010). Many of the workers who have entered care work occupations in the Global North have been those who are disadvantaged in some way in addition to gender—by virtue of poverty, migration status, or racial-ethnic status. In the United States, for example, almost 30 percent of domestic workers are foreign-born and over 20 percent of nursing aides are African-American (Duffy 2011).

The cultural scripts around care, combined with the structural vulnerabilities of care jobs, have combined to create powerful barriers to the care sector's being seen as part of the next frontier of the labor market for all. So, while globally, the demand for care workers continues to increase, the devaluation of this labor and the unique vulnerabilities of its workers undermine the future of care work as a labor market sector and threaten basic worker rights, gender equality, and the ability of societies to provide for their growing care needs.

Global Migration of Care Workers

One of the ways that countries in the Global North have met some of the expanding demand for care workers is through flows of migrant workers from the Global South. Once working in the receiving country, these workers' status as both care workers and migrant workers creates a type of double jeopardy, making them extremely vulnerable to exploitation. The outflow of women who do both paid and unpaid care work simultaneously exacerbates the already-gaping care deficits in their home countries. Global migration, driven by economic forces as well as by violence, is a fact of modern life. However, the current institutional and structural organization of migration related to care work is part of the problem rather than part of the solution.

International migrant flows of women workers to fill care jobs is not a new phenomenon. In 1900, over one-quarter of domestic servants in the United States were foreign-born; an additional 18 percent came from families where at least one parent was foreign-born (Duffy 2011, 23). These immigrant women, primarily from Ireland, were spurred on by famine and desperation in their homeland, as well as by the targeted efforts of the United States to recruit more women to address the servant shortage in the booming industrial cities of the Northeast. Immigration scholars have long argued that workers' and families' decisions to migrate are driven by a combination of "push" factors in the sending country and "pull" factors in the receiving country. In the globalized economy of the twenty-first century, the push and pull factors for some care workers have shifted.

Sociologist Saskia Sassen (2002) has identified two simultaneous processes that have shifted the dynamics of global migration in the context of globalization. The first is the creation of "global cities," which concentrate the power and resources at the center of global corporations in a small number of large cities around the world. The concentration of high-income professionals who run these companies creates an increased demand for low-wage service workers to support their work and lifestyles. This dynamic exacerbates the specific forces already discussed, creating growing demand for domestic workers, childcare workers, and elder care workers in the Global North, a significant "pull" factor for workers from the Global South.

The second key process of globalization identified by Sassen is the creation of "survival circuits" that link the survival of national economies in the Global South to the export of workers through migration. Sassen argues that the expansion of multinational companies and the increasing influence of multinational organizations have exacerbated the dependence of economies in the Global South on those in the Global North. Many countries find themselves deeply in debt and forced by international banks to adopt structural adjustment policies that eviscerate social services and public infrastructure at home in order to pay debts to wealthier countries. One way that debtor countries have found to allow their national economies to survive is to export workers, who send home remittances in the form of hard currency (Sassen 2002). In 2014, the total amount of remittances to developing countries reached $427 billion, more than three times the amount of official development assistance (World Bank 2016). Thus, women in the Global South are "pushed" into migration by not only individual economic hardship, but a national interest in reaping the fruits of their exported labor.

While it is a particularly dramatic example, an examination of the Philippines is an illustrative case to demonstrate that current patterns of migration among care workers are more than simply the result of a set of individual worker and family decisions, but rather the consequence of global forces stemming from the institutional interests and policies of global corporations, national governments, and multinational organizations. In 1982, the Filipino government established the Philippines Overseas Employment Administration (POEA) to organize and supervise the export of nurses and maids to high-demand areas such as the United States, the Middle East, and Japan and other highly developed Asian countries. Governments in receiving countries also cooperated in facilitating the immigration of Filipina workers. For example, the US government in 1989 passed the Immigration Nursing Relief Act to allow for the importation of nurses to meet the growing demand for these workers (Sassen 2002). Today, an estimated 8.1 million Filipinos live and work in other countries, almost 10 percent of their home country's population. Since the early 1990s, the majority of these migrant workers have been women. And over one thousand government-licensed recruitment agencies continue the work begun by the POEA (Asis 2006). In the United States, Filipinos are one of the largest groups of foreign-born workers (McNamara and Batalova 2015), and are overrepresented among nursing aides and domestic workers (Duffy 2011).

For highly developed countries, immigrant care workers have become a key part of meeting growing care needs. These workers face multiple layers of vulnerability. In the United States, foreign-born workers make up 17 percent of childcare workers, 22 percent of nursing aides, orderlies and attendants, 14 percent of registered nurses, and almost 30 percent of physicians and surgeons (Duffy 2011). The gendered dynamics of devaluation discussed above, joined with the precariousness of immigrant status, exposes migrant care workers across the socioeconomic spectrum to high risk for being subordinated or exploited. Nannies, elder care givers, and other domestic workers—that group who face perhaps the most extreme levels of vulnerability already—are often undocumented, making their ability to resist mistreatment very limited (Hondagneu-Sotelo 2007; Parreñas 2001). Scholars have shown that immigrants working in long-term care or health care face a "double isolation" due to their migrant status combined with the antisocial hours and demands of care work (Bourgeault 2015). Even among physicians, on the whole a much more privileged group than these other workers, it has been shown that immigrants are constrained by their dependence on their employers for visas to take on undesirable shifts and/or specialties (Bhalla 2010).

Racial dynamics have also always been present in care work relationships, with women of color and immigrant women often expected to serve the care needs of white and upper-class families regardless of their own family needs (Duffy 2011). The editors of *Global Dimensions of Gender and Carework* have argued that "far from creating new opportunities that work against historical patterns of race, ethnic, and class discrimination, globalization through the mechanism of gendered care work may, in fact, propel these nation-specific patterns into new and formidable systems of global stratification" (Zimmerman, Litt, and Bose 2006, 27). As women migrate to perform care work in other countries, they become part of the entrenched racial and class hierarchy of care within the receiving country. Evelyn Nakano Glenn (2010) has documented how these gendered and racialized expectations, combined with the global forces discussed above, create a system in which the journeys and the labor of many migrant care workers must be seen through the lens of coercion.

In addition to creating problematic conditions for care workers, the mobility of caring labor also has crucial implications for exacerbating the care deficit in labor-exporting countries. Arlie Hochschild (2002) has described "global care chains" like the one in which Rowena Bautista is a link. Rowena works as a live-in nanny in a suburban home in Washington, DC. Her own two children live in her native Philippines with their grandmother and twelve other family members. Because the grandmother works as a teacher, she has hired Anna de la Cruz to cook, clean, and care for the children. Anna's own teenage son is left in the care of her eighty-year-old mother-in-law. Similar global care chains stretch from Mexico to California, from Cape Verde to Italy, from the Philippines to Dubai, and from Thailand to Japan. The global supply chains that characterize the twenty-first century world economy have stark human consequences when the commodity in that supply chain is care.

While the examples of mothers leaving children behind are especially poignant, the gaping care deficits in sending countries are exacerbated by the migration of care workers across the socioeconomic spectrum. Nicola Yeates (2010) has described global nursing care chains in which "the United States draws nurses from Canada; Canada draws nurses from the United Kingdom to make up for its losses to the United States; the United States draws nurses from South Africa to fill its own vacancies; and South Africa draws on Swaziland." Importantly, these global care chains embody much more complex migration patterns than the simplified South-to-North transfer in Sassen's model. In fact, South-to-South migration is equally common (UNDP 2015). However, as Yeates points out, while many countries simultaneously import and export nurses, poorer countries tend only to export these and other care workers. So, the biggest deficits tend to be at the "ends" of these chains, in those countries and regions that are the poorest.

As an example to demonstrate the scale of the impact of care worker migration on sending countries, between 1999 and 2002 the number of foreign-trained nurses based in the United Kingdom more than doubled. This migration occurred against the backdrop of an already-dramatic differential in access to nursing care. In the United Kingdom the nurse-to-population ratio during this period was 847 nurses per one hundred thousand persons. That ratio was sixty-six per one hundred thousand persons in Nigeria and 129 per one hundred thousand in Zimbabwe, two of the major sending countries (Zimmerman, Litt, and Bose 2006, 17).

In its current form, the migration of care workers intensifies the care deficits in the Global South by extracting the paid and unpaid labor of the women who perform most of this work. Although the path is perhaps less direct, contemporary patterns also exacerbate care deficits in the Global North by contributing to the cyclical devaluation of caring labor and those who do it. And in neither region do current institutional structures of migration promote the development of sustainable long-term work and livelihoods in the care sector.

Building the Future of Care Work: Policy and Values

Like the green energy sector, the care sector has the potential to be an important source of jobs and livelihoods while simultaneously addressing one of the major social problems of our time. Making this happen will require concerted action on the part of national, regional, and local policymakers as well as multinational actors. Building a robust care sector that meets the changing needs of people around the globe while providing stable livelihoods to care workers will require increasing public investment in the care sector, bringing all care workers under the umbrella of national and international labor regulations, and managing migration policy to support care workers and care needs worldwide. Ultimately, there is a need for a profound cultural and structural transformation that breaks the cycles of the devaluation of care.

Increase Public Investment in the Care Sector

Elsewhere in this volume, Juliana Martínez Franzoni has argued that the universal provision of social services is a critical component of building a society in which every member has the opportunity to enjoy a minimum standard of living that is unlinked from his or her employment status. Fundamentally, this is a proposal to provide publicly funded care to all members of a society—as children, in old age, and in ill health. In addition to meeting human needs, I have argued that, in the future, building a robust care sector will be a critical source of employment across the globe. While private and philanthropic organizations have an important role to play, public investment is critical for the sustainable development of this sector.

The care sector has a number of unique characteristics that make the market an inadequate tool to provide the quality and quantity of care that is needed in a society. First, like the roads and bridges of physical infrastructure, the "human infrastructure" of the care sector can be considered a public good. This means that the provision of care has societal outcomes that reach far beyond the individual directly receiving the care: "a well-educated labor force, healthy and productive adults, security in illness and old age, and the general well-being of the population" (Duffy, Albelda, and Hammonds 2013, 150). In the absence of the collectivization of the costs of public goods, the market fails, setting prices too high and supply too low. Second, in many sectors, economic growth is linked to productivity gains that allow individual workers to produce or accomplish more in the same amount of time. In the care sector, there is an upward boundary to productivity gains. Once a nurse has so many patients or a teacher so many students, adding more will negatively affect the quality of care substantially. This also causes market distortions, depressing wages for care workers and/or the quality of care provided (Duffy, Albelda, and Hammonds 2013).

The development of a robust care sector, therefore, depends on increased and sustained public investment across the globe. For many Global North countries, this would mean a reallocation of public funding toward the priority areas of health care, childcare, education, and social services. Research has shown that, in countries with higher proportions of care workers employed in the public sector, the wage penalties for care are lower (Budig and Misra 2010). National, regional, and local governments can begin by selectively investing in the parts of the care sector that have the greatest unmet need in their own populations, focusing on improving access to care as well as job quality for care workers. Coupled with strong public support, the private sector can also have a role in, for example, providing employer-based childcare or supporting career-advancement programs for care workers.

In the Global South, focused investment on areas that build a society's capacity to meet its care needs will lay the foundation for the development of a strong care sector. Modernizing systems of sanitation, water, and energy provision are necessary first steps in the poorest countries, while other countries need support in building schools, hospitals, and childcare centers. National and local governments, philanthropic and multinational aid organizations, and the business community can all have a role in implementing care-focused development strategies. Importantly, however, investment cannot end with the physical infrastructure, but must also include targeted policy and spending to train care workers and create the conditions for their work to be sustainable. Ultimately, again, this means the integration of the care sector as a major priority for public spending at the national and local levels.

Bring All Care Workers under the Umbrella of National and International Labor Law

Some of the most vulnerable care workers—domestic workers, home care aides, private household nannies—are not currently covered by basic labor protection laws in many countries in both the Global North and the Global South. This means that they have no wage protection as well as no legal recourse against exploitation and abuse. In some local contexts, these workers have organized to create legislation that protects them, such as the recently passed Domestic Workers' Bill of Rights in Massachusetts. This law is a model that both brings these workers under the umbrella of many existing legal protections and addresses some issues specific to working in someone else's home. Likewise, a legal change in 2014 finally brought home care workers in the United States under the auspices of the Fair Labor Standards Act. In many countries, particularly in the Global South, it will also be key to develop ways to regulate and protect the large numbers of care workers who are operating in the informal economy (UNDP 2015). Legal advances such as these are necessary to obtain basic rights for these groups of care workers and ensure that the care sector becomes a viable labor market choice.

Reform Care Policy and Immigration Policy in Dialogue with Each Other

Governments are already playing a role in the migration of care workers. With more attention to the shape of these policies, they could play a role in mitigating the harm done by current patterns of migration. Governments could structure their involvement differently to make the whole process of labor migration less coercive, and provide a well-formulated scheme to ensure security, protection, and rights for workers in the receiving countries. The United Nations Development Programme has recommended that multinational organizations play a stronger role in managing global migration. Care work is an area that is ripe for this kind of intervention (UNDP 2015).

Yeates (2010) has argued that one of the most important measures that can be taken in both the Global South and the Global North to ameliorate nursing shortages exacerbated by global migration is to implement policies to improve wages and working conditions for nurses. Research has shown that policies that increase wages in developed countries have a significant impact on the retention of the domestic nursing workforce. Nonwage policies such as setting minimum staffing ratios have also had important effects on increasing both the number of nurses who stay in the profession and demand for nursing training. These kinds of wage and nonwage policies are important to implement across the care sector in receiving countries in order to create jobs that provide sustainable livelihoods and reduce the potential for exploitation of vulnerable workers such as migrants.

In sending countries in the Global South, research has shown that policies that increase compensation and improve working conditions for care workers both stimulate more entries into the occupation and decrease the number of nurses who emigrate (Yeates 2010). Again, these kinds of policies need to be implemented across the sector—for childcare workers, teachers, nurses, social workers, home care aides, and others. They address the underlying reasons for care worker shortages and will fundamentally transform the coercive nature of much contemporary care worker migration. Simultaneously, immigration policy needs to be reformed to support workers' freedom of movement in ways that acknowledge the benefits to both sending and receiving countries.

Break the Links in the Cycle of the Gendered Devaluation of Care

This is an ambitious policy goal, as deeply embedded norms and practices are slow to change. However, it is absolutely critical. As long as care work is viewed as anything less than valuable and skilled labor, it will not be rewarded and recognized appropriately. Policymakers must craft policy that both raises the value of the care work done by women and encourages men to participate more fully in paid and unpaid care. Only then can care be transformed from women's responsibility to a responsibility shared by all of society.

Parental leave policy in Sweden provides a good model of how deliberately crafted policy can lead to behavioral and normative change. Sweden implemented a generous paid parental leave policy many decades ago, only to find that it was having an unintended consequence. Although the policy was designed to be gender-neutral, in practice, the overwhelming majority of parental leave was being taken by women. This pattern was, in fact, creating increased gender inequities in paid work, as women who took longer breaks in their careers were significantly disadvantaged upon reentering the paid labor force. So Swedish policy was changed to require a certain amount of the leave to be taken by fathers in cases where both parents were present. Within a decade, the number of fathers taking leave had increased dramatically. Research has shown that fathers who take leave continue to contribute more hours to parental care even once the leave has ended (Zimmerman 2015).

Targeted policies that support unpaid care and encourage men's participation raise the value of this work by providing economic and cultural recognition. Public policy has a huge role to play in shaping the paid care labor force as well. A large proportion of care work in the Global North is publicly funded. In countries such as Britain and Canada, large federally funded programs support the health care workforce. In many countries, schools are publicly supported, in some cases extending down to early childhood. Mental health and social services also depend on government funding in some form to operate. This level of investment gives government policy the potential to influence the wages and working conditions of care workers strongly, as well as to encourage occupational integration across gender and race.

The Future of Work and the Care Sector

Some authors in this volume have argued that technological innovation and the development of artificial intelligence threaten to erase many jobs as we know them. Other authors have stated that one of our responses to these changes should be to unlink livelihoods from jobs by providing guaranteed universal access to basic incomes and basic services. In an important sense, the care sector is where these ideas come together. Although technological innovation has had important impacts on how care workers do their jobs, these jobs are far less likely to be fully automated than other sectors of the labor market. And many of the basic services that members of a society need are, in fact, care services—childcare, health care, education, elder care. There is an opportunity here to meet the needs of all members of a society while providing a source of employment for large numbers of workers. It may be that with the disappearance of jobs in other labor market sectors, the shape of care jobs changes even more dramatically than I have suggested here—so that more people have jobs that take up less of their time, for example. But the care sector is fundamental to not only the future of work, but standards of living around the globe.

Part II

RISKS AND REPERCUSSIONS

Alternative Futures

6

Taskers in the Precariat

Confronting an Emerging Dystopia

Guy Standing

Probably never in the history of capitalism has its core trend changed so fast. The labor process is being transformed in several ways simultaneously, among them the technological disruption of traditional occupations, new regulations promoting flexible labor, the globalization of labor transactions and competition, and the emergence of digital "tasking" platforms.

These developments have created a new and rapidly expanding "precariat" class, consisting of millions of people obliged to accept a life of unstable labor and living, without an occupational identity or corporate narrative to give to their lives (Standing 2011, 2014). And the amount of unpaid "work" is rising relative to the amount of paid "labor," as more people work away from fixed workplaces and outside fixed working hours, or with jobs that pay only when "on-task," ignoring travel time (in the case of, for example, care workers), waiting time (drivers), security check time (Amazon warehouse workers), and so on.

The precariat has been growing all over the world with the spread of flexible labor practices and the associated economic insecurity. Latterly, its rise is being accelerated by the explosion of digital tasking platforms such as Uber (ride-hailing), TaskRabbit (domestic chores), and Amazon Mechanical Turk, which distributes microtasks to remote online workers. The McKinsey Global Institute (MGI) has estimated that what it calls "online talent platforms" could add 2 percent to global GDP between 2015 and 2025, creating seventy-two million full-time equivalent jobs (Manyika et al. 2015). While the heroic assumptions involved mean that little faith should be held in this precise figure, it does indicate the scale of the developments.

Digital tasking platforms work as online marketplaces, matching buyers and sellers of labor. The platforms make their money from taking a cut of each transaction, though some offer or require additional services that they themselves provide, for a fee. For instance, Uber provides insurance coverage for its drivers while they are transporting fares. Most platforms for services have two features: they deal in short-term tasks (assembling a flat-pack wardrobe, writing a newspaper article) and the people supplying the services use their own equipment and assets (cars, homes, tools).

Many platforms claim to belong to a new "sharing economy" that is boosting efficiency and incomes through increased utilization of underused assets. However, they are in fact expanding the scope of commodified labor and the amount of unpaid "work-for-labor," as we shall see. They all bypass the firm as traditionally understood. They are creating "platform capitalism."

By late 2016 Uber, the app-based taxi service, had over a million drivers worldwide and was operating in more than five hundred cities in seventy countries. Airbnb, initially designed for a casual rental market and enabling people to let rooms in their homes on a short-term basis, had over three million listings, ranging from spare beds to castles, in sixty-five thousand cities and 191 countries, and had more rooms on its books than some of the world's largest hotel chains.

Some platforms are in direct competition with older forms of service. These include Uber, its US rival Lyft, and imitators elsewhere such as GrabTaxi in southeast Asia, Ola in India, and Didi Kuaidi in China. BlaBlaCar, a French start-up originally called Covoiturage, is a car-sharing platform that enables drivers making long journeys to reduce the cost by "selling" empty seats.

Other companies put buyers in touch with providers of services rang-ing from housecleaning (Handy) to valet parking (Luxe), grocery delivery (Instacart), drink delivery (Drizly), and dogsitting (BorrowMyDoggy). Deliveroo delivers meals to your door; TaskRabbit undertakes domestic tasks and errands; Thumbtack finds professionals to supply services, from installing a kitchen to teaching yoga. It is a misnomer to call this the "sharing economy." These digital platforms are labor brokers, often tak-ing 20 percent or more from all transactions.

"Crowdwork" platforms also act as labor brokers, providing a digital labor exchange through which organizations ("requesters") post online tasks, often split into small, sometimes micro tasks, which workers ("taskers") then bid for. These platforms charge 10 percent or more per transaction. The pioneer in microtasking was Amazon Mechanical Turk (AMT), set up by Amazon in 2005, but there are now dozens of crowd-work platforms, among the biggest being Upwork, PeoplePerHour, and CrowdFlower.

ClickWorker, based in Germany, boasts eight hundred thousand "click-workers" in 136 countries and big-name clients such as Honda and T-Mobile. Lancers, a Japanese platform, had 420,000 registered workers in 2015. The Japanese crowd-labor industry body aims to increase the number of crowdworkers nationwide to ten million by 2018 and twenty million by 2023 (Jackman 2015).

Founded in 2009, by 2016 Uber had become easily the most valuable American company of its generation; its implied valuation of $70 billion in late 2016 was higher than that of 80 percent of firms in the S&P 500 stock market index, including General Motors and Ford. Airbnb, after just eight years of existence, was valued at $30 billion in March 2017.

Uber has become so emblematic that, early in the 2016 US presidential campaign, Republican primary candidate Jeb Bush ostentatiously rode in an Uber taxi to signal his support for the company and the company's support for him. In a speech flagged as laying out her economic plan, Democratic candidate Hillary Clinton was more equivocal, promising to "crack down on bosses misclassifying workers as contractors." We will come back to that.

Although for every platform that becomes a household name, dozens fizzle out or remain as "micro" as they began, overall they are expanding phenomenally fast, generating more than US$25 billion in revenues in

2016. A common attitude was summed up by Bob Bahramipour, CEO of Gigwalk, which recruits taskers for brief projects in retail, merchandising, and marketing. He told the Associated Press (2013), "You can hire 10,000 people for 10 to 15 minutes. When they're done, those 10,000 people just melt away."

Taskers in the Precariat

MGI estimates that 20 to 30 percent of the workforce in the USA and western Europe—up to 162 million people—are working in the "gig economy." Nearly half of these people rely on such work for their primary income (Manyika et al. 2016). A 2016 survey commissioned by Upwork and the misnamed Freelancers Union found that fifty-five million people, or more than one in three US workers, had freelanced online or offline in the previous year. Of those, a quarter relied wholly on this type of labor, about half mixed part-time freelancing with part-time or casual employment, and fewer than a fifth were "moonlighters" with conventional jobs (Upwork and Freelancers Union 2016).

Another study (Katz and Krueger 2016) estimated that 16 percent of the US workforce were doing temporary "gig" or contract work as their main job in 2015, nearly double the proportion of twenty years earlier. Moreover, the increase of "alternative work arrangements" appeared to account for all net employment growth in the US economy since 2005. While the study estimated that only half a percent of all US workers were providing services through online platforms, the number was said to be growing rapidly.

This could well be an underestimate. In the UK, a 2016 survey suggested that one in ten working-age adults had done tasks contracted through online platforms in the previous year, and over a third of those said that this was their sole or main source of income (Huws and Joyce 2016).

Digital platforms are building a new "putting-out" system and eroding old forms of service delivery, just as the original putting-out system of supplying materials to independent home workers eroded medieval guilds. They are leveraging change in all the sectors they are penetrating, with underappreciated spillover effects. For instance, in the USA,

Uber's rise has hit Medallion Financial, which makes loans to Yellow Cab drivers to buy their licenses ("medallions"). The price of medallions has tumbled as Uber has taken business from licensed taxis and many drivers have been pushed into default on their loans, potentially threatening the ability of Medallion Financial to lend to future would-be licensed taxi drivers.

The On-Demand Concierge Economy

We can differentiate between three categories of tasker. The first consists of those in the gig—or, more cruelly, "concierge"—economy, performing services such as taxi driving, cleaning, handiwork, or delivery, commissioned through digital platforms.

The digital platforms earn high incomes at their taskers' expense. Uber takes 20–30 percent of each fare, plus a booking fee in some cases, and dictates fares and routes. Airbnb nets 9–15 percent on every booking. TaskRabbit charges 30 percent of the task fee (15 percent for repeat bookings) and obliges the client to pay an extra 5 percent for its insurance guarantee scheme. The revenues gained from these transaction fees far outweigh the cost of services provided by the platform—development and maintenance of the technology, administering booking and payment systems, insurance, and so on.

The platforms insist that taskers are not employees but independent contractors, and so are not covered by labor law entitling them to a range of benefits and legal protections. In the USA, these include the minimum wage, overtime pay, expense reimbursement, rest breaks, health and safety rules, workers' compensation, unemployment compensation, employer contributions to social security, and protection against discrimination. Nor are they allowed to unionize. Because antitrust law treats contractors as businesses, bargaining collectively is considered a cartel. (In 2015, Seattle passed a law granting independent contractors the right to unionize, but in April 2017 it was suspended by a federal judge pending legal challenges by the US Chamber of Commerce and about a dozen Uber and Lyft drivers backed by the antiunion National Right to Work Legal Defense Foundation and the Freedom Foundation.)

Uber goes to great lengths to justify the independent contractor label, describing its drivers as part-time "driver-partners" who choose to provide rides using its platform. TaskRabbit's support center poses the rhetorical question "Do Taskers work for TaskRabbit?" and gives its answer:

> No, they do not. Taskers are local entrepreneurs and independent contractors who work for themselves. TaskRabbit simply provides the platform for Clients and Taskers to meet. We vet and background-check all Taskers before allowing them onto the platform to ensure they are professional and reliable individuals.

This is disingenuous. Most taskers are neither entrepreneurial nor independent; few build a business based on queuing for iPhone buyers, as some are tasked to do. But it would be equally wrong to call them "employees" in the classic sense; they are not directly supervised, own the main means of production, and, in principle, have control over their working time. However, they are not self-employed, either. They depend on the labor broker (platform) to obtain tasks and are subject to rules, such as wearing a T-shirt with the company logo or accepting a certain number of tasks. Yet, like the self-employed, they bear most job-related costs, including transport, repairs and maintenance, and insurance for accidents and ill-health.

Ongoing court cases in the USA and elsewhere, claiming that taskers are employees, highlight the inadequacy of the old dichotomy of "employee" and "self-employed." This is a new form of labor and categories should be adjusted accordingly. "Freelance" is a misnomer, as is "independent worker" (Harris and Krueger 2015), since most taskers are not "free" or completely independent. "Dependent" contractor is more apt than "independent." But the term "tasker," as in doing tasks, conveys the phenomenon more pithily.

In June 2015, the California Labor Commissioner ruled that Uber's control of pricing, tipping, driver ratings, and type of car made it a de facto employer. A decision to classify Uber drivers and other taskers as employees would hugely reduce the platforms' income by increasing their operating costs. Indeed, it would destroy their business model. This is why, despite appealing the California ruling and other court decisions, including an adverse ruling by a UK employment tribunal, Uber has tried to settle cases out of court in return for maintaining drivers' status as independent contractors. Some smaller US platforms have nevertheless decided to treat their taskers as employees and are still in business, including Shyp (shipping), Munchery (meal delivery), and Luxe (valet parking). Lawyers for Uber drivers and others seeking employee status argue that these platforms can afford to operate on slimmer margins.

While it seems preferable to make taskers a separate category, some platforms do behave in key respects like employers, dictating terms, controlling quality, and disciplining taskers deemed to have fallen below set standards. Uber requires drivers to accept at least 80 percent of drive requests (Hullinger 2016). TaskRabbit has moved from a system in which taskers bid for posted tasks to one that assigns them to tasks at an hourly rate. They then have thirty minutes to accept or reject the task. Those failing to accept a certain percentage of tasks within a certain period, or failing to respond within thirty minutes, can be "deactivated," with reactivation requiring successful completion of a reeducation quiz. Too many slips result in a tasker's being removed from "the community" altogether. As one Facebook comment put it, "Anyone left working for TR [TaskRabbit] is an indentured servant. . . . You are not growing your own business; you are growing TR as a business" (cited in Garling 2014).

Taskers are also subject to control through customer ratings posted on their profiles. For instance, Uber drivers must maintain a rating of at least 4.6 out of five "stars." This is a new form of sweating: a sad, low-cost way of inducing self-exploitation. Ratings are not just a feedback mechanism; they are a means of monitoring and disciplining, without the need for a supervisor. The platform is part of the panopticon state in which surveillance is automated. Ratings are pernicious, as they impose constant regulation and do so with little transparency or accountability. An Uber driver may be rated poorly for a slow journey due to heavy traffic, for refusing to break the speed limit, or for a difference of opinion, perhaps on a matter of politics, sports, or religion. The client may be in a bad mood, or be prejudiced against certain ethnic groups. The ratings take seconds, but may have drastic implications for the tasker, leading to loss of income and future opportunities. If several customers give the driver a low rating, he or she will be deactivated. There is no due process, no means of appeal.

The relationship is supposed to be symmetrical, in that customers can rate taskers and vice versa. Thus, Handy commented:

> Handy is a transparent platform that takes care of every need in the home. As part of that transparency, we offer a two-way rating system so independent professionals can offer feedback on how a job went and customers can do likewise. This incentivizes excellence on both sides of the supply and demand equation, provides constructive feedback for professionals and customers, and opens up more lines of communication to ensure the best possible experience in the home (Dzieza 2015).

This claim of rating equality does not reflect the reality. The consequences of a subpar rating for a tasker are much more severe than a poor rating would be for a customer. Some Uber drivers have been deactivated without notice and forced to pay for a "training class" approved by the platform in order to be reactivated. Some platforms do not deactivate, but downgrade taskers receiving subpar ratings, so that they come lower down the listings when searches are made. This is a powerful control mechanism.

In an impressive show of erudition, California judge Edwin Chen cited Michel Foucault in his 2015 ruling that Uber had a case to answer in a class-action suit brought on behalf of drivers claiming they should be classified as employees. Remarking that the ratings system gave Uber a "tremendous amount of control over the 'manner and means' of its drivers' performance," he noted Foucault's words in *Discipline and Punish* that a "state of conscious and permanent visibility assures the automatic functioning of power."

As Judge Chen pointed out, ratings make the relationship between the platform and tasker look more like a conventional employment relationship. And when deactivating or downgrading is done without notice or warning, it is equivalent to being fired. If US courts eventually rule that platforms such as Uber and TaskRabbit are employers, use of ratings to deactivate or discipline taskers could also fall foul of Title VII of the Civil Rights Act, which forbids discrimination on the basis of sex, race, color, national origin, or religion.

Another issue raised by tasking is the erosion of professionalism. Uber is again an exemplar, since it has attracted high-profile protests from taxi operators claiming unfair competition in just about every city it has entered. Depending on the regulations in force, Uber crafts its business model to try to ensure its drivers are not subject to the rules applying to conventional taxis. In London, for instance, traditional cabbies must drive only authorized vehicles ("black cabs") and pass a "knowledge" exam involving knowledge of every street in central London.

Cities wishing to protect traditional taxis have been hitting back, by classifying Uber and other app-based services as conventional taxis or devising regulations to constrain their operations. In London, however, the Competition and Markets Authority has attacked regulations proposed by Transport for London as anticompetitive, suggesting lower standards for black cabs instead. And Uber and others are finding ways to operate within the new rules, or are operating on the old basis pending lengthy court appeals. The threat to professional standards remains.

Disputes about standards are bound to arise whenever amateurs provide a service that hitherto was the exclusive preserve of those with qualifications or membership in an occupational community. Hotel and bed-and-breakfast organizations have attacked Airbnb, saying its "hosts" have an unfair advantage because they do not need to comply with fire regulations or taxes on overnight stays. In New York, Airbnb has been accused of encouraging illegal leasing and landlordism (Streitfeld 2014). Amateurism is a route for cheapening labor and increasing the rental income of the platforms.

Taskers fit into the precariat: they lack income security, labor security, and an occupational trajectory. They must do a lot of work-for-labor, unremunerated, beyond formal workplaces. Uber, among others, has tried to give the impression that most of its drivers are earning extra money to supplement a regular income. It seems rather that, globally, millions of taskers are scrambling for odd jobs and are otherwise unemployed or in low-paid activities. They are on-demand servants for the elite and salariat. The concierge economy is part of the Second Gilded Age.

Taskers in Cloud Labor

A second group of taskers consists of those doing online tasks. Initially, this sphere was dominated by low-level microtasks, epitomized by Amazon Mechanical Turk (AMT). However, online tasking has moved upmarket to cover many forms of professional work, such as accountancy, legal research, medical diagnosis, and design. Professional tasking platforms include Upwork, Freelancer.com, and PeoplePerHour. In California, UpCounsel provides online legal services and handles its taskers' finances and document management. UpCounsel's CEO sees this as the start of "the virtualization of professional services" (Wadhwa 2015).

The numbers involved in cloud labor are large and growing fast. AMT has an estimated half a million taskers available at any one time. In 2016, Upwork, formed in 2014 through a merger of Elance and oDesk, had twelve million registered "freelancers" on its site from 180 countries, connected to five million client businesses. Australia's Freelancer.com claims nearly twenty-four million registered users either posting tasks or seeking them.

The business models vary. Microtasking platforms are based on extreme Taylorism—the division of labor into components in which the manager does the thinking, the laborer the doing. It is clouded (literally) in euphemisms, such as the term used to describe the units of work, HITs (Human Intelligence Tasks). Many pay only a few cents apiece. A worker must do a lot of HITs to make a little money. One survey in 2012 found that AMT taskers in the USA had done, on average, over nine thousand tasks, and their Indian counterparts more than 6,500 (Kittur et al. 2013). These figures are indicative of how minute the tasks typically are.

Microtaskers are probably the most exploited and most likely to self-exploit of all taskers. Their work is usually allocated at a set rate per task, which is often extremely low. Tasks may turn out to be more complex or time-consuming than taskers were led to believe. In practice, they have no means of redress, should the requester avoid paying by claiming, falsely, that the work was not of sufficient quality, or simply failing to pay. As Michael Bernstein, who leads a Stanford University project on crowdsourcing, put it, "AMT is notoriously bad at ensuring high quality results, producing respect and fair wages for workers, and making it easy to author effective tasks" (cited in LaPlante and Silberman 2015).

Requesters and broker platforms often seem to forget that the tasks are being done by real people with real needs and emotions. Lukas Biewald, CEO of CrowdFlower, which specializes in collecting, cleaning, and labeling data, revealed his true attitude in a moment of hubris when telling an audience, "Before the internet, it would be really difficult to find someone, sit them down for ten minutes and get them to work for you, and then fire them after those ten minutes. But with technology you can actually find them, pay them the tiny amount of money and then get rid of them when you don't want them anymore" (cited in Marvit 2014).

Even though a majority of taskers so far have been in rich countries, reflecting access to reliable internet connections, cloud labor is globalizing. Pay rates reflect the fact that tasks can be done equally well by someone in Bangalore or Accra as in Boston or Amsterdam. In that respect, among others, platforms are undermining the ability of workers to obtain decent wages.

On-Call Employees

A third group of taskers consists of employees, with employment contracts, who are called upon only as the employer requires and paid accordingly. These taskers, on zero-hours, on-call or "if-and-when" contracts, or on "flexible" or "just-in-time" schedules, are remunerated only for hours they work on contracted tasks. In the United States, 10–16 percent of employees have irregular or on-call schedules. According to federal data, two-thirds of food-service employees, half of all retail workers, and 40 percent of janitors and cleaners have, at most, a week's notice of when they will be working (Stone 2017).

Time and money spent on work-related activities that on-call workers must undertake in order to do those tasks—providing their own uniforms or means of transport, for example—often go unrecognized and unremunerated. So-called flexible schedules oblige those on such contracts to be on permanent standby, unable to plan, not knowing if they will obtain paid labor or how much. Some are doubly exploited, forbidden to take other jobs or prevented from enrolling in training programs in case this affects their availability.

Occupational Dismantling

Digital platforms and their legions of taskers are eroding notions of employee and employment, and the body of labor-related entitlements and protections built up during the twentieth century. They are also accentuating the dismantling of occupational communities. For hundreds of years, occupational guilds defined working life, setting standards, codes of ethics, means of training, and sources of social protection. They stood against the market. The neoliberal agenda aims to dismantle them, and the on-demand economy is both a consequence and an accelerator of that. The costs include the withering of occupational ethics and routes of social mobility through professions and crafts.

Taskers have the potential advantage of flexible working. But they are being used to undermine professional qualifications, further marginalizing the time-honored concept of the professional and craft community. One of the least-analyzed aspects of the neoliberal agenda has been the reregulation of occupations, including the great professions. In particular, there has been a shift to state licensing, with an avowed intention to protect consumers, not those inside the profession or craft. A third of US occupations now require practitioners to be licensed (and pay a hefty fee for the privilege).

Trade unions are not the only labor bodies to have been weakened by the neoliberal onslaught. Outsourcing and automation are further accelerating the deprofessionalization of services and increasing the class fragmentation of professions, making it more difficult to move from lower to higher echelons. Some analysts have gone further, arguing that automation will—and should—largely displace the professions (Susskind and Susskind 2015). Thus, in 2014, forty-eight million Americans used online software rather than professionals to do their tax returns, and the most popular US legal service is legalzoom.com, an online advice and do-it-yourself document-drafting service. Ebay and PayPal process over sixty million disagreements each year using "online dispute resolution" software that helps settle disputes without involving lawyers.

The prospect that the professions will be dominated by automated near-equivalents should alarm us. The issue is not just loss of income for those in professions and crafts. Occupations have been vital communities and zones of rights throughout history, involving more than just delivery of a commodified service. They impart ethics, collegial empathy, and a culture of learning and questioning of received wisdom. Machines and software cannot do this.

An automated service may implement the conventional wisdom more accurately and consistently. It will deliver the norm. A community of human professionals delivers services distributed around the norm. This allows for the historical reality that, in every professional service, today's conventional wisdom can become tomorrow's obsolescent practice. What seems odd today often becomes a new norm tomorrow.

Automation and Heteromation

While the technological revolution is disrupting occupations, it is worsening the distribution of income by extracting income from labor and work for the benefit of labor brokers. This is reducing the number and range of high-paying jobs, directly by increasing the division of labor into smaller, cheaper tasks, and indirectly by weakening the bargaining position of those competing with taskers.

The combination of digital technologies and platform capitalism is also affecting the character of work and labor. It is reducing the number of defined jobs by shifting to tasks done by people who are neither employees nor independent contractors. At the same time, it is also increasing the number of activities counted as jobs in our misleading labor statistics. By being commodified—made into market transactions—some forms of work previously done privately (or not at all) are being turned into jobs, or tasks for others to do.

On-demand shopping, queuing, cleaning, and so on boost phony "employment," pleasing politicians, but in reality merely substituting hired servants for the same work as before. If people order their shopping and delivery online, rather than do it themselves, the "work" of shopping is converted into someone else's "labor." The same goes for activities that hardly count as work," such as dog-walking. This is another reason why the claim that technology is displacing labor is misleading. The concierge economy is generating more labor.

To complicate matters, digital platforms are also increasing the amount of unpaid work that does not count as labor, by creating forms of work previously not done at all and by converting some forms of paid labor into unpaid work. As a mass phenomenon, this is unique to the twenty-first century. Taskers must do many forms of work, unpaid, that would have been paid as labor in an equivalent conventional job. For instance, task rabbits are paid for tasks, but not for all the extra work they do around those tasks, such as buying, cleaning, and maintaining tools. Uber drivers must spend time and money looking after their vehicle and pay for their own fuel.

Meanwhile, the new technologies are inducing additional work, captured by the ungainly term "heteromation." The classic example is provision of personal information by online users that gives the technology companies free data for building their moneymaking services. The work may be regarded by those doing it as productive or personally rewarding— participation in social media, for example. But the distinctive character of heteromation is that the platforms gain from the work of others through the ability to "insert human beings within technological systems in order to allow the system to operate in intended ways" (Ekbia and Nardy 2012). As the vice president for research of Gartner, a technology consultancy, aptly said in 2012, "Facebook's nearly one billion users have become the largest unpaid workforce in history" (cited in Ekbia and Nardy 2014). By the end of 2016, the number of Facebook users had risen to 1.9 billion.

Unsolicited training is another form of unpaid work encouraged by the new technologies and growth of the precariat. Often in desperation, people take online courses in several subjects, induced by advertisements, sweeteners, encouragement, or insistence by employment offices. This work is partly speculative; there is no guarantee it will lead to any income or employment. Nor is it necessarily beneficial in other respects; there are always opportunity costs in using time and money for one thing that could be used for something else.

There is also the financial cost involved and the likelihood of "pig cycle" effects: a shortage of pigs (marketable skills) leads to price rises for pigs (wage opportunities for those with the skills), which leads farmers to invest in more pigs, which leads to a glut of pigs and falling prices (wages and job opportunities). Unlike pigs, the skills may have become obsolete by the time they have been expensively obtained.

Regulate Labor Brokers

Digital labor brokers are here to stay; there is no going back to earlier employment relations. Unions and activists should not repeat the reaction to labor flexibility policies in the 1980s and 1990s, when unions refused to negotiate and simply resisted, eventually conceding on more unfavorable terms. Had they negotiated for a new social compact when they had sufficient strength to do so, insisting on basic security for all in return for flexibility, there would be much less insecurity for those performing labor today.

The on-demand economy requires new forms of regulation, redistribution, and social protection to redress the growing imbalances and inequities. These should start with something basic. Every period in which labor and work have been transformed has led to an overhaul of statistics to represent reality. This matters, since statistics orient public debate and policy thinking. Crowd labor, new forms of labor triangulation, and growth of the precariat make current official statistics even more "unfit for purpose."

Where taskers are contractors working primarily for one company and required to comply with its rules and standards, there is a case for calling them employees, as the California appeals court decided in the case of FedEx drivers. But any distinction between contractors and employees will be arbitrary. Instead of trying to shoehorn tasking into the dichotomous classification of contractor or employee, taskers should form a separate category. For instance, Harris and Krueger (2015) have proposed that "independent workers" in the gig economy should be covered by employment discrimination laws, have the right to organize, and have social security contributions paid on their behalf—but they would not be entitled to the minimum wage, and on-demand companies would not have to pay unemployment insurance or workers' compensation.

While these specific proposals can be argued over, some general principles apply. In particular, it is imperative to strengthen taskers' collective bargaining capacities. Tasker associations should be set up, as separate entities or within occupational bodies. (Stone 2017 cites existing models, including in the airline, entertainment, and freelance sectors.) Certainly, the emergence of taskers will intensify friction between groups of workers; there is not and never has been a unified working class. The divergence of interests is why a "collaborative" bargaining system is needed, for bargaining between complementary or substitute occupational groups, not just between employers and employees (Standing 2009). On one side are employers, requesters, and labor brokers; on the other, employees, taskers, and freelancers. Why should only employees be covered by the protections built up in the twentieth century? Anybody doing any kind of work should have the same rights and entitlements.

The platform labor brokers claim that they are only providing technology to put clients in touch with "independent contractors" of services. Thus, Uber and its rival Lyft say they are technology, not transport, companies. They thereby avoid paying payroll taxes for taskers and they do not provide nonwage benefits that employees are supposed to receive, including equipment needed to do their job, paid holidays, company pension contributions, and, in the USA, medical insurance. In return for their intermediary role, the brokers typically take 20 percent of earnings. But they are free-riding on the public, because taskers fallen on hard times will need state benefits for which the brokers do not pay.

For that reason, among others, there should be a levy (tax) of, say, 20 percent of companies' earnings from labor broking, or a levy for each tasker they contract. Brokers should also provide insurance coverage, including accident insurance, for taskers while on jobs contracted through their platforms. If this is a sharing economy, as its advocates claim, costs, as well as benefits, should be shared.

As an emerging "profession," labor brokers should be registered and required to join an association that develops ethical codes and monitors their conduct. In the UK, nearly forty online businesses, including Airbnb, Zipcar, and TaskRabbit, have formed a trade body, Sharing Economy UK, which has drawn up a consumer code of conduct setting standards for staff training, safety, and complaints procedures intended to promote good practice. But if standards can be set for consumers, they should also be set for the treatment of taskers.

Codes of ethics and good practice should be drawn up, with tasker involvement. These should include written contracts between broker and tasker, a right for taskers to know and correct information about them held by the broker, a ban on blacklisting taskers who complain or sue for compensation, and due process restraints on use of customer ratings. Brokers should also ensure that taskers are paid promptly for contracted tasks.

To protect taskers and raise their income, several other reforms are essential. Occupational licensing must be rolled back. In the USA, more than one thousand occupations are now subject to licensing, most unnecessarily. Barbers, bartenders, manicurists, massage therapists, florists, interior designers, and upholsterers are among the occupations for which some states require licenses, usually involving obligatory study or "training," examinations, and payment of a high fee (Carpenter et al. 2012). Rather than protecting the public, licensing is all too often motivated by the desire to restrict entry into the occupation and boost the incomes of incumbents (Nunn 2016).

The insurance industry dominates licensing, transferring risks, uncertainty, and costs onto workers and enabling licensing boards to block or punish people, usually without due process. Labor brokers and the precariat should be united in wishing to see less licensing. It is a means of restricting the right to practice forms of work, and thus of lowering earning opportunities for many competent people.

Licensing should be limited to occupations that involve externalities and dangers, as in the case of surgeons and architects. Otherwise, collective self-regulation should be revived. There should be more reliance on accreditation: that is, belonging to an association that testifies to its members' competence or experience. Unlike licensing, accreditation is voluntary, and customers can choose whether to use an accredited or nonaccredited professional. For all professions, an international accreditation system should be constructed, with standardized rules.

Taskers who are on call, on zero-hours contracts, or subject to "flexible" schedules set by the firm should be compensated for inconvenience and insecurity through, for instance, "standby bonuses" as in Germany, or given a base salary or retainer. They should also be allowed to do other work, with no exclusivity clauses in their contracts. All taskers should have the right to decline tasks demanded with less than twenty-four hours' notice, without loss of pay or opportunity, to allow them to gain more control of their lives.

Taskers should have a right to legal advice on contracts and disputes, paid partly by contributions from labor brokers. They should be required to make a small contribution, to discourage frivolous actions. But access to legal advice would encourage both sides to make agreements transparent and standardized as far as possible.

Of course, regulation can only do so much. Elsewhere, it is argued that what is needed is a new income distribution system founded on a universal basic income, paid to each individual regardless of labor status

(Standing 2016, 2017). The twentieth-century distribution system, which prioritized jobs and welfare benefits linked to jobs, has broken down irretrievably. Real wages have stagnated for decades throughout the industrialized world, due in part to globalization that has tripled the world's labor supply and promoted offshoring and the growth of international supply chains. Tasking is only an extreme form of the flexible labor practices that have burgeoned in the neoliberal quest for "competitiveness" pursued by almost all Western governments.

This is not the place to go into the broader arguments for basic income. However, a system anchored on a basic income would be of special benefit to taskers, as well as the precariat more generally. Giving taskers basic security would help to increase their bargaining power vis-à-vis labor brokers and employers, strengthen their individual and collective voice, and enable them to refuse tasks with low pay or poor working conditions.

One way of funding a basic income is through democratically controlled sovereign wealth funds, built up from levies or taxes on rental income derived from exploitation or ownership of assets, including natural resources, buildings, financial assets, and intellectual property. The cut taken by intermediaries on third-party transactions is another form of rental income, based on ownership of the exchange or platform on which those transactions take place. Thus, all or part of the levy on digital tasking platforms recommended here could be paid into a sovereign wealth fund, alongside other contributions, that would help finance a basic income.

The platform capitalism taking shape is not a sharing economy. It is not wholly parasitic; it offers new and/or more efficient services, and it is commodifying spheres that were outside the market economy. But it is transformative, contrary to the contention of defenders of the old labor system, such as Larry Mishel, president of the Democrat-leaning Economic Policy Institute in Washington, DC, who has dismissed its impact as "trivial" (Mishel 2015). It is transformative directly, by generating tasking labor for millions, and indirectly, through its impact on traditional suppliers of services. Even if a majority of taskers are doing tasks part-time, their numbers are growing rapidly, scaring competitors into making concessions (Hall and Krueger 2015). Moreover, having used official revenue data in support of his "trivial" claim, Mishel then undermined it by noting that "failure to report income is very common among independent contractors."

In one respect, the on-demand economy reverses a capitalist mantra. Instead of being owned by capitalists, means of production are "owned" by the taskers—the precariat. The platforms maximize profits through ownership and control of the technological apparatus, protected by patents and other intellectual property rights, and by the exploitation of labor through tasking and unpaid work.

As platform-based tasking expands, it will be appreciated just how isolated the precariat is in this zone, in constant competition with one another. The atomization drives down wages and transfers costs, risks, and uncertainty onto the precariat. So far, at least, taskers have had minimal means or opportunities to coalesce.

These forms of labor intensify pressure to commodify all aspects of life. Intensifying self-exploitation is a sad way for the precariat to respond to adversity. It is how those experiencing declining wages and living standards cover up the decline, for a while. But when sweating spreads to taskers, the threat to wages and working conditions for all workers grows. The precariat's vulnerability today is a threat to all of us tomorrow.

7

AUTOMATED BUT COMPENSATED?

Technological Change and Redistribution in Advanced Democracies

David Rueda and Stefan Thewissen

Technological change is widely regarded as one of the main drivers of long-term economic development (Romer 1990). By complementing occupations with certain skill profiles while making others redundant, it structures employment and significantly shapes the occupational structure (Goldin and Katz 2008; Oesch 2013; Ford, this volume). Technological innovations can have far-reaching social implications that differ across occupations. For Karl Marx, technology contributed to the creation of a "reserve army of the unemployed" who allowed capitalists to reduce the wages of the working classes. More optimistically, technological change enables specialization and skill upgrading, which facilitates a move away from routine labor (Erikson and Goldthorpe 1992; Iversen and Cusack 2000; Wren 2013).

Current and recent technological innovations are strongly connected to computer-based information technology. Its momentous implementation in the last few decades has been spurred by significant real price declines in computing power (Autor, Levy, and Murnane 2003). Computers can perform routine tasks that are well-defined and repetitive and complement complex and more ambiguous abstract task structures. They have a limited effect, however, on interpersonal service tasks. These routine occupations tend to occupy the middle of the educational and wage distributions. The risk of automation, therefore, cannot be captured by income or educational lines, but rather involves a process of polarization, affecting ordinary households (Spitz-Oener 2006; Autor, Dorn, and Hanson 2015). More generally, by affecting certain occupations and industries, it entails an income risk that is unequally shared among the population (Thewissen and Van Vliet forthcoming).

The employment and wage effects of technological change have been relatively well-examined. Studies report significant decreases in the share of employment and wages of routine occupations (Autor, Levy, and Murnane 2003, 2015; Goos, Manning, and Salomons 2014; Michaels, Natraj, and Van Reenen 2014). Job loss among occupations prone to automation might even significantly expand in the upcoming decades (Frey and Osborne 2017; Susskind and Susskind 2015). In an influential contribution, Ford (2015) argues that a basic income guarantee should be adopted by states to cope with the threat of a "jobless future." Yet, technological change has not received much attention in political science. This is surprising, given the expected effects on income inequality and risks—two factors that play an important role in a discipline dominated by questions of distribution and welfare state risk mitigation (Pierson and Castles 2006). Inequality is frequently invoked as a key determinant of societal outcomes ranging from electoral politics to conflict. The idea that insurance motivations are a significant determinant of redistribution has become prominent in the recent comparative political economy literature. Moreover, whether or not individuals exposed to technological change demand redistribution by the state as a way to cope with their increased income insecurity is a precondition to understanding the political plausibility of policy solutions, including a basic income scheme.

In this chapter, we discuss the causal chain from technological change to income risks and inequality, redistribution preferences, and redistribution. We first discuss these connections, which serve as our theoretical underpinning to link individual risks to macro outcomes. We also show evidence that the extent to which an individual has a routine occupation makes her most vulnerable to the restructuring effects of information technology. At the country level, we report a positive relationship between the levels of routine task intensity and income inequality. From there, we move on to the main part of our analysis and show that technological change is an important determinant of redistribution preferences. This suggests that there is demand for government redistribution as a way to cope with increased uncertainty and inequality. And yet, further examination suggests that this demand has not translated into higher levels of actual redistribution. This paradox might be the result of a failure to convert demand into actual redistribution outcomes further down the political chain. We conclude with some general implications.

The Politics of Redistribution

Inequality is frequently invoked as an explanation for a number of crucial issues in political science. It is often considered a determinant of processes as diverse as the decline of electoral turnout (Verba, Nie, and Kim 1978; Rosenstone and Hansen 1993), the increase in the support of extreme-right parties (Betz 1994), and the likelihood of political conflict (Lichbach 1989). Recently, and for good reason, the political causes of inequality have received an increasing amount of attention. Focusing on the American case, Bartels (2008) has shown the spectacular increase in inequality over the past thirty-five years to be the product of policy choices in a political system dominated by partisanship and particularly receptive to the preferences of the wealthy. Hacker and Pierson (2011) coincide not only in the appreciation of the attention that policymakers pay to the rich in America, but also about the fact that politics is the main factor behind inequality ("American politics did it").

The challenges posed by inequality are mitigated by redistribution in industrialized countries. Redistribution can take place to actively mitigate income differences, or to promote redistributive social insurance. Since its emergence, the welfare state has been profoundly connected to the protection of people from labor market risks. In the words of Peter Baldwin (1990, 3), "Social insurance provided the tools with which to reapportion and moderate the effects of natural and manmade misfortune."

The (often implicit) model behind much of the work on comparative politics and political economy starts with redistribution preferences.

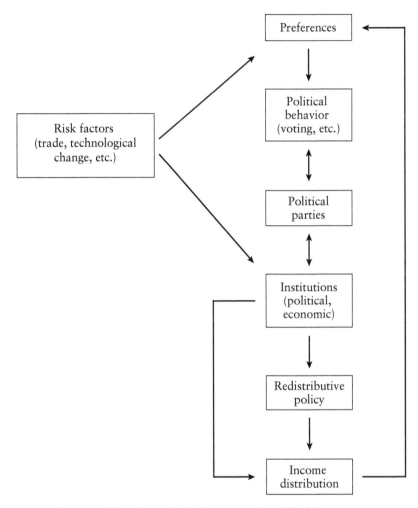

Figure 7.1 The politics of redistribution in industrialized democracies

Taking Beramendi and Anderson (2008, 12) as inspiration, one can think about this model as being represented by figure 7.1.

In this figure, the starting point is a set of redistribution preferences that affect how individuals behave politically. Their political behavior (whether voting or other, less-conventional forms of political participation) then affects, and is in turn affected by, the actions of political parties and other political agents. Political parties then affect—and again, are themselves affected—by the nature of institutions. The literature on comparative politics and political economy often focuses on political (such as the electoral or party system, the relationship between legislatures and executives, or the nature of government) or economic institutions (for instance, the nature of labor markets or welfare state regimes). These institutional arrangements are often understood to constrain political agents in their ability to design and implement policy, which then affects the income distribution within a society and also (going back to the beginning of this causal chain) the redistribution preferences of individuals. At different points in the chain, a number of factors can intervene: for example, trade openness may be considered an important determinant of redistribution preferences or of coordination in labor markets, or European integration an important limitation affecting the autonomy of partisan economic policy. Equally important among these exogenous factors is technological change.

We can use the structure of figure 7.1 to think about how redistributive policies addressing technological change might come about. We can think both about the demand for redistribution (individual preferences for compensation and insurance emerging from technological change) or the supply of redistribution (how, or whether, these preferences are eventually translated into policy). Our research focuses on the demand for redistribution and whether it is affected by the challenges embodied by technological change. The concept that preference for insurance against job risks can fuel preferences for redistributive social protection plays a prominent role in the comparative political economy literature. But, as far we know, technological change has not yet been recognized as an occupational threat in the redistribution preferences literature.

In the traditional political economy literature, redistribution preferences are a function of material self-interest (Meltzer and Richard 1981). The Meltzer-Richard model assumes that the preferences of the median voter determine government policy and that the median voter seeks to maximize current income. More recently, scholars have questioned the idea that material self-interest motivations should be limited to a measure of present income. This approach distinguishes an insurance component of redistribution preferences that incorporates an intertemporal element in material self-interest. Individuals will insure against uncertain future income levels and will therefore favor social protection when they are exposed to an increased risk of job or wage loss. As these forms of social security (such as unemployment benefits or social assistance) are redistributive, redistribution preferences for individuals exposed to these risks will be high (Sinn 1995; Moene and Wallerstein 2001; Iversen and Soskice 2001, 2009; Rehm 2009).

Our point of departure is to explicitly recognize an occupational hazard, independent of the level of income, that translates into higher preferences for nonmarket protection. We want to emphasize that the risk of job or wage loss depends on the occupational level of routinization. The implication is quite distinct: we expect an occupation's level of routine task intensity to positively affect preferences for redistribution.

In other words, to begin at the beginning of figure 7.1, we first need to know whether there is a connection between the exposure to the risks emerging from technological change and the demand for redistribution. The question will then be whether demand is translated into redistributive policy. We start with the first of these and examine who bears the brunt of technological change—thus, which people we would expect to increase their demand for redistribution following their exposure to this risk.

Technological Change as an Occupational Risk

Current technological innovations involve an occupational risk for individuals that depends on the degree to which their occupation is susceptible to automation. The ease of automation increases when an occupation contains more routine tasks. Individuals are risk-averse and favor more redistribution to insure against the risk of automation when the routine task intensity of their occupation is high—or, differently put, the routine task intensity of an occupation positively predicts the level of an individual's redistribution preferences.

We further propose that there are factors moderating the (positive) effect of routine task intensity on preferences for redistribution. The importance of routinization as a determinant of nonmarket insurance preferences will increase in the degree of sectoral risk exposure and the level of present income. We view income as a variable that accentuates the preferred level of insurance for individuals holding more routine occupations. If an individual has relatively more to lose from technological change, then this risk will become a more decisive factor in preferred levels of nonmarket protection. We hypothesize that routinization becomes a stronger predictor of redistribution preferences for individuals employed in sectors more exposed to technological change as a result of an increased actual risk of job or wage loss (e.g., Michaels, Natraj, and Van Reenen 2014; Thewissen and van Vliet forthcoming) and as a consequence of the increased visibility of this risk (as more individuals employed in the same sector are exposed to automation). Sectoral differences in risk exposure have been frequently examined in studies of insurance preferences (e.g., Rehm 2009; Walter 2010). Yet, occupational factors are generally seen as more important determinants of nonmarket protection preferences than sectoral ones. Human capital is more tied to an occupation than to an industry, and occupations are considered to be more important socialization factors (Oesch 2006; Rehm 2009; Kitschelt and Rehm 2014).

Current innovations in information technology are generally considered to have strong and dissimilar effects across occupations (Goldin and Katz 2008; Oesch 2013; Wren 2013; Susskind and Susskind 2015). They complement individuals with abstract or personal tasks, while individuals in routine occupations face an increased risk of being substituted by capital (Autor, Dorn, and Hanson 2015). Routine tasks can be partitioned into step-by-step rules and do not require cognitive or service skills that are difficult to automate (Goos and Manning 2007; Goos, Manning, and Salomons 2014). But it is important to emphasize that some routine tasks susceptible to automation (for example, bookkeeping) might well be complex and require extensive educational training. Because of this, innovations in information technology do not affect occupations linearly across educational lines. In fact, routine occupations tend to lie in the middle of the educational and income distribution (Oesch 2013).

Advances in information technology have been found to have affected the occupational structure of industrialized democracies significantly in the last couple of decades. Oesch (2013) finds a decrease of relative employment of between 29 and 41 percent in routine occupations in Denmark, Germany, Spain, Switzerland, and the UK from around 1990 to 2008, while employment in nonroutine analytical and interactive occupations increased by 23 to 41 percent. Michaels, Natraj, and Van Reenen (2014), using data for the United States, Japan, and nine European countries between 1984 and 2004, report that strong polarizing effects of information technology account for a quarter of the growth in relative demand toward nonroutine high-skilled labor. Goos, Manning, and Salomons (2014) analyze the period between 1993 and 2010 in sixteen Western European countries and show that technological change and offshoring can account for three-quarters of the observed increase in high-skilled nonroutine work and decrease in medium-skilled routine employment. (See also Autor, Levy, and Murnane 2003 and Spitz-Oener 2006 for single-country studies on this topic.) Interestingly, these studies all find much weaker or insignificant effects of international trade and offshoring once the impact of technological change is accounted for.

To illustrate that individuals holding routine occupations are most exposed to the risk of wage or employment loss from automation, we use the routine task intensity (RTI) index from Goos, Manning, and Salomons (2014), who rely on Autor and Dorn (2013) and Autor et al. (2015). Goos, Manning, and Salomons (2014) distinguish between routine, manual, and abstract task inputs, derived per occupation from the *Dictionary of Occupational Titles.* The RTI index measures the log routine task input per occupation, minus the log manual and abstract task inputs, so that the measure increases the relative importance of routine tasks vis-à-vis manual and abstract tasks. As the RTI index gauges the task structure of an occupation, it does not vary across countries and time. Goos, Manning, and Salomons (2014) rescale these actual measures to mean 0 and standard deviation 1 in their sample. Measures are available at the two-digit occupational International Standard Classification of Occupations (ISCO)-88 level, a scheme to classify occupations in a comparable fashion across countries and time.[1]

Another occupational measure of the degree of RTI comes from Oesch (2013). Oesch codes occupations at the four-digit ISCO-88 level into multiple nonroutine and routine occupations, drawing on Spitz-Oener (2006), who also differentiates between routine, manual, and abstract (or analytical and interactive) tasks. These occupational categories can be combined into a dummy equal to 1 if an occupation is routine, and equal to 0 if otherwise. This indicator and the continuous variable from Goos, Manning, and Salomons (2014) are highly correlated (0.73). As we have more variation for the continuous Goos, Manning, and Salomons RTI index, we use this one as our benchmark and the Oesch (2013) dummy as a sensitivity test.

The European Social Survey (ESS) provides us with a standardized occupational identifier at the four-digit ISCO-88 level for 2002–2010 and ISCO-08 for 2012. We recode the 2012 wave into ISCO-88 definitions using the International Labour Organization (ILO) four-digit correspondence table.[2] By means of this occupational identifier, we can link individuals to the RTI index of Goos, Manning, and Salomons (2014). Our analysis draws on ESS surveys between 2002 and 2012 for the seventeen Western countries for which at least two waves of information are available.[3]

To obtain a better understanding of what type of occupations score high and low on the RTI index, we will first explore the relationship between the index and both education and income.[4] Table 7.1 lists the occupations ranked by their level of RTI. We can see that, on average, nonroutine occupations have a higher wage and educational level. Yet, these relationships are not very strong; middle-paid and middle-skilled occupations, in particular, have high values of RTI (Autor, Levy, and Murnane 2015; Goos, Manning, and Salomons 2014). This is also reflected in relatively low correlations between the RTI index and equivalized income (–0.13) and educational level (–0.17). General managers have the least routine occupation, a profession with above-average wage and skill levels, but the second-least routine are drivers and mobile-plant operators, low-skilled, low-paid occupations. The most routine occupations are customer service and office clerks and precision workers. These middle-skilled occupations require relatively few cognitive or interpersonal skills and can be partitioned into step-by-step rules fairly easily.

Following the earlier cited papers (Autor, Levy, and Murnane 2003; Spitz-Oener 2006; Goos, Manning, and Salomons 2014; Michaels, Natraj, and Van Reenen 2014), we can see by looking at changes in employment headcounts and wages using ESS data that holding routine occupations is an occupational risk. Table 7.1 shows that, within the relatively short period between 2002 and 2012, nonroutine occupations (with a negative RTI score) saw, on average, an increase in their employment share and a higher increase in their wage compared to routine occupations (with a positive RTI score).

Table 7.1 Levels and changes in employment shares and income for occupations ranked by their level of routine task intensity (RTI)

	ISCO	RTI	Average years of education	Equivalized income		Employment shares	
				2002 average (dollars)	% change 2002–2012	2002 average	ppt change 2002–2012
Nonroutine		-0.75	14.35	29,530	17.26	64.34	3.63
General managers	13	-1.52	13.44	29,667	10.44	3.44	-0.52
Drivers and mobile-plant operators	83	-1.50	11.32	20,531	23.54	4.09	-0.32
Life science and health professionals	22	-1.00	17.71	36,571	14.97	2.31	0.99
Physical, mathematical, and engineering science professionals	21	-0.82	16.52	36,716	12.62	4.73	0.71
Corporate managers	12	-0.75	15.16	41,161	5.33	7.07	1.46
Other professionals	24	-0.73	16.61	34,721	16.69	7.23	1.21
Personal and protective services workers	51	-0.60	12.34	20,987	21.57	10.13	1.40
Other associate professionals	34	-0.44	14.15	29,263	19.34	10.82	-0.01
Physical and engineering science associate professionals	31	-0.40	13.93	27,171	25.19	5.37	-1.09
Life science and health associate professionals	32	-0.33	15.03	26,423	18.77	4.14	-0.17
Extraction and building trades workers	71	-0.19	11.59	21,619	21.41	5.01	-0.03

(*Continued*)

Table 7.1 (Continued)

	ISCO	RTI	Average years of education	Equivalized income		Employment shares	
				2002 average (dollars)	% change 2002–2012	2002 average	ppt change 2002–2012
Routine		**0.83**	**11.74**	**22,071**	**13.94**	**35.66**	**-3.63**
Sales and services elementary occupations	91	0.03	10.92	18,935	6.02	4.67	0.53
Models, salespersons, and demonstrators	52	0.05	12.16	21,384	19.65	4.39	0.16
Stationary-plant and related operators	81	0.32	11.64	24,685	10.93	1.16	-0.25
Laborers in mining, construction, manufacturing, and transport	93	0.45	11.03	19,533	0.28	2.22	0.18
Metal, machinery, and related trades workers	72	0.46	11.98	21,002	34.85	6.09	-1.90
Machine operators and assemblers	82	0.49	11.18	18,670	12.48	3.37	-0.41
Other craft and related trades workers	74	1.24	10.33	18,790	26.92	1.88	-0.61
Customer services clerks	42	1.41	12.92	25,492	3.72	1.88	0.56
Precision, handicraft, printing, and related trades workers	73	1.59	12.37	26894	7.51	0.96	-0.20
Office clerks	41	2.24	12.86	25326	17.07	9.05	-1.70

Notes: The figures show for nonroutine (negative RTI score) and routine (positive RTI score) the average values for RTI, years of education, equivalized income, and income changes, and the sums for employment shares and employment changes. Calculations are based on the countries for which information for both 2002 and 2012 is available (i.e., all except Austria, France, Greece, Ireland, Luxembourg, and Spain).

Technological Change and Demand for Redistribution

Having argued that technological change is an occupational risk for people in routine occupations, the next step is to examine whether individuals in routine occupations indeed demand more distribution for insurance motives. How should we measure redistribution preferences? There is no perfect way to do this but the ESS contains a question designed to directly capture what we aim to explain: whether or not an individual supports government redistribution. Respondents are asked whether they agree or disagree on a five-point scale to the following statement: "The government should take measures to reduce differences in income levels." This variable is recoded to capture support for government redistribution. Our final measure contains the following categories: 1: Disagree strongly; 2: Disagree; 3: Neither agree nor disagree; 4: Agree; and 5: Agree strongly.[5] This question is the only one tapping into social policy preferences available in all waves of the ESS. It is frequently used in studies seeking to explain redistribution preferences (Rehm 2009; Burgoon, Koster, and van Egmond 2012; Burgoon 2014; Kitschelt and Rehm 2014; Rueda 2014; Wren and Rehm 2014; Häusermann, Kurer, and Schwander 2015).

To better view the differences in redistribution preferences across occupations, we generate a binary measure for support for redistribution equal to 1 if an individual agrees or agrees strongly with support for redistribution (see also Rehm 2009; Wren and Rehm 2014). In figure 7.2, we rank the occupations on their level of RTI, again distinguishing between occupations with a negative RTI index score (nonroutine, N) and a positive RTI index level (routine, R). We can see that, on average, individuals in routine occupations have higher levels of support for redistribution. In both groups, support for redistribution increased over time.

Figure 7.2 offers an intuitive picture of the relationship between RTI and redistribution preferences. A more systematic analysis of how the risks emerging from technological change affect the demand for redistribution with regression analysis at the micro level yields a comparable picture. We discuss the results and intuition here; the technical details are further explained in Thewissen and Rueda (forthcoming).[6] We use data on 63,100 individuals in seventeen Western European countries between 2002 and 2014. The dependent variable is the question on support for

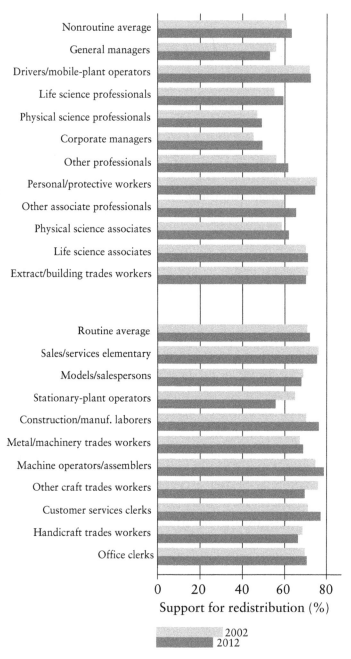

Figure 7.2 Support for redistribution across occupations in 2002 and 2012. Calculations are based on the countries for which information for both 2002 and 2012 is available (i.e., all except Austria, France, Greece, Ireland, Luxembourg, and Spain). Author's calculations based on ESS (See also Thewissen and Rueda forthcoming).

redistribution used above, and our main interest is whether the routine task intensity of an individual's occupation predicts this.

A number of factors have been identified in the comparative political economy literature as relevant in determining redistribution preferences (e.g., Rehm 2009; Burgoon 2014; Rueda, Segmueller, and Idema 2014). We include these variables to assess the influence of RTI. At the individual level, we include income, education, age, religiosity, gender, trade union membership, and whether the individual is unemployed; we also include social spending as a percentage of gross domestic product (GDP) and the unemployment rate at the country level. Consistent with previous findings in the literature, we find that poorer individuals favor higher levels of redistribution than do richer ones. This is in line with our expectations based on the Meltzer-Richard model. Furthermore, being less-educated, older, female, unemployed, nonreligious, and a trade union member each increase the likelihood of approving that the government reduce income disparities (Rehm 2009; Burgoon 2014). The results do not show significant effects from social spending or the unemployment rate.

Most importantly, our findings indicate that RTI is positively associated with redistribution preferences. This result provides empirical support for our hypothesis that individuals in routine occupations favor more redistribution to insure against the increased risk of job or income loss. In Thewissen and Rueda (forthcoming), we present a battery of sensitivity tests on the robustness of the results presented above. These include ideology and controlling for occupational risks such as skill specificity, offshoring, and migration; we test the robustness of our results for different sample definitions (including all individuals, employed individuals, and Eastern European countries, and years other than 2012 or times of crisis, and dropping countries, years, and occupations one by one). We also control for other factors at the country level: present levels of redistribution, the ex ante level of market inequality, the level of employment protection legislation, and the unemployment benefit replacement rate. We use different model specifications to account for the fact that individuals are nested within countries in our dataset. Finally, we conduct a series of sensitivity tests using different indicators for RTI and income. We use the Oesch (2013, 156) coding to generate a dummy variable for routine occupations and find that, with this indicator, the effects of RTI on redistribution preferences become stronger. Furthermore, we employ alternative definitions for real income.

Having found a robust positive effect of RTI on redistribution preferences, we continue by addressing the role of income and sectoral exposure as factors that can strengthen the association between RTI and preferences for redistribution. We find that income itself is always negatively associated with preferences for redistribution: richer individuals prefer less redistribution on average. This fits with the material self-interest logic (Meltzer and Richard 1981). Yet, income can moderate the effects of RTI on preferences for redistribution, as richer individuals have relatively more to lose from job loss due to automation. Our empirical results in Thewissen and Rueda (forthcoming) support this line of reasoning.

We also find that sectoral exposure to technological change strengthens the positive effect of the occupational level of routine task intensity on redistribution preferences. (See also Nübler, this volume; and Duffy, this volume.) Manufacturing, financial intermediation, and electricity, gas, and water supply are sectors containing, on average, relatively large volumes of routine work across our sample, and can therefore be considered to be exposed to technological change. Interestingly, public administration is also relatively exposed to RTI, which illustrates the substantive difference between RTI and offshoring. Exposure is low in hotels and restaurants, agriculture, and fishing, and also in health and social work. This corresponds to their large shares of manual and interpersonal work. While we find positive associations between our dependent variable and the interaction of the RTI index and sectoral exposure, it is also the case that the constituent element of sectoral exposure itself is negative, while the constituent RTI index variable remains positive. (See details in Thewissen and Rueda forthcoming) This seems to suggest that sectoral exposure by itself is not an important driver of preferences for public insurance. This finding corresponds to Rehm's (2009) that occupational factors matter more for insurance motivations. Still, our results indicate that sectoral exposure accentuates the effects of occupational hazards on individual preferences for nonmarket protection.

Having found a positive association between RTI and preferences for redistribution, we should also interpret its size. As we show in more detail in Thewissen and Rueda (forthcoming), the effect of RTI on redistribution preferences is larger than the effect of other often-mentioned occupational risks in the literature, including skill specificity (Cusack, Iversen, and Rehm 2006) and offshoring (Walter 2010, 2014). Having specific skills is an occupational risk, as it reduces opportunities for reemployment, whereas individuals in offshorable occupations could lose from international trade.

Inequality, Redistribution, and the Political Supply Side

The previous section provides evidence in line with the hypothesis that individuals in occupations prone to automation prefer more redistribution. In terms of our causal chain, the evidence suggests that technological change increases demand for redistribution. The next question is whether this demand eventually produces higher levels of actual redistribution, and therefore lower levels of disposable income inequality. We have to emphasize here that this is a challenging question to analyze. First, for the demand side we can rely on individual-level data, whereas here we have to move to a country design, giving us many fewer observations. Second, it might take time before demand translates into actual policy, and before policy takes effect. Third, if an individual loses her middle-paid job because of technological change, she might move to a lower-paid but less-exposed occupation. This could lead to higher levels of income inequality and redistribution, but a lower average RTI score. If this dynamic effect is strong, a simple association between exposure to technological change and inequality underestimates the effect. Fourth, multiple factors in addition to technological development produce inequality, including globalization, a gender wage gap, and a lack of trade union influence in wage bargaining (Atkinson 2015). Fifth, there can be other reasons for higher levels of redistribution across countries potentially unrelated to technological change, such as the level of unemployment due to economic shocks, the demographic composition, or the (neoliberal) political culture within a country.

With these caveats in mind, we start in figure 7.3 with a stylized scatter-plot reflecting the average degree of RTI and the amount of redistribution at the country level. The measure of redistribution is the reduction in the Gini coefficient from market to disposable income, measured as absolute Gini points (Atkinson 1997; Korpi and Palme 1998; Kenworthy 2011, chap. 6). For consistency, we use the countries and time frame covered in the earlier part of our analysis. To maximize observations, we have to rely on the Solt (2014) inequality database.

Given the pervasive substitution effects of information technology on routine occupations (and its influence on income inequality), we would expect industrialized democracies to provide redistributive social insurance against the increased risk of employment and wage loss represented by technological change. However, figure 7.3 suggests that higher levels of exposure to the risks emerging from technological change are correlated with lower rather than higher levels of redistribution in the countries in our sample. This could even suggest—though we have to be very careful not to draw unwarranted conclusions for the reasons discussed at the beginning of this section—that a rise in demand for redistribution coming from increased exposure to technological change comes with a decline rather than an increase of redistribution.

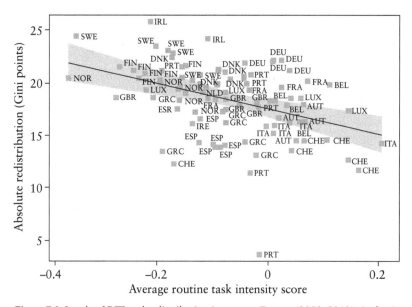

Figure 7.3 Levels of RTI and redistribution in western Europe (2002–2012). Author's calculations based on Solt (2014) and European Union Labour Force Study.

We can also gain some insight into the effects of routinization on the distribution by comparing the levels of average exposure to RTI to levels of disposable income inequality for the countries for which we have data. We would expect technological change to affect earnings inequality (directly, when someone loses his or her job, or through wage competition), while the effects on disposable income inequality should be mitigated by the generosity of the welfare state. Below, we explore the relationship between average RTI and the Gini index.

Figure 7.4 reflects the relationship between levels of RTI and disposable income inequality. Consistent with the message of the previous paragraphs, the graph seems to suggest that higher levels of exposure to the risks emerging from technological change are, in fact, correlated with higher levels of income inequality.

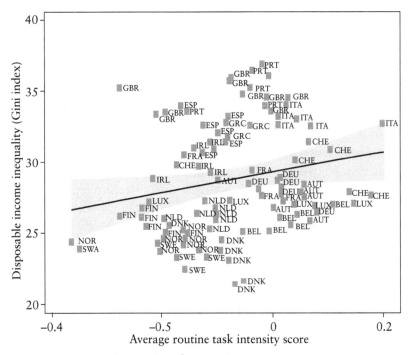

Figure 7.4 Levels of RTI and income inequality in western Europe (2002–2012)

Source: Author's calculations based on Solt (2014) and European Union Labour Force Study

Figures 7.3 and 7.4, taken together, produce a political puzzle. While exposure to the risks emerging from technological change comes with unequally distributed income risks, overall exposure is not associated with more redistribution. This could imply that the demand for redistribution found earlier does not translate into actual higher levels of redistribution to protect and compensate the workers affected by these risks.

Conclusions on the Political Economy of Technological Change

In this final section, we summarize our main findings and explore some initial political economy arguments that could help us understand the relationship between technological change and inequality and, therefore, the puzzle of redistribution in the figures.

We have argued in this chapter that current technological innovations in information technology involve a substantial employment risk for individuals holding routine occupations by facilitating the ease of automation. We find that individuals in routine occupations respond to this risk by preferring higher levels of redistribution as a means of nonmarket insurance. Even though technological change is widely considered to be a key occupational driver with large distributive effects, whether it influences the preferred level of redistribution has not been subject to inquiry in the comparative political economy thus far. Indeed, our analysis suggests that, on average, the routine task intensity of an occupation has a larger positive effect on the preferred level of redistribution than do other risks described in the literature, in particular offshoring and skill specificity. Our chapter's main take-home message is that the relationship between technological change and redistribution demand is extremely robust.

Next, we showed that the effect of exposure to technological change on an individual's redistribution preferences goes up when that person has more to lose from automation. In other words, richer individuals might, on average, favor lower levels of redistribution preferences, but the impact of RTI on preferences for nonmarket protection increases. This view of income can be seen as more nuanced than existing perspectives where income has only a separate direct effect, which might be negative because of material self-interest (Meltzer and Richard 1981), or positive when insurance is a normal good (Moene and Wallerstein 2001), implying that individuals demand more when their income goes up. We have also shown that the effect of routinization on redistribution preferences increases if an individual is working in a sector exposed to technological change. By introducing sectoral exposure as a moderating variable, we combine an occupational and sectoral side of risk exposure and complement our individual approach with a factor that can be more sociological and group identity–related.

Even though we find ample evidence for a higher demand for redistribution from employees exposed to the risk of automation, we do not see that exposure to technological change goes hand-in-hand with higher levels of redistribution to mitigate these risks. We conclude, therefore, that the apparent failure to provide redistribution as protection and compensation for technological change enters the political process further down the causal chain, as redistribution demands fail to be converted into redistribution outcomes. A productive direction for future research would be to explore which factors in figure 7.1 contribute to the failure of turning the demand for redistribution into policy. In many industrialized countries, leftist parties have failed to include redistributive policies in their electoral platforms because of the influence of centrist median voters (or the tendency of the poor to turn out to vote less often than the affluent). In others, institutional factors (does proportional representation make a difference?) or structural ones (do globalization and international openness weaken the political power of labor?) may be part of the picture. An additional hypothesis might be that the propensity to vote goes down for individuals affected by technological change.

What are the implications of our chapter? Our point of departure is the labor economics literature's finding depressed wages and employment levels for occupations more susceptible to automation; we find the same stylized patterns in our data. Yet, we identify political challenges that emerge from this. We show that these economic risks shape the preferences of individuals for additional insurance—but we question whether these preferences translate into actual protection. Given the increased demand for nonmarket protection, a key policy challenge is how such a protective system can be generated—by, for instance, providing social insurance or training possibilities to smooth labor transitions—and how these institutions themselves affect the occupational risks discussed here.

Our chapter comprises a political puzzle shedding doubt on whether policy implications might come about because of technological change. On the one hand, we find solid evidence that the technological revolution can induce citizens to demand redistributive policies. However, as we do not yet see a positive association at the country level between exposure to technological change and actual levels of redistribution, the supply to satisfy the demand for redistribution seems to be lacking. This would hamper the possibility for introducing schemes such as a basic income (Ford 2015) to support affected citizens' living standards. In addition to thinking about possible policy solutions, we should also devote attention to how these policies might come about—and, in particular, to how these can be supplied.

In this concluding section, we should also point to weaknesses of this chapter's methodological design. The section on the demand for redistribution is built on survey data, rather than an experiment where individuals are randomly assigned to occupations. One might argue that individuals self-select into occupations, leading to possibly confounded causal interpretations of our results. This reasoning would imply that risk-averse persons who already have higher preferences for provision of public insurance choose occupations less-exposed to risk. Second, it could be that individuals in routine occupations increased their redistribution preferences, lost their jobs because of automation, and moved to nonroutine occupations while keeping higher levels of preferred nonmarket protection. Unfortunately, we cannot directly test for this, as we do not have micro panel data at our disposal. Yet, both of these arguments predict a negative association between the degree of routine task intensity and the preferred level for redistribution, militating against our statistically significant findings of a positive association. It might be, however, that because of these counteracting effects, we underestimate the effect of RTI on preferences for redistribution.

There are a number of interesting lines of future inquiry we would like to note. First, in this chapter we allow the risk of automation to differ across occupations, depending on their degree of routine task intensity.

We devote less attention to country-specific patterns, depending on, for instance, the amount of investment in research and development, or qualitative educational factors that potentially shape how individuals cope with technological change. Second, our findings point toward the possibility of cross-class coalitions between low-wage individuals in non-routine occupations and high-wage individuals holding routine occupations in support of a redistributive welfare state (Häusermann, Kurer, and Schwander 2015). This has potential implications for our understanding of individuals with secure current and future employment versus those without, and political mobilization. Whether these coalitions materialize should be subject to further research.

8

The Crisis of the Liberal International Order

Technological Change and the Rise of the Right

Vinnie Ferraro

> That aspect of the modern crisis which is bemoaned as a "wave of
> materialism" is related to what is called the "crisis of authority."
> If the ruling class has lost its consensus, i.e. is no longer "leading"
> but only "dominant," exercising coercive force alone, this means
> precisely that the great masses have become detached from their
> traditional ideologies, and no longer believe what they used to
> believe previously, etc. The crisis consists precisely in the fact that the
> old is dying and the new cannot be born; in this interregnum a great
> variety of morbid symptoms appear.
>
> —Antonio Gramsci, *Selections from the Prison Notebooks*

The deterioration of the market value of labor in richer parts of the world
has been steady over the last forty years. Some poorer states, such as India
and China, have enjoyed dramatic increases in the market value of labor
during that same period. However, even they are beginning to experience
a weakening of labor markets. Globalization has been the driving force of
this trend, but the logic of globalization and its more recent ancillary, robotization, will ultimately create a world not of rich and poor nations, but of
a unified rich elite and an undifferentiated mass of disenfranchised citizens.
For self-protection, that elite will divert the anger and despair of those citizens away from policies designed to enhance the market value of labor into
the destructive forces of nationalism, xenophobia, and authoritarianism.

That outcome was hardly predicted in 1991 when the last ideological competitor to the liberal world order, socialism, collapsed. (An earlier competitor, fascism, had been vanquished by war in 1945.) Economic activity conducted along classical liberal lines—market values determined by supply and demand, limited government intervention in that market, and reasonably stable currencies—was supposed to usher in an increasingly more comfortable and efficient world. Indeed, the idea of progress is central to the political attractiveness of market capitalism. There was, in the years following the collapse of the Berlin Wall in 1989, a sense that liberalism had "triumphed." Francis Fukuyama (1992) wrote that "liberal democracy may constitute the 'end point of man's ideological evolution' and the 'final form of human government,' and as such constituted 'the end of history.'"

That outcome had also been predicted earlier. The world had witnessed a similar wave of globalization in the late nineteenth century. Both periods were marked by dramatic changes in transportation and communications technologies, which had the effect of creating global, not local, supply chains. In both periods, a new economic power had arisen—the United States in the nineteenth century and China in the twentieth—that upset previously well-established supply chains. And both periods experienced dramatic surges in income inequalities within certain socioeconomic groups.

The nineteenth-century wave of globalization ended with World War I. Its collapse has been well documented and articulated by Kevin H. O'Rourke and Jeffrey G. Williamson in their 1993 book *Globalization and History: The Evolution of a Nineteenth Century Atlantic Economy*. They argue,

> The impact of the railroad and the steamship was reinforced by political developments after 1860 as European economies moved rapidly toward free trade. The world was becoming a much smaller place, and to an observer in 1875, it must have seemed as if it was going to get a lot smaller. Yet nothing is inevitable. History shows that globalization can plant the seeds of its own destruction. Those seeds were planted in the 1870s, sprouted in the 1880s, grew vigorously around the turn of the century, and came to full flower in the dark years between the two world wars (93).

This chapter argues that, in many respects, the current global economy mimics the O'Rourke and Williamson pattern. The pattern, however, is just a heuristic device. As compelling as some of the similarities between the two periods may seem, there are some very important differences as well. The nineteenth century contended with two billion people, the twenty-first century, nine billion. No one in the nineteenth century regarded human activity as a decisive element in the global climate; the twenty-first century must address the urgent perils of climate change. The blood-and-soil nationalism of the late nineteenth century ushered in a devastating world war, a calamity avoided thus far in the twenty-first century. Finally, in the earlier time, the human intellect was regarded as singular. Humans in the future must wrestle with artificial intelligences of considerable powers.

Moreover, the pattern places too much emphasis on the process of globalization as the motor force of the reaction implied by O'Rourke and Williamson. The backlash against the liberal system of market capitalism has existed since it emerged: the desire to resist the commodification of social life so brilliantly explained by Karl Polanyi in *The Great Transformation* (1944) and described by him as the "countermovement" to market capitalism. That resistance is a parallel structure to globalization and it exists not only as a response to global economic intrusions on social life, but also in response to purely domestic consequences of market forces. Market capitalism has always had winners and losers—that outcome is not unique to globalization. The critical difference between the earlier period and now is that globalization has accelerated the process of losing and deepened it to include the former winners.

Finally, the pattern reflects a fundamental contradiction in the modern world system. The liberal systems of market capitalism and representative democracy operate in completely different realms. Market capitalism is truly universal. For it to operate most efficiently, the factors of land, labor, and capital should have no national identities. Representative democracy requires an emotional identity that has evolved in a profoundly parochial manner in the agency of the nation-state. The contradiction between global and local interests exists for all systems that purport to be universal. Marx may have believed that the proletariat had no homeland, but World War I and Stalin belied that claim. The nation-state has a hold on the minds of people that, in times of distress, can easily override the clinical self-interest assumed by the market. Dani Rodrik (2011) accurately described these tensions in his analysis of what he called the "trilemma": that democracy, sovereignty, and globalization cannot interact simultaneously.

The Rise in Income and Wealth Inequality in the World

There are wide variations in liberal practices in the world. The social democracies of Europe are at one end of the spectrum. At the other end are societies that adhere to stricter market rules. The United States is an example of the latter. The differences are important, but they also are narrowing. This chapter focuses on the practices of the United States because its policies better illuminate how a state can be managed to serve the self-interest of a small group of people. Since 1971, the market has worked to benefit an increasingly shrinking share of the population. According to the Pew Research Center (2015), "'middle-income' Americans are defined as adults whose annual household income is two-thirds to double the national median, about $42,000 to $126,000 annually in 2014 dollars for a household of three. Under this definition, the middle class made up 50% of the U.S. adult population in 2015, down from 61% in 1971."

Middle-class income has "trickled-up." After the Great Recession of 2008–2009, the shift of income to higher-income groups was astonishing: "For the United States overall, the top 1 percent captured 85.1 percent of total income growth between 2009 and 2013. In 2013 the top 1 percent of families nationally made 25.3 times as much as the bottom 99 percent" (Sommeiller, Price, and Wazeter 2016).

Inequality was not a contentious political issue in post-1945 America until the Great Recession exposed the political foundations of inequality. The bailouts of institutions that had induced the crisis by their exorbitantly risky behavior highlighted inequality by linking it directly to a political process. Gradually, greater attention has been paid to the question of income inequality, and the scholarly commitment to addressing that question was significantly boosted in 2014 with the publication of Thomas Piketty's book *Capital in the Twenty-First Century*.

The earlier economic debates on inequality had centered on whether the traditional description of inequality—the Kuznets curve—was accurate. Named after the economist Simon Kuznets, the curve represented the rise of inequality as farmers moved into cities in the early period of industrialization, and its steady decline as industrialization matured and the forces of democratization created an economic safety net. Questions have arisen because the safety net has recently proven to be inadequate (Acemoglu and Robinson 2002).

Why has the safety net failed to address inequality? Democracy has been derailed by rich elites who have used their economic power in the political process to further concentrate their wealth. Over time, the accumulation of wealth creates the means to prevent the state from taxing it. The public good of a robust economy becomes the private good of a small number of people. Elites rarely, if ever, interact with the less fortunate in substantive ways. Rather, they develop rationalizations to explain the failures of the poor. Similarly, the poor have only a rough idea of how "rich" the rich have become over the last forty years. The scale of the discrepancy between the very rich and the not-rich today defies imagination.

The ability of elites to redefine the public good in terms of their private interest is not historically unusual. It is very difficult to measure how this redefinition occurs, but there are many studies that suggest that the influence of elites on legislative outcomes is decisive. Two Princeton scholars, Martin Gilens and Benjamin I. Page (2014), assert, "When the preferences of economic elites and the stands of organized interest groups are controlled for, the preferences of the average American appear to have only a minuscule, near-zero, statistically non-significant impact upon public policy" (575). The historical record suggests that when wealth becomes highly concentrated, public policy is determined more by the interests of the elites than by those of the majority.

Even those who do not believe that income inequality is, in and of itself, a problem were flummoxed by the consequences of liberalizing the American economy since the 1970s. In October 2008, Alan Greenspan, the former chairman of the US Federal Reserve, testified to the House Committee on Oversight and Government Reform. When asked to explain how the behavior of several financial institutions led to the financial collapse of 2008, Mr. Greenspan told the Committee, "Those of us who have looked to the self-interest of lending institutions to protect shareholders' equity, myself included, are in a state of shocked disbelief." Self-interest is the bedrock of liberalism, but liberal theorists used the term in a social, not a personal, context. Self-interest is not selfishness. Self-interest includes a concern for the long run, a regard for those with whom one will interact over time, and actions that will create a well-functioning economy that will be shared by all. In other words, liberalism's ultimate objective is the public good; individual freedom is simply a means to that end.

Mr. Greenspan should not have been surprised that lending institutions involved in the subprime mortgage crisis did not care about the public good, or even about the interests of their shareholders. The chief executives of those institutions had carefully insulated themselves from the consequences of their actions. Mr. Greenspan was remembering a time when investment banks were privately owned and profits and losses were borne almost exclusively by the partners in the firm. That circumstance assured that the self-interest of the partners was closely identified with the viability of the firm over the long term. That world ended when the investment banks went public. Once the link between private and public loss was severed, the executives of those firms could assure themselves of generous compensation, even if the firm itself suffered a loss or went into bankruptcy. The loss was shifted to the shareholders, or, in the most extreme case, to a central bank or sovereign government. Selfishness no longer required self-interest if compensation committees and shareholders were passive or co-opted. The executives had eliminated all personal risk to their behavior.

This circumstance was never envisioned by the classical liberal theorists: the public good was never something that should be privatized. For them, it was inextricably tied to the social universe in which capitalists and democrats were born, had children, lived out their lives, and died. Current day pseudo-liberals are fond of quoting Adam Smith's *Wealth of Nations*. They would be better advised to read Smith's *Theory of Moral Sentiments* (1759), which warns of the dangers of accumulating wealth without due regard for the society that collectively creates the condition for that wealth: "This disposition to admire, and almost to worship, the rich and the powerful, and to despise, or, at least, to neglect persons of poor and mean condition . . . is . . . the great and most universal cause of the corruption of our moral sentiments" (66). The present age has deliberately chosen to disregard his advice, and in so doing has compromised the economic progress once promised by the original liberal theorists.

The ideology of neoliberalism is not self-executing. The Kuznets curve suggests an inherent internal dynamic in the political economy of the market, which can correct the tendency toward greater inequality. That suggestion is misleading. Democratization can lead to greater measures to protect the poor, but it can also lead to measures that heighten inequality. The United States passed through a similar period in the late nineteenth and early twentieth centuries in which incomes and wealth were concentrated among a very few. The Great Depression, which the nation took several steps in the New Deal to avoid repeating, was a consequence of that concentration. Those steps were not automatic, nor were they part of an endogenous economic dynamic: they required concerted political effort. But the New Deal validated the link between inequality and political action predicted by Kuznets.

The path to the Great Recession of 2008–2009 was also laid down by a series of political decisions, such as the repeal of the Glass-Steagall Act, to undo the protections of the New Deal. In this process of deregulation, democracy was not used to benefit the greater good. The impact of these decisions was amplified significantly by the accelerating process of globalization, which opened even greater opportunities for capital while weakening the power of labor by essentially doubling the available workforce from about 1.5 billion to three billion people.

This freeing up of capital was not restricted to the United States. Relaxing government regulation, reducing taxation, fostering the free movement of capital, and emphasizing economic growth instead of economic development were the mainstays of the liberal economic order designed by the USA in 1944 in the Bretton Woods institutions: the World Bank, the International Monetary Fund, and what we now call the World Trade Organization. The collapse of the Soviet Union and the decisions in the 1990s by both China and India to adhere to the rules of these organizations created, for the first time in human history, a truly universal market for capital.

These institutions have fostered liberal ideology and been marketed under different rubrics: structural adjustment programs, the Washington Consensus, austerity, and neoliberalism. This ideology is externally imposed at a moment of weakness in a nation-state's economy, whether that weakness is a debt crisis, a sustained payments imbalance, or a sharp uptick in poverty. In most cases, the policies have been imposed on poor states. But neoliberalism can also be self-imposed. The deep unwillingness of the United States to consider tax increases to support its less well-off residents is a political choice. The objective of these choices is to disarm the power of the state to restrict the freedom of those who own capital.

The American experience was mirrored globally. Poorer countries had had austerity programs enforced on them by the International Monetary Fund and the World Bank for many years and their effects have been, at best, mixed (Easterly 2005). More recently, richer countries have had austerity programs imposed on them as well, as conditions for sovereign debt relief. For example, since 2008 Greece has received three rounds of assistance from international organizations. In return, Greece cut its government budget, raised taxes, and reduced pensions and services. The quality of life there has deteriorated. Its austerity programs were imposed so that wealth could be transferred from the ordinary Greek citizen to the banks that hold Greek debt. The programs are designed to protect the interests of the rich at the expense of the poor.

Overall, the global economy has grown prodigiously over the last forty years. In many countries, such as China, economic growth has lifted millions out of poverty. (Dieter Ernst provides a more detailed analysis of China and the process of technological change in chapter 9 of this volume.) However, globalization has also punished labor by facilitating the use of the lowest-cost labor linked into a global supply chain that knows no boundaries of time and space. Those who rely on the market value of labor to survive are being economically disenfranchised, and robotization is likely to aggravate that trend.

From 1990 to 2009 the share of labor compensation in national income in twenty-six of the thirty OECD countries declined from 66.1 to 61.7 percent (ILO 2013). This decline occurred despite rising productivity in most of these economies, a shift from traditional patterns where labor's share increased as productivity increased. This shift has been noted by MIT professors Erik Brynjolfsson and Andrew McAfee in their book *Race against the Machine* (2012) and attributed to increasing automation in the workplace. Oxford researchers Carl Benedikt Frey and Michael A. Osborne (2013) estimate that 45 percent of US employment is susceptible to computerization. More recent research suggests that the impact of robotization might be even more significant than expected (Acemoglu and Restrepo 2017). The chapters by Martin Ford and Irmgard Nübler in this volume give more detail on the issue of how robotization will affect employment.

The current wave of technology is different from previous waves. Technology has often had the effect of reducing the need for human labor and, by and large, these reductions have allowed humans to pursue more productive and less dangerous activities. Usually there is a period of transition as the new technology displaces workers, but, over time, the increase in economic activity has created new opportunities for more creative work. Historically, more jobs have been created by technological innovation.

This time, however, the changes will be different.

First, the changes will affect more people. When the Luddites protested the introduction of technology, their numbers were quite small and the textile factories were not very large in contrast to today. For example, in 1980 the Parkdale Mills in South Carolina produced 2.5 million pounds of yarn every week with two thousand workers. It now employs 140 workers (Clifford 2013). Similar job displacements will occur in countries such as China. Because robotization expands productivity as much as twenty times per worker, the phenomenon will have a dramatic effect on the country's industry (Middlehurst 2015). Even low wages cannot compete with no wages.

Second, the jobs created by this technological revolution will likely be for highly skilled workers. It is hard to imagine what kind of jobs will be created for unskilled workers by the robotization revolution, although that possibility cannot be discounted. It is harder to imagine societies comprising only individuals with the aptitude or the inclination to develop higher skills. It is also difficult to imagine the sustained societal commitment necessary to raise skill levels for all. There are very few reasons to believe that the declining share of labor in national income will do anything but continue.

Finally, earlier periods of change occurred when there were existing social and economic alternatives for the technologically dispossessed. Think of the differences in the United States between the technological waves of the late nineteenth century and today. Families were once more tightly integrated and social groups were deeper and more willing to cushion the blow of unemployment. There were also more ways to keep oneself alive without an industrial job. Farming and other means of subsistence were still viable for many and housing was less expensive. At other times of technological change, unions were strong enough to cushion the impact of dislocation. Today, only the state and private charity offer shelter from hard times.

There is no need to answer the question of whether robotization will bring about the end of jobs. That question is impossible to answer and the wrong question to ask ("Automation" 2016). As Mignon Duffy and Robert Pollin argue persuasively in this book, there are very large numbers of potential jobs serving infrastructure, the environment, and social needs. The correct question to ask is "how do we pay for these services?." The neoliberal response has always been that only jobs associated with private profit should command an income. That response has assured us all of an unlimited supply of Pet Rocks, but does nothing to assure that we can all drink clean water. David Rueda and Stefan Thewissen address the issue of compensation in chapter 7 of this volume.

It also matters little to the unemployed that the future might be brighter for employment. Robotization may, in fact, create more jobs in the long run, but future economic payoffs do nothing to diminish the political effects of lost jobs. Workers must pay a mortgage this month, or a tuition bill this semester, or a doctor's bill this week. Relatively few individuals can afford the luxury of a long-run perspective.

The Political Consequences of the Declining Market Value of Labor

Returning to the O'Rourke and Williamson historical pattern, it is not surprising that the world is currently experiencing an antiglobalization backlash, as occurred in the nineteenth century. Globalization has created what Guy Standing calls the precariat, and its politics are ones of resentment and anger.

At the end of the nineteenth century, that anger and resentment was channeled into an intense feeling of nationalism, aggravated by a morbid fascination with the emerging "science" of eugenics. Most people relied heavily on the identities created by familial, occupational, and local ties to give themselves a sense of their place in society. The process of globalization created a world quite separate from these traditional markers, and it was very difficult for many people to find their place and a sense of meaning in the new world. Nationalism and race were the surrogates offered up by the political elites at that time, surrogates that ultimately led to World War I and the brutal racial policies practiced against Jews, Roma, Chinese, and Ethiopians by the Axis allies in the interwar period and World War II. These elites exploited the insecurity of ordinary citizens and defined "enemies" who were tangible, but remote from the actual roots of the alienation.

In his book *Escape from Freedom*, Erich Fromm explained how the greater freedoms afforded by the new technologies of the nineteenth century—the telephone, the telegraph, the railroad, etc.—increased the anxieties of many citizens. The trauma of World War I and the consequent economic disruptions caused by hyperinflation and depression deepened these anxieties to the point where citizens offered up their freedom to authoritarian leaders who promised security and certainty rooted in power, racial identity, and order. The growth of totalitarian regimes, both fascist and communist, crushed the nascent liberal institutions painstakingly developed by Europe and plunged the world into another devastating war.

The economic conditions that led to the rise of totalitarian regimes in the twentieth century are similar to the conditions in the world after the Great Recession of 2008–2009. The slow economic and political deterioration of liberal institutions since 2009 is palpable. The Pew Research Center (2016) has been polling American voters on their attitudes toward the federal government since 2014 and the results of the polls have been consistent and sustained: "Currently, 22% of registered voters say they are 'angry' at the federal government, while 59% are 'frustrated' and 17% 'basically content.'" The approval ratings for the US Congress hover at abysmally low levels. More broadly, there seems to be a declining faith in the efficacy of democracy as a way of addressing the problem of economic and political deterioration.

Voters in Europe and the United States have moved away from traditional parties in an anxious hunt for alternative approaches, and there is little ideological coherence to the platforms of these new parties. Parties have sprung up that have explicitly derided traditional politics, such as the Best, the Pirate, and the Dawn Parties in Iceland and the Five Star Movement in Italy. New parties with nationalist agendas have emerged in Europe: the United Kingdom Independence Party in Great Britain, Golden Dawn in Greece, the National Front in France, the Progress Party in Norway, the Freedom Party in the Netherlands, the Northern League in Italy, the Alternative for Germany Party, the Danish People's Party, the True Finns in Finland, the Sweden Democrats, the Jobbik Party in Hungary, and the Freedom Party in Austria. In the United States in 2016, Donald Trump marketed his position as a genuine outsider to traditional politics. Bernie Sanders mounted a very robust campaign as a political outsider to what he regarded as a compromised system.

This massive reshuffling of "politics as usual" indicates that many voters have given up on traditional parties. There are two threads to the new politics that genuinely challenge the liberal hegemony over politics: a deep-seated distrust of the economics of globalization and a profound aversion to its social manifestations, what might loosely be called multiculturalism. Both threads suggest that voters are defining their interests increasingly in national, racial, and ethnic terms. And both threads are profoundly inconsistent with liberal values.

The xenophobic response is not limited to the United States and Europe. One can find elements of this mood in the success of the Bharatiya Janata Party in India, the election of Rodrigo Duterte in the Philippines, the growing authoritarianism of Turkish president Recep Tayyip Erdoğan, and the coalition-building efforts of the Likud Party in Israel. Australia has gone through six prime ministers in nine years. Russian president Vladimir Putin has tightened his personal control over the Russian state. Chinese president Xi Jinping is consolidating his political power in a manner reminiscent of Mao Zedong. The enthusiasm for the liberal international order we witnessed in 1991 after the dissolution of the Soviet Union has dissipated almost completely.

The precariat know that many corporations have moved their production facilities abroad and that trade agreements, beginning with the North American Free Trade Agreement, facilitated the movement of their jobs overseas. The blame for their situation rests on a vaguely articulated "system" that seems rigged against their interests. That feeling deepened tremendously during the financial crisis of 2008, when hundreds of thousands of people lost their homes while bankers responsible for that crisis kept compensation packages that seemed massively unfair and disproportionate. Moreover, the "system" paid out hundreds of billions to preserve those banks, but allocated virtually nothing for the ordinary citizens who lost their homes and their pensions.

However, the "system" does not have a face. Citizens in liberal economies believe that alternatives, such as socialist economies, are antithetical to freedom and cannot deliver robust economic growth. Faced with the prospect of rejecting neoliberalism, the precariat lacks a viable alternative to support. Its members nonetheless understand that the current system has abandoned them. And, in truth, it has. According to Justin R. Pierce and Peter K. Schott (2012), "U.S. manufacturing employment fluctuated around eighteen million workers between 1965 and 2000 before plunging 18 percent from March 2001 to March 2007" (2). Ultimately, many US corporations created many more jobs abroad than they did at home: "During the 1990s, American multinational companies added 2.7 million jobs in foreign countries and 4.4 million in the United States. But over the following decade, those firms continued adding positions overseas (another 2.4 million) while cutting 2.9 million jobs in the United States" (Harrison 2013).

Whom should the workers blame for the loss of their jobs? Presidents Clinton, Bush, Obama, and Trump? The companies that moved the factories? The people who bought cheaper goods at Wal-Mart that were manufactured in China? Or policymakers who truly believed that freer trade is always the correct policy?

The Politics of Anger

The point at which a citizenry believes that the political and economic system lacks legitimacy is a moment of great danger to any polity. It is the point described by the quotation from Antonio Gramsci at the beginning of this chapter when the elite rules by coercion and not by authority. The long-term stability of any polity is determined by the extent to which most citizens are governed by an ideology to which they conform voluntarily.

This loss of faith lies in the seemingly "irrational" actions of the precariat, favoring policies that ostensibly damage their "real" interests: opposition to free trade, suspicion of immigrants, and hostility toward minority ethnic, racial, and religious groups. These stances violate many of the precepts of liberalism, such as the free movement of capital and labor and the prohibition against discrimination. The corruption of liberalism, however, should first be laid at the feet of the elites. The precariat is hardly irrational; that label belongs to those who believed that people would calmly accept a declining standard of living.

The anger of the precariat is directed toward elites who hold themselves above the rules but insist that others follow them scrupulously. The elites have managed to create a situation in which they write the rules governing their own behavior in a manner that maximizes their self-interest. Jane Mayer's book *Dark Money* (2016) outlines the rather sordid fashion in which US politics have changed recently as wealthy individuals have decided to intervene directly in the writing of laws. One of the more extraordinary aspects of the financial crisis of 2008–2009 was the extent to which activities that most people regard as clearly fraudulent, such as the marketing of collateralized debt obligations constructed to fail, did not land anyone in jail. More revealing is that these were not, in fact, illegal—public officials had made sure that such activities could not be punished by law.

It is no wonder that many citizens are rejecting traditional elites and looking for an alternative. But the alternatives offered have nothing to do with the problem of inequality. Those offered by the elites are meant to distract the precariat. Much of the political rhetoric of neoliberalism is simply an intra-elite war where the interests of the precariat are means to the end of protecting the interests of capital. Is there a real difference between the Republican and Democratic Parties to an American member of the precariat? When the Socialist president of France pushes through a revision of labor laws rejected by every major union in 2016, one wonders what the party labels stand for. In the current environment, the political elites benefit even if the damages caused by inequality are not addressed, as long as the elites stay in power. The average net worth of an official in Congress is $1.03 million, twelve times the net worth of the average American household (Gerencer 2015). Campaign finance laws make it possible to win elections without really serving the public interest.

Political elites understand the truth of Thomas Hobbes's proposition that, if one wishes to wield power over others, one should make the people know fear. Mobilizing fear and hate is an old political tactic. It is difficult to accomplish when the daily lives of citizens hold the promise of a brighter future. It is remarkably simple when a population has deep anxieties about the present and what is to come. There is little question that much of the world's population now exists in that latter state. Ambitious leaders have used fear to mobilize specific political bases, the three most common of which have been terrorism, immigration, and globalization.

First, the most dramatic fear shared by many in the world is that of terrorism, despite its very limited scope. On an almost daily basis, that fear is mentioned in most media, and whenever terrorist attacks occur, the media spend a great deal of time covering the graphic details. For the media itself have a selfish interest in exploiting those fears: higher ratings.

The right wing in the West has a dedicated mantra condemning what it calls "radical Islamic terrorism," which stokes incredible anger and hostility toward Muslims. Terror offers opportunities for the expansion of state power, and many states have restricted civil liberties in the face of those attacks. France and Belgium have declared states of emergency, which, as of this writing, have yet to expire; Russia has used the fear of Chechen terrorists to dramatically expand its police powers; and Egypt has vastly restricted various freedoms in its efforts to combat the Muslim Brotherhood. China fears the Uighurs; citizens of Myanmar fear the Rohingya; the Dinka fear the Nuer. The list could go on. The United States has departed from its traditional embrace of civil liberties even though its practices thus far remain less draconian than those of other states.

Such changes make it much easier for citizens to accept restraints on personal freedom. In the 2016 US presidential election, many commentators used the word "fascist" to describe the appeal of Donald Trump. The use of such a word to describe a single individual at a discrete point in time obscures more than it illuminates. Whatever parallels to the 1930s in Germany may seem appropriate to describe the United States in 2017, one is well-advised to be more careful in such characterizations. Donald Trump is not Adolf Hitler, the United States is not Germany, and 2017 is not 1933. As Umberto Eco (1995) said in his essay on fascism, "Mussolini did not have any philosophy: he had only rhetoric." Nevertheless, one should never think that the long liberal traditions of the United States and Europe insulate them from the possibility of a descent into authoritarianism. Sinclair Lewis explored that possibility in his 1935 novel *It Can't Happen Here*. Before it happened, very few Germans ever believed that their country would be ruled by someone like Adolf Hitler.

There is no reason to believe that the descent into authoritarianism is inevitable. Liberal sentiments and institutions remain strong in some states. The outcomes of national elections in Austria in 2016 and the

Netherlands in 2017 suggest that right-wing parties are not automatic winners. The legal setbacks to the proposed "Muslim ban" by the federal courts in the United States in 2017 indicate that individual rights can still be protected. And, even though British citizens decided to leave the European Union, voters in Scotland and Northern Ireland remained committed to the multilateral institution. It is difficult to deny, however, that public support for liberal institutions and values seems to be fraying.

Second, antiglobalization sentiment was aggravated by a long-festering debate in the United States and Europe about immigration. Despite considerable evidence to the contrary, there is a widespread belief that immigrants take away jobs from citizens, exploit the welfare system, and lower wages. Immigrants are sometimes easy to identify, and recent immigrants are usually unconnected from the traditional centers of power, political or economic. They therefore constitute a vulnerable and easily targeted sector of the population, serving as a useful scapegoat for the economic malaise of the precariat.

Anti-immigration sentiment melds easily into the terror fear, and the syncretic relationship between the two is a powerful political force. It is not easy to identify "others" in the United States and in Europe, but frightened populations easily transform certain signals, such as the wearing of a turban or hijab or an accent or differently colored skin, into concrete threats. That transformation is made even easier when the knowledge base of the citizenry about other cultures is limited or distorted. Politicians exploit these fears by speaking in stereotypical terms, which take on meanings that are far removed from reality. When the Swiss People's Party wanted to communicate an anti-immigrant message, it simply used a picture of a minaret to make the point. In the United States, anti-immigrant sentiment is expressed with the fatuous phrase "sharia law," even though there is virtually no evidence of any significant group in the United States pushing that agenda, or that the people who use that phrase have any idea about what it means.

Additionally, "the other" is often defined in terms of an imaginary people. The dominant group in the United States has always been, and, to a large extent, remains white, Christian, male, and heterosexual, even though the country's population scarcely conforms to those attributes. Populism often applies a soporific to history: "white" ignores the history of discrimination against peoples from southern Europe or Ireland, as well as the heavy legacies of slavery in the United States; "Christian" ignores the rabid anti-Catholicism of the Protestants in the Know-Nothing Party and the Ku Klux Klan; and the histories of women and gays and lesbians remain conspicuously invisible. In the United States, it is relatively easy for both the elites and some of the politically disenfranchised to adopt a caricature of the "American" people.

Third and finally, globalization itself becomes an enemy of the people. Antiglobalization comes in two flavors: a left critique that blames companies for sending jobs overseas and a right critique that blames trade pacts signed by the government. For some, the difference is important. For many others, however, the distinction is irrelevant. Populism does not have an economic agenda or any use for traditional parties. In the United States, the election of Donald Trump suggests that the neoliberal agenda of the Republican Party, particularly with respect to taxes, will be pursued aggressively even as nonliberal protectionist trade policies are also pursued. If the right-wing Marine Le Pen becomes president of France, it is likely that left-leaning policies will prevail. Consistency is not necessary for populist politics; anything that protects the nation is justified. Politics is merely the instrument of the nation. Its enemy is the state that embraces globalization. Populism's objective is the destruction of those elements of the state that support globalization, and it matters little to the populist whether those policies are right- or left-wing. For the populist, mainstream parties are always invested in the perpetuation of the state over the interests of the people.

From this perspective, the world itself is a threatening place and the only place of safety is in the company of fellow citizens who share the same values. This sentiment exposes the profound contradiction mentioned earlier between the universal claims of market capitalism and the parochial claims of the nation-state. Nationalism offers a more tangible alternative to neoliberal abstractions. The neoliberal claim that everyone is better off with free trade rings hollow in the ears of the precariat. When one has lost a job, it is difficult to accept that fate as a means to enrich others, particularly when those others are enriching themselves by eliminating jobs. Nationalism creates a shared fate and that belief brings comfort to those who think that they are being besieged by strangers.

Possible Futures

The liberal international order is now more threatened than it was in the struggle against fascism and communism in the twentieth century. Those contests were against external threats and were conducted in the unfortunately familiar terrain of normal nation-state competition. The challenge today is internal and a crisis of faith and authority—issues that cannot be resolved by a resort to armed force. There are a variety of ways this crisis might unfold.

First, the world can abandon the liberal order and turn toward authoritarianism and balance of power politics as an alternative to the liberal, multilateral order. This alternative seems to be the most likely in 2017 as the United States, under the leadership of President Trump, is signaling that it intends to withdraw from its role as the prime supporter of the global liberal order. Without the hegemonic leadership of the United States, the world will revert to the O'Rourke and Williamson pattern, which led to a world war and a Great Depression. The disarray of the interwar period suggests that world order is not self-regulating and needs a powerful champion.

Nationalism is overriding essential norms of the 1945 order. The American decision to invade Iraq in 2003 without the sanction of the UN Security Council undermined the multilateral framework of that order, and the election of Donald Trump as president, with his agenda of bilateral trade agreements and reduced commitments to international organizations, signals the end of US support for the liberal international order. The surge in nationalism in Russia, evidenced by its moves in Georgia and Ukraine, and in China, marked by extravagant maritime claims made in the East and South China Sea, induce countervailing nationalist impulses in surrounding countries. As many scholars have noted, not many in Europe foresaw the cataclysm that was to unfold in 1914. In the early twenty-first century, there is not yet much discussion of a great war, but there are certainly many potential flash points in the Middle East, in the Baltics, in Eastern Europe, and in Southeast Asia that could trigger an unanticipated war (Kofman and Sushentsov 2016).

The economic pressures that led to the Great Depression are also paralleled in the contemporary period. A huge technological transformation has increased productivity to an incredible degree; a dynamic new economic power has arisen—China in the late twentieth century in many respects mimics the rise of the United States in the late nineteenth—that has created new economic relationships and unsettled well-established ones; and the specter of underconsumption has been brought about by the reduced purchasing power of previously well-employed citizens and the concentration of wealth at the very top of the income brackets. Income distributions in the late 1920s look very much like income distributions in the 2010s.

The earlier period also introduced the world to two new ideologies, both of which evolved into totalitarian regimes: Communism emerged after the October Revolution in 1917 and *fasci* began to form in 1915. These ideologies were not spawned by the Great Depression, but rather by war. Inequality was not itself the trigger for totalitarian ideologies—the insecurity, loss of faith, and the failure of leadership exposed by World War I were sufficient for many people to reject liberalism. But inequality amplifies those conditions. Once the Great Depression occurred, many in the United States believed that both fascism and communism were attractive alternatives, even though World War I had not ravaged the liberal consensus there as it had in Europe. As of 2017, no new ideology has emerged to bring the coherence to the nationalist movements necessary to frame a new world order. They remain diffuse, united only by their rejection of the liberal world order, and offering little more than a return to balance of power politics.

An economic collapse and a descent into authoritarian politics is the most likely endpoint of current neoliberal policies that remain unresponsive to the populist and nationalist challenge. These policies have emphasized reducing the costs of production at the expense of supporting demand for those products. Consequently, the market now overproduces and the evidence of deflationary pressures is undeniable. Stimulating demand is the correct response, but the opposition of the elites to tax increases to pay for fiscal policies to increase demand in the market renders that strategy nugatory. The opposition to tax increases is both ideological and structural. Some elites foolishly believe that their wealth will insulate them from the negative effects of an economic depression despite the overwhelming historical evidence to the contrary. The structural basis for opposition to raising taxes to achieve a redistributive effect is that the redistributive effect is a collective good. Raising overall demand in a market economy potentially raises the demand for a competitor's product, and in a highly competitive market it is more rational to avoid that risk and hope that other competitors take the losses to their profits to stimulate demand. As of 2017, there is virtually no reason to believe that any redistributive fiscal measures are possible in any of the major market economies and thus the most likely outcome is an economic implosion.

The second possible future is the reform of liberalism in ways that inspire hope and confidence. Again, there is a historical parallel to this course of action. The New Deal stimulated the US economy by redistributing wealth through the tax mechanism. The panoply of programs under the New Deal was remarkable, and the opposition to the new economic framework was formidable and fierce. But the exigencies of the moment were also compelling. Slowly, and somewhat chaotically, incomes rose, until the Federal Reserve raised interest rates in 1937 in an ideological reversion to neoliberalism.

Government intervention in the economy is far less heretical now than it was in the 1930s. Most governments now accept a role in redistribution; the part it plays in building infrastructure and providing health and educational services is accepted and expected. Nonetheless, the resistance to raising taxes is profound. Even tax increases that are carefully crafted to include only the very wealthy are opposed by many citizens because they believe that every tax increase is in some sense a Trojan horse. And the rich are incredibly well-organized to oppose any meaningful tax increases.

A reform of liberalism must involve redistribution of wealth and income. The current system of welfare payments is viewed by many as chaotic, bureaucratic, and subject to political whims. It is also inadequate for the needs of many. In its place, some countries, such as Switzerland and Finland, have raised the possibility of a guaranteed annual income, a policy that had many advocates. As attractive as the proposals may seem, it is difficult to imagine their adoption. When the Swiss held a referendum on a guaranteed income of 2,500 Swiss francs per month, 77 percent of the voting population rejected the proposal. Poorer countries have more opportunity to think systematically about social policy, as pointed out by Juliana Martínez Franzoni and Diego Sánchez-Anocochea in chapter 11.

It is also difficult to imagine Franklin Roosevelt's success in passing New Deal programs being replicated in the current global political environment. The opposition to higher taxes is significantly better organized now than it was in the 1930s, the loopholes to avoid higher taxes have become ubiquitous in the unreadable tax codes, and the ability to shelter income and wealth from taxes has become more routine and institutionalized. Moreover, with the ability of capital to move freely anyplace on the planet, raising taxes in one nation-state will require a concerted multilateral effort to be successful. That level of cooperation is virtually impossible in a world of rising nationalism and xenophobia.

Some analysts are rethinking neoliberal policies. Different approaches to trade are being discussed (Prestowitz 2016). *The Economist* extended a mea culpa on the issue of free trade after the vote in Great Britain to leave the European Union: "Proponents of globalisation, including this newspaper, must acknowledge that technocrats have made mistakes and ordinary people paid the price" ("Politics" 2016). The International Monetary Fund also published a paper suggesting that neoliberalism has been "oversold" (Ostry, Loungani, and Furceri 2016). All this questioning, however, has yet to cohere in a systematic way. Even if the technocrats and academicians were to come up with a viable alternative to neoliberalism, it is not clear that the political and economic elites who profit from the blind application of neoliberalism would be willing to make that change.

The third possible future is to reconceptualize a dominant ideology and construct a new world order—built, perhaps, on the best aspects of liberal thinking but with more emphasis on social responsibilities and less on personal freedom. Liberalism evolved when roughly 750 million people inhabited the planet, when virtually everyone was involved in agriculture, and when most human activity had minimal impact on the global environment. The social good was always present in the minds of the early liberal thinkers, but was more obvious and palpable when people lived in small villages and everyone knew each other. It is far more difficult to identify in a world of seven billion people, where much interaction is anonymous, and when the means to privatize important goods such as fresh water, clean air, and security are becoming more effective.

Liberalism may be an important, but incomplete, phase in human history. It required new ways of thinking about the human condition such as private property, clear checks on the use and abuse of state (and religious) power, and a radical reconceptualization of nature and humanity's place in it. These changes were critical to the progress humanity has made over the last five hundred years. But discontent with liberal society, with its refusal to take the distribution of income and wealth as a serious problem as well as its willingness to tolerate the abuse of power in the name of freedom, has never gone away, and those concerns are only becoming more acute. Polanyi's countermovement has never disappeared and its complaints have never been answered.

For example, one of the principal pillars of liberal thought—private property—will be seriously questioned. It is unlikely that private property will be abolished, but the untrammeled freedom of individuals to "own" valuable or dangerous resources will probably be restrained. Climate change will be the leading wedge for this ideological revision. There are trillions of dollars of hydrocarbon reserves currently owned by fossil-fuel companies. At some point, the world will have to say that these resources cannot be extracted. That declaration will expropriate property, replicating the similar politically difficult, but correct, decision that had to be made when slavery was abolished. Other environmental concerns will also limit how resources such as fresh water can be allocated. The public good will be the critical element of how private property must be redefined.

The liberal international order is threatened from the inside, as is usually the case with empires of thought. There are other orders being advanced: China, for example, desires to enjoy the economic freedoms of the market without the concomitant political freedoms of democracy. Some societies place significantly less emphasis on material progress and others a high priority on order and stability. But the liberal international order is not being eroded by these alternatives. It is being eroded because its "center cannot hold." The words William Butler Yeats wrote in "The Second Coming" to describe the sense of loss brought on by World War I are as prophetic in 2017 as they were in 1919: "The best lack all conviction, while the worst / Are full of passionate intensity."

Part III

The Global South

Challenges and Opportunities

9

Advanced Manufacturing and China's Future for Jobs

Dieter Ernst

China provides interesting new perspectives for research on the employment effects of the New Technological Revolution. While much of this research has focused on the United States, Europe, and Japan, this chapter explores how China's push into advanced manufacturing and services through robots and other new disruptive technologies might affect the country's future for jobs.

For China, moving up the value-added chain is a response to its slowing economy and the increasingly severe economic and social costs of the established export-oriented manufacturing model. Despite massive investments in production, infrastructure, and R&D on a scale and at a speed never seen before, much of China's industry is still stuck in very basic manufacturing and low value-added services. Slow productivity growth and limited innovation capacity remain widespread outside a handful of large companies and regional clusters of excellence. A major demographic crisis is looming and wages are rising, while companies complain about a scarcity of skills needed to move up the value-added chain.

Three questions are at the center of this chapter: (1) Will China be able to improve its competitiveness through productivity-enhancing innovation, while at the same time creating enough quality jobs?; (2) What are the strengths and weaknesses of China's bold strategy to upgrade manufacturing and services through flexible automation and computer-based network integration?; and, most importantly, (3) Are policies in place to improve employment effects and wage incomes and to create the specialized, knowledge-intensive skills needed to upgrade into advanced manufacturing and services and further close the innovation gap?

After decades of rapid-fire growth, China has reached a level of development where catching up through an investment-driven "Global Factory" model based on low-wage production is no longer sufficient to create long-term economic growth and prosperity. Serious constraints on environmental, human, and financial resources imply that economic growth based on scale expansion is running out of steam, depressing China's economic growth. The closer it has moved to the technology frontier, the less scope there is for imitation and low-level incremental innovation. Of critical importance now is that Chinese firms adopt, absorb, and develop advanced manufacturing technologies.

At the same time, severe headwinds are constraining the country's growth. International trade, a primary source of China's rise, has fallen to its lowest level since 2009, and continues to languish. Since the turn of the century, a declining labor force, rising wages, and skill bottlenecks are eroding its international competitiveness. As a result, corporate profits, export competitiveness, and asset prices have slumped.

To break out of this growth impasse, China's leadership has decided to leapfrog into advanced manufacturing and services. Two policy initiatives are the expression of that ambition: the China Manufacturing 2025 plan (MIC 2025), and the Internet Plus plan (IP). Both seek to promote innovation-driven development using robots, 3D printing, Big Data, and the integration of manufacturing and services through the mobile internet. In line with the Thirteenth Five-Year Plan, the goal is to upgrade China from a "big industrial country" to a "powerful industrial country."

China is likely to emerge over the next decade as a major user and producer of robots and other advanced manufacturing technologies. In addition, its push into advanced services will be invigorated by the increasing role played by its largest firms, which can draw on ample financial resources and close government contacts. However, China continues to lag well behind advanced economies in R&D on major frontier technologies and in high-impact invention patents. The country still has a long way to go to develop the broad portfolio of management and innovation capabilities needed to implement the above transition.

Part One of the chapter singles out China's comparative advantage in manufacturing and the extraordinary size of its economy, which explain why China has not followed Dani Rodrik's pattern of "premature deindustrialization" (Rodrik 2015), neither in output nor in employment. Outside of mining, metals, textile and apparel, manufacturing in China has continued to act as an employment absorber until 2015. However, China is now beginning to face a major demographic crisis which is resulting in labor shortages and steep rises in wages.

Part Two provides a brief overview of the objectives of the MIC 2025 and the IP plans to address rising labor costs by moving up the value chain. The analysis highlights formidable challenges, as a large part of China's industry is still at the level of industry 2.0, i.e. mainly assembly lines. China's leadership recognizes those challenges, but fails to address fundamental weaknesses related to innovation capacity, employment generation, skills and labor market conditions.

Part Three of the chapter assesses China's current position and capabilities in advanced manufacturing technologies (with a focus on robots). China has moved ahead in a very short period of time, substantially narrowing the innovation gap that separates it from the US and other advanced countries, as well as from neighboring Asian competitors. And yet, the country still may need a decade or so to catch up with global industry leaders. Arguably the most problematic weakness of both the MIC 2025 and the IP plans is an almost exclusive focus on technology, and a failure to collect data on possible impacts of advanced manufacturing and services on jobs, skills, income and inequality. Such data, however, are absolutely necessary to explore China's Future for Jobs.

To reduce this knowledge gap, Part Four reviews newly available data for China on unemployment, income inequality, skill requirements and the development and quality of service jobs. These data document that official statistics underestimate China's unemployment rate and that the inequality of income is rising. These data also show that there is a glaring shortage of the necessary skills (especially for soft and vocational skills), as well as well-paying knowledge-intensive service jobs. Forging ahead in advanced manufacturing thus will face major hurdles, as long as these critical bottlenecks in skills are not addressed.

China's push into advanced manufacturing coincides with the "new normal" of a lengthy industrial slowdown. Thus far, its service sector does not provide a sufficient number of knowledge-intensive and well-paying jobs. This is bound to constrain the growth of household incomes and consumption. Any such slowdown in income may eventually begin to constrain the service sector, too, as the profit squeeze in manufacturing companies and declining worker income lead to a decline in investment in and consumption of services. In order to avoid this "worst-case scenario," it is necessary for both MIC 2025 and the IP plan to be based on realistic projections of employment effects, wage incomes, skill requirements, and other labor market impacts.

China Is Different

As its per capita income is still a fraction of that in advanced countries, China qualifies as a developing country. However, it is very different from other developing countries. Its comparative advantage in manufacturing, combined with the extraordinary size of its economy, makes it unlikely that China will follow Dani Rodrik's (2015, 3) pattern of "premature deindustrialization." This concept implies that manufacturing begins "to shrink (or is on course for shrinking) at levels of income that are a fraction of those at which the advanced economies started to deindustrialize." According to Rodrik, most developing countries tend to be small in global markets for manufacturing, and hence act as price takers. "As price takers . . . these developing countries may have 'imported' deindustrialization" (22), especially if they lack a strong comparative advantage in manufacturing (4).

On both accounts, China clearly does not fit this pattern. Since opening up to the international economy in 1978, China has seen rapid growth of industrial manufacturing and exports, followed by massive investments in its innovation system. As a result, it has become a serious global competitor, not only in terms of price, but also technology. China now competes head-on with the United States and other advanced countries across a wide array of industries, including R&D-intensive sectors.

In addition, due to its size, this country was able to develop a broad industrial base. This sets China apart from Korea and Taiwan, where initial plans for broad-based economic growth were soon abandoned for specialization in sectors of comparative advantage, with Taiwan, in particular, serving niche markets around the world.

What distinguishes China is that massive investments in the country's R&D infrastructure and higher education were combined with the country's deep integration into Global Production Networks (GPNs) and Global Innovation Networks (GINs). A proxy for its high degree of GPN integration is that 44 percent of its exports are produced under so-called processing trade arrangements, in which imported inputs are assembled into exports. Another indicator is that two-thirds of China's production of goods and services are intermediates, which is substantially higher than the world average.

As for integration into GINs, China is the largest "net importer" of research and development and the third most important offshore R&D location (after the United States and the UK) of the three hundred top R&D spending multinationals. China is thus deeply integrated, albeit still unevenly, into the international circulation of technological and managerial knowledge needed to enhance its absorptive capacity. In 2013, 385 of the top five hundred R&D spenders had R&D activities there, up from 195 in 2009, making China the most popular global location for the top five hundred spenders in this area to set up an R&D center.

Despite its deep integration into international trade and global networks, there are as yet no signs of significant specialization. "Across virtually all industries in China, the optimal firm size—the firm size with lowest per-unit production costs—is below market demand. I.e., there is sufficient market demand in every sector of the economy for several firms to co-exist and compete." As a result, "one can expect to see ongoing investment across virtually every sector of the Chinese economy" (Holz 2015). In short, China is unlikely to experience premature deindustrialization any time soon.

China also differs from advanced countries. According to Robert Z. Lawrence and Lawrence Edwards, manufacturing employment in the

United States and other leading industrialized countries has followed a pattern of "employment deindustrialization," growing more slowly than employment in the overall economy, due to a "combination of productivity growth, demand for goods, and international trade" (2013, 5). By contrast, China's manufacturing industry has until recently acted as an absorber of employment. While the country's manufacturing employment came down by eighteen million, or almost a fifth, between 1995 and 2000, this decline was driven primarily by an aggressive restructuring of the state-owned enterprise sector. But, once the effect of this reform receded, manufacturing employment rose steadily, not only in absolute numbers but also as a share of total employment. From 2002 to 2013, the number of manufacturing workers in China surged by an incredible 27,699,736, whereas in the United States 2,952,000 manufacturing workers lost their jobs during the same period.[1]

Nonetheless, a significant displacement of manufacturing jobs has occurred since 2014, with most of it concentrated in the mining and metals sectors (troubled by excess capacity), and the textile and apparel sectors as their exports decline. Mining and metals lost 1.4 million workers over 2014 and 2015; China's labor ministry expected an additional 1.8 million job losses in 2016. Textiles and apparel shed around four hundred thousand jobs each year in 2014 and 2015 (Cui 2016a).

At the same time, China is facing a major demographic crisis that is now beginning to affect labor supply, productivity, and income distribution.[2] According to the National Bureau of Statistics (NBS), the working-age population declined by almost 3.5 million people in 2012. China is experiencing a nationwide labor shortage and steep rises in worker wages, including for immigrant workers (Cai 2013). There is still some debate about the precise timing of this shift to a labor shortage. A 2013 working paper by the International Monetary Fund, for instance, expects the Lewis turning point in China to emerge between 2020 and 2025 (Das and N'Diaye 2013).

Since around 2005, China has experienced a massive rise in unit labor costs in the manufacturing industry. Compared to an index of 100 in 2000, unit labor costs rose to an index of 240. This contrasts with a decline in the US index over the same period to around 88, and a much smaller increase in Korea's, to 120.[3] In response, Chinese factories are shedding workers to curb rising costs, despite output growth fueled by domestic orders (Wang and Feng 2016).

As China is now facing a looming labor shortage and rising wages, this might imply that its main focus should be on productivity-enhancing innovation and that job creation and related labor market issues might not be the country's main challenge. This precisely is the approach selected by the Chinese government. This narrow focus on productivity-enhancing innovation, however, comes at a significant cost, as will be demonstrated in the rest of the chapter.

Objectives and Strategy

Since the Third Plenum, China's leadership has emphasized the need to upgrade the manufacturing industry beyond catching up with global industry leaders, by forging ahead in advanced manufacturing. Emblematic of the shift to an innovation-driven development model are two complementary policy initiatives:

- A ten-year plan issued by the State Council on May 19, 2015, entitled "Made in China 2025," (MIC 2025), which focuses on upgrading the country's manufacturing industries through the use of productivity-enhancing advanced manufacturing technologies such as robots, 3D printing, and the Industrial Internet.[4]
- On July 4, 2015, the State Council unveiled its Internet Plus (IP) plan, aiming "to integrate mobile Internet, cloud computing, big data, and the Internet of Things with modern manufacturing, to encourage the healthy development of e-commerce, industrial networks, and Internet banking, and to help Internet companies increase their international presence."[5]

Both plans share three fundamental objectives: to a) upgrade China's industry through flexible automation and computer-based network integration with knowledge-intensive services; b) expedite investment in required digital infrastructure (in order to enhance network convergence, accelerate fiber-optic network construction, and improve broadband speed, while strengthening cybersecurity); and c) strengthen the capacity of domestic firms to develop intellectual property rights for critical core technologies, materials, components, and software, and for scaling up cost-effective production and incremental innovations.

Below, I present a brief review of the still fairly vague policy statements about the IP plan followed by a more detailed outline of objectives and implementation priorities of the MIC 2025 plan.

The Internet Plus (IP) Plan

China has the world's largest internet population (sixty-five million people), with 85 percent (fifty-six million) using mobile devices to connect to the internet. In 2015, it overtook the United States to become the world's largest e-commerce market. However, with an internet penetration rate of 50.3 percent in 2015, China still has ample room to catch up with Korea's record internet penetration rate of 85.1 percent.

Given this huge market potential, it is hardly surprising that large firms (both Chinese and multinationals) are the main drivers behind the IP plan, while the government somewhat belatedly discovered the internet as a new growth engine. Main drivers on the business side are China's immensely powerful internet companies and system integrators, the so-called BATs (Baidu, Alibaba, and Tencent); leading consumer electronics companies such as Midea, TCL, Haier, and Konka; and mobile telecom and smartphone companies. The dynamic behind the IP plan is driven primarily by intense competition between online and offline commerce channels, and in particular among the BATs and Alibaba's rival JD.com. In fact, leading global players such as SAP, Microsoft, IBM, and Oracle have now discovered the China internet market, which is projected to reach more than $1 trillion over the next five years. In short, the IP plan provides a chance for the Chinese government to piggyback on a wave of corporate internet penetration strategies. This sets this plan apart from MIC 2025, which is the brainchild of the government.

In July 2015, the State Council released the *Guiding Opinions on Promoting the Development of Internet Plus* to deepen the integration across industry and services.[6] China's IP plan follows closely Germany's Cyber-Physical Systems initiative and the US Industrial Internet Consortium.[7] The IP plan describes, in fairly general terms, requirements, targets, action plans, and support policies. Eleven key "Internet Plus" actions include entrepreneurship and innovation; collaborative manufacturing; modern agriculture; smart energy; inclusive finance; public services; efficient logistics; e-commerce; convenient transportation; green ecology; and artificial intelligence. In addition to this laundry list, the *Guiding Opinions* include twenty-five relevant supportive measures, categorized into five parts.

Because business has aggressively signed on to the IP plan, its economic impacts are likely to be substantial, including the development of 5G mobile communication technologies and infrastructure for broadband and mobile communications (especially in remote regions in China's midwest and "smart cities" in the mideast); the spread of big data and cloud computing in related industries such as health, education, and financial services; wearable mobile devices; and the Internet of Things. In addition, the release of a second government report, *Guiding Opinions on Promoting the Healthy Development of Internet Finance* shows that China seeks to create a more certain environment for internet finance companies to grow.

As for implementation, the IP plan lists a total of sixty-five corresponding development tasks and specifies the respective leading responsible ministries. To fit with the timeframe of the Made in China 2025 plan, the IP plan is to complete an initial implementation phase by 2018 and reach full completion by 2025.

The "Made in China 2025 (MIC 2025)" Plan

A primary objective is to upgrade China's industry through flexible automation and computer-based network integration. MIC 2025 was drafted by the Ministry of Industry and Information Technology (MIIT) over two and a half years, with input from fifty experts from the China Academy of Engineering and the Chinese Academy of Sciences, as well as around one hundred experts from industry and research institutes. Issued by the State Council on May 19, 2015, MIC 2025 has the full support of China's leadership. Vice Premier Ma Kai heads the leading small group that is responsible for effective implementation.

The focus of MIC 2025 on advanced manufacturing represents a volte-face in China's development strategy. Five-Year Plans since 2007 had previously emphasized the expansion of the service sector, in line with then-fashionable initiatives in the United States. The Twelfth FYP (2011–2015) had targeted the service sector to become the single biggest contributor to GDP by 2015. However, by that time the pro-service tide had already started to ebb in the rest of the world. In 2011, the Obama administration launched its Advanced Manufacturing Partnership, while Germany formally adopted its Industrie 4.0 initiative. MIC 2025 moves beyond science and technology and seeks to upgrade all stages of China's industrial supply and demand chains.

MIC 2025 is most closely linked to Germany's Industrie 4.0 initiative, which seeks to integrate factories, research labs, and service providers across domestic and global supply chains through flexible automation and the Internet of Things in industrial manufacturing. Germany has the advanced technology needed, and thus is China's preferred partner. The design of MIC 2025 also draws on other international benchmarks that pursue similar advanced manufacturing upgrading strategies.

The challenge for China's industry is that it is still in transition from Industry 2.0, which is mainly assembly-line work, to Industry 3.0, which uses more industrial automation, electronics, and IT. Today, only about 60 percent of Chinese companies use industrial automation software such as Enterprise Resource Planning; the internet adoption ratio by Chinese small- and medium-sized enterprises is only 25 percent (Heng and Trenczek 2015). To reduce this huge gap, MIC 2025 encompasses upgrading objectives for process management and logistics, R&D, intellectual property rights, and technical standards.

MIC 2025 addresses several overriding objectives: a big push in firm-level industrial innovation capacity (focused on R&D and patents); quality improvement and accelerated productivity growth and quality; an expansion of informatization and digitization of industry; and "green development," focusing on reductions of energy consumption, water usage, and pollution. In order to implement these objectives, MIC 2025 seeks to provide a new framework for coordinating industrial support policies to overcome a persistent gap in technological, management, and innovation capabilities across the gamut of China's manufacturing industry.

Improved policy coordination is considered to be particularly important in order to reduce the fragmentation of decision-making across government agencies and between the central government and local governments. There is a broad consensus that improved coordination is essential to overcome deeply entrenched disconnects between industry, academia, and government. As an important step in this direction, MIIT has brought together fourteen state-run associations from different sectors and created a voluntary quality management standard for automated and intelligent manufacturing.

MIC 2025 highlights ten priority sectors for China's push into advanced manufacturing: 1) new advanced information technology; 2) automated machine tools & robotics; 3) aerospace and aeronautical equipment; 4) maritime equipment and high-tech shipping; 5) modern rail transport equipment; 6) new-energy vehicles and equipment; 7) power equipment; 8) agricultural equipment; 9) new materials; and 10) biopharma and advanced medical products. For each of these priority areas, the plan provides objectives, albeit still on a quite general level.

In essence, MIC 2025 is meant to address China's rising labor cost challenge. To achieve this goal, it seeks to boost labor productivity through an increased use of robots and through network-based upgrading of the entire industrial value chain and related services. A 7.5 percent annual growth of labor productivity is projected until 2020, and from then on an annual growth of 6.5 percent. This will require a reversal of China's long-term productivity slowdown from almost 9.5 percent during 2007–2012 to an estimated 6.7 percent for 2015 (Conference Board 2015, 16).

A report from the US Manufacturers Alliance for Productivity and Innovation concludes that MIC 2025 is likely to produce substantial improvements in manufacturing productivity (Bledowski 2015). In short, China's MIC 2025 and IP Plans appear to be focused almost exclusively on the nation's productivity challenge. But, as we will see below, both fail to address major unresolved challenges related to jobs, skills, and other labor market issues.

China's Push into Advanced Manufacturing—What Is Missing?

To assess China's prospects in advanced manufacturing, it is important to recall that much of its industry is still stuck in very basic manufacturing. Many of these factories will not survive the next ten years without major upgrading of facilities and production processes. No doubt, this constitutes a huge potential for industrial upgrading, provided China's policies are flexible, explorative, and open to necessary changes. Most importantly, these policies need to move beyond the low-wage model of the country's export-oriented industrialization.

Ever since it opened up to the world economy under Deng Xiaoping, China has developed its industrial technological capacity at record speed. Despite this unparalleled achievement, however, its innovation capacity continues to lag well behind comparator countries. At 1.98 percent, its R&D intensity in 2015 was much lower than that of Korea (3.60 percent), Japan (3.40 percent), Germany (2.85 percent), and the United States (2.78 percent) (IRI 2016, 2). China's energy consumption per unit of GDP (0.26) is much higher than that of the United States (0.16), Korea (0.18), or Germany and Japan (each 0.11) (Shao 2015). Of particular concern, both for the electronics and the car industry, are China's weak capabilities in high-end molds and dies. For these essentials, it continues to depend on imports from Japan and Germany.

In what follows, the analysis will first examine evidence about China's persistent innovation gap and assess its current use and production of robots and related capabilities. The attention then shifts to the arguably most problematic weakness of both the MIC 2025 and IP plans—a dearth of robust data on employment, skills, and other labor market issues.

A Persistent Innovation Gap   Since 2000, China has made massive investments in R&D infrastructure on a scale and at a speed never seen before (Ernst 2011). It has increased spending in this area roughly 10 percent each year—a pace the country maintained even during the 2008–2009 recession. This sustained commitment to a rapid expansion of R&D sets China apart from the crisis-induced cuts in the United States and Europe. And, with the exception of Korea, Taiwan, and Singapore, no other emerging or developing country has ever even contemplated such a big push.

Today, China is the world's second-largest investor in R&D. It is one of the four leading countries in science and technology publications, with particular strengths in materials science, analytical chemistry, rice genomics, and stem-cell biology. Within materials science, China is especially strong in nanotechnology, ranking third (after the United States and Japan) in the number of publications in this subject; the Chinese Academy of Science is ranked fourth for nanoscience citations (after the University of California, Berkeley; MIT; and IBM). Additionally, China is ranked among the top five global R&D leaders in high-tech industries such as energy (both nuclear and renewable), satellites and spacecraft, commercial aircraft, automotive (especially electric cars), supercomputers, and life sciences (especially genetics), and it is rapidly catching up in high-speed rail, information and communications technology, and defense and security.

Yet, China's gap in innovation capacity persists. The country's leadership is very conscious that it continues to lag well behind the United States in R&D on major breakthrough technologies, in critical capabilities (both management and technological), and in accumulated portfolios of high-impact invention patents.

As China's GDP growth declines, its R&D investments are also bound to slow down. In addition, its barriers to innovation remain substantial, including severe quality problems in education, plagiarism in science, a fragmented innovation system (prone to rivalries among different government agencies and between the central government and local governments), and barriers to entrepreneurship and private R&D investment (Ernst 2015, 2011). Access to high-quality data is critical for networked advanced manufacturing. China's push into advanced manufacturing will face major impediments as long as access to data resources remains highly unequal, and as long as questions remain about the reliability of the data that the government has made available in the public domain.

As for research on advanced manufacturing technology, China has invested quite some effort, but progress thus far has been limited. A Fraunhofer Institute study finds that Chinese researchers have patented important inventions in key advanced manufacturing technologies, including wireless sensor networks, embedded systems, low-cost robots, and big data ("Study" 2015). In terms of the number of patents filed for Industry 4.0 technologies, it finds that China is one of the largest players, especially for data networks and big data. China may emerge over the next decade as a producer of some of those technologies. It is unclear, however, whether it has the capacity to develop commercially successful advanced manufacturing technology platforms.

In short, despite all its achievements since the 1980s, China's catching up in advanced manufacturing technology is a hard struggle that is measured in decades rather than years. But this challenge is different from that faced by Sisyphus in Greek mythology, who was forced to roll an immense boulder up a hill, only to watch it come back to hit him, repeating this action for eternity. For China, this struggle to move up the value-added chain has become a powerful catalyst for mobilization.

Robots Are All the Rage, but Where Does China Really Stand?   Robots—in particular, the flexible and autonomous variety—are supposed to play an important role in the MIC 2025 plan. Let us look at China's official data on the use and local production of robots, and on the progress made toward autonomous robots.[8] From 2009 to 2014, sales in China of industrial robots increased by an annual average of 59 percent. In 2014, the sales volume reached about fifty-seven thousand units, around one-quarter of total global robot sales. That year, the Chinese Robot Alliance (CRIA) reported that twenty-nine manufacturing sectors in China were using robots, up from twenty-six in 2013. For 2015, the growth of robot sales is estimated at 25 percent, with the growth rate of domestic robot suppliers' sales estimated at over 40 percent.

With an estimated operational stock of 262,900 multipurpose industrial robots in 2015, China has rapidly caught up with Japan (297,200) and is now slightly ahead of the three North American nations (259,200). The media have reported widely on prestige projects such as the Swiss ABB robot project in the Zhuhai High-Tech Zone (the largest industrial robot R&D and production base in southern China) and the all-robot manufacturing plant in Dongguan. According to industry observers, many factories in the Pearl River Delta, the heart of China's world factory, are investing in robots, as labor shortages bite and local authorities face the need to spur innovation to counter the economic slowdown.

China still has a long way to go to catch up in the use of robots. Take robot density—robots per ten thousand employees—which is a key performance indicator. The current global leader in industrial robotic automation is South Korea, with 478 units, followed by Japan (314) and Germany (292). At 164 units, the USA currently occupies seventh place in the world. China is currently in twenty-eighth place, with just thirty-six units.[9]

On the supply side, China remains heavily dependent on foreign technology: 75 percent of all robots used there are purchased from foreign firms (some with assembly lines in China), and the country remains heavily dependent on imports of costly core components from Japan. The latest count reports 107 Chinese companies producing robots, but many of the end products have low quality, safety, and design standards.

However, China is now making a concerted effort to catch up in the development of robotics patents. While its share in total robotics patents in the year 2000 was only 2 percent, that figure had risen to 37 percent by 2011. Korea's share stood at 17 percent in 2011, while Japan's fell from 45 percent in 2000 to 10 percent in 2011 (Keisner, Raffo, and Wunsch-Vincent 2015, 24). Between 2000 and 2012, the countries with the highest number of filings were Japan, China, Korea, and the United States.

China will continue to bolster the development of a domestic robotics industry, according to a new robotics technology roadmap released in April 2016 by the government for the Thirteenth Five-Year Plan period (2016–2020) ("China" 2016). China aims to have three to five internationally competitive domestic robotics companies by 2020. By that time, the country is also expected to achieve a robot density of at least one hundred industrial robots installed per ten thousand employees, with the high-end manufacturing sector having a robot penetration rate of 45 percent. To achieve its development goals, the Chinese robotics industry will have to increase its self-sufficiency in the production and design of key components and R&D in the generic technologies necessary to make the transition to smart robotics.

The government and its companies are persistent, and it is reasonable to expect slow and steady gains in this area. In about five to ten years, China's robot industry is likely to produce industrial robots that are on par with those from Germany and Japan.

Employment and Other Labor Market Data

China's employment and labor market data are poor and unreliable. The official employment statistics provided by the National Bureau of Statistics (NBS) are organized in such a way that it is quite tedious to construct proxy indicators for newly created manufacturing jobs, layoffs, or wages and income. To navigate through the maze of fuzzy and sometimes conflicting information, I have relied on interviews with China-based industry experts and researchers.

The first important point is that manufacturing still acts as an employment provider. Research conducted by Judith Banister for the US Bureau of Labor Statistics (BLS) shows that China's manufacturing employment showed a continual increase over the 2002–2009 time period, rising from 85.9 million in 2002 to 99.0 million in 2009. As Chinese employment grew by about 15 percent over this seven-year period, manufacturing employment in other countries covered by the BLS was stable or declined. China's 2009 manufacturing employment was much greater than manufacturing employment in any other country: in 2009, for example, manufacturing employment was about 14.2 million in the United States, 10.8 million in Japan, and 7.8 million in Germany (Banister 2013).

More recent data from the Conference Board International Labor Comparisons Program (which has taken over the discontinued BLS research) show that China's manufacturing employment has further increased by almost 15 percent, from 98,998,570 in 2009 to 113,577,801 in 2013, the latest year available (The Conference Board 2016). From 2003 to 2014, China's NBS reports, total urban manufacturing employment doubled and the share of the urban workforce employed in manufacturing rose from 15 to 20 percent. These data do not include the significant manufacturing employment in rural areas.

In China, manufacturing still acts as an employment absorber. While the share of manufacturing in GDP declined from 32.5 percent in 2003 to 29.9 percent in 2013, the share of persons employed in manufacturing increased from 27.9 percent in 2005 to a record-breaking 29 percent in 2015. In the same year, manufacturing absorbed a much lower share in Germany (19.8 percent), Japan (16.9), Korea (16.6) and the United States (10.3) (Shao 2015).

Nonetheless, manufacturing will not generate the fifty million jobs needed by 2020 in Chinese cities, according to the Plan on Human Resources and Social Security of the Thirteenth Five-Year Plan (cited on the official website of the State Council).[10] A government work report, delivered by premier Li Keqiang at the legislative annual session on March 5, 2016, adds that, for 2016 alone, "China aims to create at least 10 million new urban jobs and keep the registered urban unemployment rate within 4.5 percent."[11] As for information on how this goal would be achieved, Premier Li's work report offers only one sentence, without providing any details: "China's fast growing service industry is expected to take the baton of job creation."

Interviews with China-based scholars and industry experts conveyed one overriding message—that Chinese policymakers have largely neglected employment effects and other labor market issues when designing their grand visions of industrial policy.[12] A frequent explanation for the lack of robust employment projections is that the top leadership level is dominated by engineers, who "mostly do not understand the economy. . . . [They are] used to the idea that the rural area of China is such a huge pool for the resource of low cost labor—the labor can come or disappear automatically depended on whether you need it."[13] Furthermore, the concept of MIC 2025 "is relatively new for China and the 'political talk' was developed only in the first quarter of 2015." According to another well-placed source from within the government, administrative inefficiencies and interagency rivalries may also play a role in explaining the scarcity of serious data on expected employment effects of MIC 2025 and related plans.

In short, Chinese policymakers have failed to base their push into advanced manufacturing on robust projections of possible employment effects and other labor market issues. This is problematic. After all, advanced manufacturing will produce sustainable economic and social benefits only if it creates a sufficiently large number of well-paid quality jobs, whether directly in manufacturing or in related industrial services.

China is not alone in struggling with the trade-offs between productivity-enhancing innovation and employment. Economists have long since discussed this knotty issue. For instance, in the 1817 edition of *On the Principles of Political Economy and Taxation*, David Ricardo argued that, over the long run, growing demand should compensate for temporary job losses. But in a revised edition in 1822, he reversed his original position, arguing that mechanization would prove "often very injurious" to workers.

John Maynard Keynes, in his masterful essay "Economic Possibilities for Our Grandchildren," published in 1930, famously argued, "We are being afflicted with a new disease, namely technological unemployment. This means unemployment due to our discovery of means of economising the use of labour outrunning the pace at which we can find new uses for labour." A possible solution was sketched out in Evsey D. Domar's 1946 classical treatise "Capital Expansion, Rate of Growth, and Employment," but successful implementation is still eluding us. Domar states that productivity growth that leads to cost reduction alone is insufficient. Innovation needs to increase as well the value of output through improvements in product performance. In other words, income-generating productivity growth is necessary for employment growth. But this inserts a qualitative aspect into the discussion of innovation and employment; i.e., this will work only if workers possess the necessary skills and if pay is sufficient to motivate them to improve product and service performance.

New Data on Unemployment, Income Inequality, Service Jobs, and Skills

As we saw, the publicly available data provide no robust projections of future job creation in China. Nor are projections of critical skill requirements available in the public domain. In addition, the data related to the labor market that are available are often subject to doubt. Without such detailed and reliable data, it will be difficult to implement the nation's bold push into advanced manufacturing and advanced services.

In China, the unemployment rate measures the number of people actively looking for a job as a percentage of the labor force, a measure that differs from those used in most OECD countries. China's official unemployment rate, as reported by the Ministry of Human Resources and Social Security, has remained practically constant since 2003, slightly below the 4.1 percent mark—a quite surrealistic "achievement" for an economy that has grown at lightning speed with drastic changes in its composition. Collecting data on the real amount of manufacturing unemployment, however, is considered to be quite sensitive, almost as sensitive as research on labor conflicts.

Fortunately, new data are now available that help reduce the gap in our knowledge. In what follows, I present new data on unemployment and income inequality, highlight China's skills bottleneck, especially for soft and vocational skills, and explore whether service jobs might compensate for the slowing growth of manufacturing jobs.

Lifting the Veil on China's Real Unemployment and Income Inequality

A recent NBER working paper calculates, for the first time, China's unemployment rate from 1988 to 2009 using a more reliable, nationally representative household survey (Feng, Hu, and Moffitt 2015). The unemployment rates calculated by the NBER study differ dramatically from those supplied in official data. The NBER unemployment rate averaged 3.9 percent from 1988 to 1995, when the labor market was highly regulated and dominated by state-owned enterprises, but rose sharply during the period of mass layoff from 1995 to 2002, reaching an average of 10.9 percent from 2002 to 2009. The study estimates that the actual unemployment rate in the latter period averaged nearly 11 percent, while the official rate averaged less than half that. The NBER data also seem to be much more consistent with what is known about China's labor market and how it has changed over time in response to structural changes and other significant events.

The NBER paper estimates that labor force participation rates (which are not available in official statistics) declined throughout the whole period, particularly from 1995 to 2002 when the unemployment rate increased most significantly. While China's unemployment rate has soared since the mid-1990s, labor force participation has dropped: it averaged 83.1 percent around 1995, fell dramatically during the transition, and stabilized at around 74 percent during the 2002–2009 period. Young people were hit especially hard by the layoffs during the 1995–2002 period. The labor force participation rate of young men and women, with and without college educations, all fell by more than ten percentage points.

China's leaders are particularly concerned about the high unemployment rate among university graduates, which has apparently been rising over the last few years. The Chinese Academy of Social Sciences reported a graduate unemployment rate of 12 percent in 2010, while foreign observers estimate that it may be as high as 27 percent (Lee 2014). The 2014 China's Household Finance Survey jointly conducted by Texas A&M University and China's Southwestern University of Finance and Economics found that 16.4 percent of university graduates between the ages of twenty-one and twenty-five were unemployed, whereas the rate for those in the same age bracket who dropped out before middle school was only 4.2 percent (quoted in Lee 2014).

The quite significant diversity in employment outcomes reported in the NBER study might well reflect the increasing inequality of income that China has experienced since the turn of the century. A recent study for the US National Academy of Sciences (NAS), drawing on newly available survey data collected by several Chinese university survey organizations, finds a rapid increase in income inequality in China's recent past (Yu and Xiang 2014).

According to the NAS study, China's income inequality not only surpasses that of the United States by a large margin but also ranks among the highest in the world, especially in comparison with countries with comparable or higher standards of living. The study argues that this inequality is driven significantly by structural factors attributable to the Chinese political system, the main structural determinants being the rural-urban divide and the regional variation in economic well-being.

In short, new data on unemployment and income inequality in China document that both reached precariously high levels well before the country started to push into advanced manufacturing and services.

China's Skills Bottleneck

For both the IP plan and the MIC 2025 plan to work, it is important to generate realistic projections of what types of skills are needed. Both plans emphasize the use of robots and internet-based information networks. China's leadership understands that both plans are bound to boost demand for workers with highly specialized skills, both in vocational and in knowledge-intensive services related to mobile communications, software, and chip design. In its National Plan for Medium- and Long-term Education Reform and Development, the government outlined plans to expand vocational education, established a target of 90 percent secondary-school enrollment by 2020, and increased investment in secondary and university education. Unfortunately, no data seem to be available in the public domain on the size of projected specialized skill requirements. This lack of reliable data constitutes an important handicap for China's push into advanced manufacturing and services.

In 2005, the McKinsey Global Institute warned about "China's looming talent shortage," emphasizing that multinational companies were finding that few graduates had the necessary skills for knowledge-intensive service occupations (Farrell and Grant 2005). Since then, the danger signals have multiplied. In a 2015 survey of 2,361 China-based employers representing over four million employees, the global recruitment firm Hays found that almost one-half (45 percent) of employers believe that a severe skills shortage has the potential to hamper the effective operation of their business in China ("China's" 2016). The most difficult jobs to recruit for in China are senior management candidates in sales, marketing, research & development, engineering, accountancy and finance, operations, technical, human resources, and information technology. According to a 2013 McKinsey study, the projected gaps are especially serious for skills that require vocational training (with a gap of sixteen million workers projected for 2020) and university education (where the projected gap is eight million workers) (Chen, Mourshed, and Grant, 2013).

A number of the experts I interviewed emphasize that the scarcity of specialized skills needed for the big push in advanced manufacturing and services is an important factor in explaining China's rise in graduate unemployment. Interviewees also report that a growing demand for IT-related specialized skills is driving up wages for workers who possess them. This demand seems to crowd out smaller domestic firms and leave the field to a few large companies, whether foreign multinational corporations or large Chinese firms such as Huawei.

For example, one interviewee reports that entry-level pay for IC design engineers is higher today in Shanghai or Shenzhen than in Taipei. It is somewhat perplexing that, despite this, leading Chinese IC design houses based in Shenzhen or Shanghai (such as HiSilicon or Spreadtrum) are competing successfully with their Taiwanese counterparts. One plausible explanation may be access to subsidies. Another may be the use of foreign (Taiwanese, US, Korean) engineers who are moonlighting in China, sometimes over the weekends. These foreign chip designers are used to working under best-practice R&D management processes, and thus may well be more productive.

Despite China's high graduate unemployment, US firms there report a lack of availability of talent as a top-ranking operating challenge (Lawrence 2015). While much of the debate has focused on the insufficient supply of required technical skills (with a focus on science, technology and engineering), the push into advanced manufacturing will increase the need for soft management and communication skills that are needed to operate and incrementally improve increasingly complex information-based factories, supply chain, and support services. In China, the primary and secondary education system is skewed "towards test preparation, leaving limited classroom time for the cultivation of analytical and creative skills. In other words, hard skills are introduced early on and strengthened over time, while soft skills are too often left to languish" (Chan 2015). Innovation research has shown that complementary soft entrepreneurial, management, and system integration capabilities are of critical importance if a company wants to successfully create, change, improve, and commercialize products, services, equipment, processes, and business models (Ernst 2009, 13 and 14).

In the end, however, vocational training may be China's most serious skill bottleneck. The country's education system fails to address the needs of the rapidly evolving labor market, especially for skills required for advanced manufacturing and services. While university graduates cannot find suitable jobs, there is a growing scarcity in many industries of well-trained and experienced skilled workers who can run smart robots, industrial 3D printers, and internet-based information networks. A recent study concludes that "China's vocational education and training (VET) system threatens the country's rise to industrial superpower status. Reform of the VET system is long overdue. Only if China succeeds in establishing a system that can be adapted to the changing requirements of companies will the dream of its political leaders to make the country an industrial superpower materialise" (Klorer and Stepan 2015, 1).

To summarize, the above proxy indicators of the increasing scarcity of specialized skills may be the Achilles heel of China's push into advanced manufacturing and services. The skill bottleneck is likely to prevent the achievement of the big upgrading plans and thus may thwart the goal of improving competitiveness. As long as we have no realistic assessment of China's skill deficit, we cannot answer a critical question: In light of the current skill deficit, how many quality jobs can realistically be created in manufacturing and services?

Will Service Jobs Compensate for the Slowing Growth of Manufacturing Jobs?

China's push into advanced manufacturing coincides with a slowdown of Chinese exports of manufactured goods. At the same time, efforts to reduce overcapacity in mines and metals and to reform the state-owned enterprise sector have displaced a significant number of manufacturing jobs. As a result, the focus of employment generation will have to shift even more than before to the service sector.

China's service sector has rapidly increased since the late 1970s: its compound annual growth rate from 1978 to 2013 was almost 11 percent. However, the percentage of GDP generated by services is still low. According to an Asian Development Bank study, China's per capita GDP in 2013 was $9,828 (in 1990 US dollars), and the share that services contributed was 46.1 percent, about 13 percentage points lower than an economy would typically reach at this level of GDP per capita (Wang Wei 2013, 236).

This raises two important questions: Will China's service sector be able to compensate for the declining role of manufacturing as a source of employment growth? And, specifically, will the economy be able to create enough quality service jobs so that domestic demand can grow, based on increasing income?

While it is beyond the scope of this chapter to answer these questions exhaustively, I offer a few observations on what might be realistic options for China to link services to advanced manufacturing.

Insights from Research on Manufacturing Services   Research in the United States and other industrialized countries leaves little doubt that robots and other advanced manufacturing technologies are bound to reduce the direct labor requirements of China's manufacturing industry (Shipp et al. 2012). Research by the US National Academy of Engineering (2012) has identified the proliferation of manufacturing services as an important source for quality jobs. By integrating manufacturing, services, and R&D, successful firms can use advanced manufacturing technologies to provide packaged solutions that combine high productivity gains with substantial job gains in complementary support services.

Another important source of quality service jobs necessary for advanced manufacturing can be found in a variety of digital infrastructure platforms, such as broadband as an enabler of new applications (e.g., cloud computing), 4G wireless communications, integrated health information systems, smart electric grids, low carbon energy information systems, intelligent transportation systems, mobile payment systems, and mobile collaborative learning systems (McDonald 2013).

What Has the Thirteenth Five-Year Plan to Say about the Reform of China's Service Industry?   Considering these insights from research in advanced countries, let us take a look at China's efforts to upgrade its service sector. A basic assumption is that, in order to sustain future growth, China's economy needs to be less dependent on fixed-asset and real-estate investment. To achieve this goal, policymakers have committed to liberalizing the services sector and expanding domestic consumption to spark new engines of growth. The 2013 Third Plenary Session of the Eighteenth Communist Party of China Central Committee (Third Plenum) outlined how China will expand the service sector so that, over time, it can rebalance investment's contribution to GDP. These recommendations focused on removing subsidies on the cost of capital, diversifying ownership of state assets, and encouraging private-sector investment in the service sector.

The Thirteenth Five-Year Plan gives even greater weight to the expansion of the service sector and its contribution to GDP and employment (NDRC 2016). As part of this plan, Premier Li Keqiang announced a new campaign on "Mass Entrepreneurship and Innovation" to encourage entrepreneurship and innovation in services to spur economic growth in China's "New Normal" economic phase of slower growth and less reliance on investment (State Council 2017). Intended outcomes of the initiative appear to include a more "level playing field" for entrepreneurs and better access to government-controlled business services such as bank loans. The intent of the government appears to be to increase availability of capital for more knowledge-intensive services that will create more employment opportunities, especially for higher-skilled workers and college graduates.

What Do We Know about China's Service Sector?   In light of these rather broad and general vision statements, what data do we have on the current status and quality of China's service sector, and on its capacity to generate quality jobs?

With a compound annual growth rate of almost 11 percent from 1978 to 2013, the service sector's share in China's GDP increased from less than 24 percent in 1978 to more than 40 percent since the year 2000. In 2013, the service sector's share in GDP for the first time exceeded the GDP share of manufacturing. And the most recent data for 2015 show that services now account for 50.5 percent of China's GDP. However, the economic contribution of its service sector remains well below the service sector share in the UK (78.4 percent), the United States (78 percent), or Germany (69 percent).[14]

The service sector is now a major source of new jobs—an estimated twenty million each year since 2011. However, according to data from the All-China Federation of Industry and Commerce, workers in the service sector have been less productive than those in industry and construction. Moreover, many of these service jobs do not pay as well as the displaced manufacturing jobs. In fact, service jobs in China fulfill a "catch basin" function—they go to people who cannot find other work (Cui 2016b).

The Thirteenth Five-Year Plan certainly goes out of its way to promote knowledge-intensive services as the necessary complement to China's push into advanced manufacturing. In reality, however, efforts to upgrade the service industry and to improve its competitiveness are constrained by heavy regulatory burdens, barriers to trade in services, policies that are still shaped by the requirements of industrial manufacturing, and major bottlenecks in the provision of the necessary skills. Given these negative framework conditions for upgrading the service sector, China's attempts to forge ahead into advanced manufacturing are likely to face major hurdles.

We have seen that China's comparative advantage in manufacturing, combined with the extraordinary size of its economy, explain why the nation has not followed Dani Rodrik's pattern of "premature deindustrialization." But now that China is pushing into advanced manufacturing and services through both the MIC 2025 and IP plans, the real challenge is to determine how this might affect China's future for jobs.

There is no doubt that China will emerge over the next decade or so as a major user and producer of robots and other advanced manufacturing technologies. A big challenge will be developing a broad portfolio of innovation capabilities needed to implement the above transition. Major hurdles, however, are an almost exclusive focus on technology in both the MIC 2025 and the IP plans, and a failure to collect data on the possible impacts of advanced manufacturing and services on jobs, skills, income, and equality.

A robust system to record such data is critically important now that China faces a demographic crisis that gives rise to a labor shortage and a steep rise in labor costs, at the same time that its industry is facing a lengthy slowdown. Some observers hope that the demographic crisis might reduce the number of decent jobs that need to be created. Others suspect that the challenge more likely will be to match skill demand and supply and to contain a further increase in inequality, as labor shortages and surpluses are likely to be distributed largely according to skills, education, and training. In the end, this is an empirical question, which requires hard data on labor market–related issues.

If China fails to upgrade the quality of the new jobs that are being created in its service sector, this might slow down the growth of household incomes and consumption. In turn, the profit squeeze in manufacturing companies and declining income of workers might lead to cuts in investment in and consumption of services. In order to avoid this "worst-case scenario," it is necessary to base both the MIC 2025 and the IP plans on realistic projections of employment, skill requirements, and other labor market impacts.

10

Light Manufacturing Can Create Good Jobs in Sub-Saharan Africa

Vandana Chandra

The digital revolution, paired with demographic change, is changing humankind and the future of work in unprecedented ways. As previous chapters of this book explain, it is rewarding workers who have the special skills and training to use digital technologies to enrich the value of the goods and services they produce. Modern technology has raised productivity and ushered in prosperity in many countries, including the BRICS (Brazil, Russia, India, China, and South Africa) and East Asia's middle-income economies. Even some poor countries that developed a critical mass of technical skills were able to narrow the gap in technology with the North and transform into Emerging Market countries. At the same time, nations with large numbers of workers who have ordinary skills or are less tech-savvy are being left behind, creating what is commonly referred to as the "digital divide." Sub-Saharan Africa (henceforth referred to as Africa) is at the lowest end of this digital divide.

Africa's lack of access to modern technologies is holding back the productivity gains that digitization typically delivers. In addition, the region's options for job creation are limited in spite of its vast natural wealth. Its resource-rich sectors are capital-intensive and weakly linked with the larger economy. Most workers rely either on agriculture or the informal services sector, where productivity and wages are both low. Further, an imminent youth bulge is set to trigger demand for 1.1 billion better-paying jobs of all skill levels.

One solution is for this region to leverage digitization to leapfrog from an informal agricultural to a modern industrial economy. But that will not be easy or quick. A digitized Africa is still very much in the future.

In the interim, Africa need not remain tied to low-productivity jobs on farms and the informal sector. It can jump-start its light manufacturing export industry, including agribusiness, to leverage globalization and create large numbers of better-paying jobs for its young people. There are valuable lessons from how Ethiopia succeeded in igniting light manufacturing; how Lesotho became Africa's largest garment exporter to the United States; how M-Pesa, a mobile money service in Kenya, enables users to transfer money through a simple text-based menu available on the most basic mobile phones;[1] and how poor Asian countries such as Bangladesh and Vietnam became leading world-class apparel and footwear exporters. These can provide Africa with an introduction to the "how-to" of large-scale job creation aided by modern—though not fully digital—production technologies. The crux of African industrialization is the low wage level that affords it a comparative advantage in labor-intensive traded goods. In export-oriented light manufacturing industries, especially the ones that use locally available raw materials, the region's low-wage advantage could be a game changer.

Yet, light manufacturing alone cannot be the panacea for millions of young African job-seekers. It is only the first step toward better-paying jobs for less-skilled youths. Long-lasting investments in STEM (science, technology, engineering, and mathematics) skills and improved access to modern technologies are still essential for Africa to boost productivity and unleash a good-jobs boom across all sectors, including agriculture and agroindustry.

Moreover, Africa, the world's poorest region, is unique in its experience. It has neither benefited from the bounties of the digital revolution nor been hit by the massive loss of mid-level jobs seen in many developed countries. For several decades now, it has been grappling with the challenges of globalization, and its demographic transition will only amplify the need for tailored policies to absorb its fast-growing and impatient youth population.

The skeptics doubt that Africa can contend with these multiple challenges and still create better-paying jobs. The optimists, easily outnumbered by the skeptics, are latching on to glimmers of hope anchored in digitally aided and dynamic industries that seem to have parachuted into the region from digitally sophisticated parts of the world. If some of these champions could emerge in Africa—in countries such as Ethiopia, Lesotho, and Kenya—in spite of the digital divide that isolates it from the world, policymakers must consider what is needed to scale and replicate them and create the better-paying jobs the continent needs. The question is whether its governments can play a role in fostering the process.

Will automation and reshoring in developed countries such as the United States constrain the development of light manufacturing and job creation in Africa? Several reasons indicate that they will not. First, reshoring is a relatively nascent phenomenon, with little quantifiable evidence to show the large-scale return of manufacturing and related jobs in countries such as the United States. Second, automation that fully replaces low-skilled labor has yet to become widespread in light manufacturing industries to the extent that low wages matter for a country to be competitive. The thin profit margin in light manufacturing makes it unviable for developed countries. These reasons create a window of opportunity for Africa to generate large numbers of better-paying light manufacturing jobs for its largely less-skilled labor pool.

For Africa to achieve sustained prosperity, there is no shortcut to bridging the digital divide. This chapter seeks to highlight how, in addition to light manufacturing, Africa can start putting in place the building blocks that will eventually trigger a digital revolution and help close the gap.

A Digital Divide Insulates Africa from the World

In an environment where Google and smart phones are ubiquitous, Africa's disconnect from the twenty-first-century world of digital technologies is inconceivable to most people. Inaccessibility to the internet is the glass wall between Africa and the digital dividends that helped all modern economies to leapfrog over what could have been decades of painstaking economic progress. In high-income economies, about 81 percent of individuals are connected to the internet and almost everyone uses a mobile phone.[2] In East Asia, Latin America, and the Middle East, between 85 and 90 percent of people use mobile phones and between 28 and 32 percent use the internet. More than half of the population in China uses the internet. The digital divide is the starkest in Africa, which has the lowest share of individuals with connectivity: on average, about 63 percent have access to a mobile phone and just 10 percent are connected with the internet. (South Asia's internet connectivity rate is similar.)

Within Africa, too, there is a huge digital divide between countries. In lower middle–income countries such as Zambia, Nigeria, or Ghana, almost 80 percent of residents have access to a mobile phone and about 12 percent are connected with the internet. By contrast, in low-income countries such as Burundi, Chad, Togo, and Niger, at most 1 percent of individuals have access to the internet (World Bank 2016b).

The digital divide is prevalent in Africa for three reasons: access to the internet, the capabilities to use it gainfully when there is access, and scale or a critical set of users and businesses that make it profitable to use the internet.

Access to the Internet Depends on Affordability and Scale

In any country, a person's decision to use the internet depends on the financial cost of connectivity. In light of Africa's low-income status, it is difficult to dismiss that the costs of accessing the internet are unimportant. In examining the consumer mobile plans sold by major carriers in each country, Hangler and Vidan (2013) found that the cheapest price per gigabyte of mobile data was $40 in Chad, $26 in Malawi and Ethiopia, $20 in Cameroon (after declining from $81), and $9 in Nigeria. By comparison, each gigabyte cost about $6 in the USA and Canada, about $1 in the UK, $0.60 in South Korea, $0.25 in Singapore, and 0.05 in Denmark. Apparently, weak competition is the main reason why the cost of accessing the internet is high in the United States.

In many countries outside Africa, urban locations and higher population density generate economies of scale that help to keep the cost of internet access low. Unfortunately, the geography and population size of most

African cities do not have this effect. Even when a region is connected to the internet, many households do not have access. In Cameroon, Ghana, Kenya, and Uganda, more than three in four users still go online in commercial internet cafés, where high costs and slow connections limit use (World Bank 2016b).

Digital Literacy Limits Use of the Internet for Information

The binding constraint to dismantling the digital divide in Africa is digital literacy, which can neither be purchased nor imported. Even when they are connected, Africans do not fully tap the potential of the internet or even mobile phones to seek information or to learn about or search for or create better job opportunities. Most use the internet as a communication device to call or text friends or family. Of the small proportion of Africans who have a mobile phone or access to the internet, only 14 percent use it to send emails and 17 percent to browse the web. The most popular uses are phone calls, social media, games, and music.

The digital divide also isolates African firms from the digitized world of global business and economic opportunity. Only 25 to 40 percent of Kenyan or Zambian firms in the manufacturing sector have access to the internet. In Tanzania, Uganda, and the Democratic Republic of the Congo, 5 to 8 percent of firms have access to and use the internet for managing inventory, selling online, or marketing. In services, with the exception of Kenyan firms, just 15 percent of companies in Congo, Ghana, Tanzania, and Uganda have access to the internet.

Digitization is effective and affordable when the scale of production is large, which requires firms to have large domestic or foreign customers and suppliers. While the size of the world market is infinite for an African firm, the size of the domestic market is small, as is the share of African exports of manufactures and services. Trading goods and services online in the domestic market is restricted, as the critical mass of connected customers and businesses needed for profitable online business is absent.

Deficits in Basic Learning Postpone Digital Literacy

Evidently, the root cause of weak digital literacy is the foundation of Africa's stock of human capital. While the financial costs of access and the availability of digital devices are relatively easy to fix, there is no mechanism that can speedily repair or replace the region's educational systems, which have not succeeded in delivering the quality of basic education essential for digital literacy. Over the past few decades, numerous systems have been designed and redesigned by African governments in their endeavor to upgrade the quality of education, but the outcomes continue to disappoint. While primary enrollment rates help it to walk in step with its peers in South Asia and other low-income countries, Africa remains the laggard in other key indicators of human capital.

This deficit in human capital is staggering and pervasive across countries and various levels of the educational and skills ladder. Basic primary knowledge that enables a child to read, write, and count forms the foundation for any type of learning at higher stages of education and is fundamental for digital literacy. Yet, with primary-school completion rates in the range of 38 to 55 percent, about one-half of Africa's student population falls short of the basic learning necessary to read, comprehend, and prepare for the first class in digital literacy, i.e., searching the internet for information (UNESCO 2013). In 2012, on a scale of 420 to 620, the mean reading scores of sixth-graders in Malawi and Zambia were lower than 440. Many of the remaining 50 percent of students struggle to complete primary school. Between 1990 and 2007, repetition rates at this level decreased from 5.3 percent to 4.8 percent worldwide. In spite of significant progress between 2006 and 2012, the average repetition rate was 8 percent in Africa, 36 percent in Burundi, and 25 percent in Comoros (UNESCO 2013). Weak foundations at the primary level adversely affect the quality of education at the secondary level. In the set of the top ten poorest performers in 2012, secondary repetition rates ranged between 26 percent in Togo and 20 percent in Chad.

As the weak foundations of primary learning penetrate youth and adult education programs, crossing the digital divide becomes a challenge for all generations of Africans. In spite of improvement in previous decades, in 2012, Africa's youth literacy rates were only 72 percent, compared to 80 to 98 percent in all other regions. The most shocking rates of youth literacy were in Burkina Faso (39 percent), Mali (44 percent), and Chad (47 percent). More than one-third of Africa's adults are illiterate. In the Gambia and Senegal, this is true of half the adult population.

For the nearly one-half of the student population who are unable to complete primary school, engaging in any form of digital learning is a lifelong challenge. The inability to read translates into an inability to browse, learn, and apply knowledge from the internet to all walks of life, and benefit from the information offered at almost no cost to the digitally literate. The skills subindex of the ICT Development Index measures information and communications technology capability, or the skills to use the internet.[3] In 2016, out of a total of 175 countries, twenty-three of the bottom twenty-five countries were African and had the lowest skills subindex, reflecting the deficiencies in reading and comprehension from primary schooling. Relative to the world score of 5.74, Niger, which ranked the lowest, had a score of 1.01. The top two African countries were Ghana (rank 120 and score 4.4) and Gabon (rank 132 and score 3.8).

Africa's Job Market Complicates Crossing the Digital Divide

The size of the working-age population in sub-Saharan Africa is projected to rise from 450 million in 2010 to 1.56 billion in 2060 (UN 2013).[4] More than half of global population growth and working-age population growth through 2050 will be in sub-Saharan Africa. This implies a youth bulge of huge proportions in the near future. Absent a sufficient number of decent jobs, the attendant potentially disruptive outcomes of youth unemployment can compromise political and social stability.

There is a vicious nexus between the digital divide that constrains African countries from leveraging new productivity-enhancing technologies to create better-paying jobs and the structure of the African labor market that makes the adoption of new technologies difficult. The opportunity costs of living on the other side of the digital divide are huge for Africa. How poor Indian farmers realized large income gains when they were digitally connected to the internet from a kiosk, e-Choupal, is an exemplar of a digital dividend that African farmers could also earn if they could only cross the digital divide.[5]

Where Africans Work

At present, Africa's labor market poses a predicament for a working-age population that needs large numbers of better-paying wage jobs that are most easily created in manufacturing, including agroprocessing, and commercial agriculture. As these sectors are also more amenable to machination and eventually digitization, their growth also offers the best prospects for enabling firms and workers to cross the digital divide. However, the present composition of the African labor markets is inimical to better-paying employment in these sectors, as their share is extremely small.

African workers currently have few job options. Of total employment, wage jobs make up at most 20 percent, household enterprises about 20 to 22 percent, and agriculture the remaining 62 percent (figure 10.1). Only 16 percent of wage-earners receive a regular wage, and most are concentrated in services and industry (Filmer et al. 2014).[6] Within the industrial sector, manufacturing, construction, and mining, which pay a decent wage, account for only 4 percent of total employment.[7] In resource-rich African countries, the share of wage jobs is only 1 percent. Household enterprises abound in rural and urban areas and are operated informally by farmers, street vendors, and food-sellers. Africa's agricultural

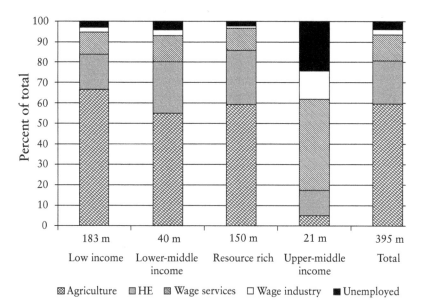

Figure 10.1 Where Africans work (2010). The numbers on the horizontal axis show the size of the labor force by age group (15–64) in millions. Numbers do not add up to 100 percent because of rounding. Resource-rich countries included are Angola, Chad, the Democratic Republic of Congo, Guinea, Nigeria, the Republic of Congo, Sudan and the Republic of South Sudan, and Zambia. Filmer and Fox et al. 2014.

sector includes subsistence farming and is largely informal. Excluding upper-middle-income countries, 80 to 84 percent of the jobs in Africa are informal, as indicated in the joint share of household enterprises and agriculture. Unemployment is almost exclusively an upper-middle-income country phenomenon.

Informal is Normal and an Obstacle to Government-Funded Digital Connectivity

Informality, which marks between 80 and 84 percent of the workers in Africa, is a severe policy challenge for governments, a deterrent for the private sector, and a direct obstacle to the adoption of digital or any modern technologies. Almost 56 to 75 percent of firms in urban and rural areas are engaged in informal commerce, which is largely low-productivity, low-wage petty trading. Invariably, informal firms are small and have difficulty in increasing their productivity through greater investment or employment. A study of seven African countries indicates that the median capital stock in urban informal enterprises is a negligible US$80 (World Bank 2012). By excluding firms from formal credit markets, informal status is a direct constraint to growth and job creation. Sutton and Kellow (2010) find that the top fifty large firms in Africa start out large and remain large.

The unrecorded and undefined nature of informal firms and informal workers makes it difficult for governments to locate them and leverage policies and programs to help them to cross the digital divide. It is equally difficult for governments to offer small-business training programs to informal firms.

Workers' Education Limits Use of Productivity-Raising Digital Technology

The educational attainment of African workers is a direct hurdle for the use of productivity-enhancing digital technologies in the workplace. In the age group of fifteen to twenty-four, more than 20 percent of employees in the "wage with contract" or best job category either have no education or have not completed primary school, and only about 40 percent have completed upper secondary or postsecondary education. In all other

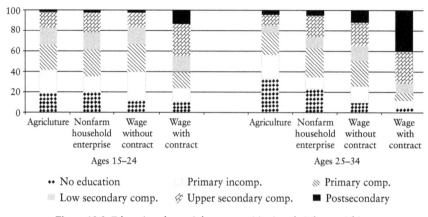

Ages 15–24   Ages 25–34

- ↔ No education   ☐ Primary incomp.   ⸝ Primary comp.
- ▨ Low secondary comp.   ⸜ Upper secondary comp.   ■ Postsecondary

Figure 10.2 Education shapes job opportunities in sub-Saharan Africa.
Filmer and Fox et al. 2014.

job categories, including "wage without a contract," up to 60 percent of employees have either no education or at best have completed only primary school.

Among older workers in the age group of twenty-five to thirty-four, "wage with contract" employees have better educational attainment: about 70 percent have either completed upper secondary or postsecondary school. Just as the quality of schooling constrains the commencement of digital literacy, educational attainment constrains workers' ability to work with digital technologies that can raise productivity in the workplace, even when they have formal wage jobs (Filmer and Fox et al. 2014).

Structural Transformation—A Hurdle for the Creation of Productive Jobs

In addition to the digital divide, the structural characteristics of the African economies have also not favored productivity-enhancing job creation. Africa has abundant natural-resource wealth stocked in many countries, but it does not foster large-scale wage job creation due to weak backward and forward linkages between the natural resource–producing and other sectors of the economy. Natural-resource production is capital-intensive and has a low employment potential. Even during commodity price booms, the spillovers from mineral or commodity production to job creation in other sectors such as manufacturing, which have a significantly larger job potential, are negative. Natural-resource booms trigger the Dutch Disease, a phenomenon that causes the relative price of nonresource goods to fall or the exchange rate to appreciate, directly leading to a decline in production and employment. The predominance of a variety of natural resources in the economies of a large number of African countries has made them especially vulnerable to frequent commodity price shocks and adversely affected nonresource exports and fostered imports. Consequently, unlike other parts of the world, Africa's manufacturing sector makes up only 11 percent of the economy, compared to a share of 32 percent in East Asia, which has some of the world's fastest-growing and prosperous economies, and 17 percent in South Asia.

Unlike the Asian economies, structural transformation in Africa has been slow and unusual. In contrast to other developing countries where jobs shifted from agriculture to more-productive urban jobs in manufacturing or services, African workers moved from less-productive agricultural jobs to less-productive urban jobs in the informal services sectors (Filmer et al. 2014; McMillan, Rodrik, and Verduzco-Gallo 2013; and De Vries, Timmer, and De Vries 2015). Manufacturing and modern services are usually swift to adopt modern technologies and create more productive wage jobs, but, as they have not scaled up in Africa, the paucity of productive and better-paying jobs is pervasive across the board.

The Vietnamese experience with structural transformation provides a stark contrast with Africa. Between 1990 and 2008, this nation's manufacturing employment grew by 8 percent, because labor moved from agriculture into more-productive urban occupations in manufacturing and services (Rodrik 2014, McCaig, and Pavcnik 2013). By comparison, in Nigeria, although the share of employment in agriculture declined by almost 20 percent, it was replaced by a 15 percent increase in the share of employment in informal households and medium-sized enterprises. There was only a 4 percent increase in the share of employment in private wage jobs. The trends in Ghana, Rwanda, Uganda, and Tanzania were similar, although on a smaller scale. In a study of a decomposition of labor productivity growth across sixteen sub-Saharan African countries during 1995 and 2009, intersectoral labor reallocation explained, on average, only about 50 percent of overall labor productivity growth.

The gains in labor productivity were the largest when labor moved out of agriculture and into manufacturing as opposed to services (McMillan and Harttgen 2014).[8]

Africa's Options for Creating 1.1 Billion Jobs by 2060

While Africa's ability to create better-paying jobs is constrained by two circumstances—youth bulge and digital divide—that it cannot alter in the medium term, it also depends on its commitment to change. Africa can do little about the imminent youth bulge that will call for about 1.1 billion new jobs by 2060.[9] It has a choice between correcting course to create more and better-paying jobs or preserving the status quo, which, by default, implies that the majority of Africans have to eke out a meager existence in the unproductive informal sector. The latter approach will likely have high social and political costs, as a bulging youth population will covet better jobs. What Africa should not postpone is immediate investments in human capital development strategies to achieve digital literacy and the skills necessary for leveraging digital technologies and raising productivity. Unfortunately, the returns on investments in human capital will materialize only in the longer term. In the interim, Africa must find other sources of better-paying jobs.

One option for job creation in the medium term is to turn to an agriculture-focused development path, which can help to create large numbers of new, but not better-paying jobs. As about 80 to 85 percent of its labor force is currently engaged in informal agriculture and household enterprises, an expansion of the agricultural sector will create more of the same jobs even if Africa's economy is booming. An increase in agricultural productivity is necessary to create better-paying agricultural jobs, but this requires the modernization of African agriculture, a longer-term phenomenon contingent on large investments in human capital development, large-scale commercialization, technological innovation, and infrastructure.

There are, however, limited agricultural opportunities that Africa can tap in the medium term by adapting simple off-the-shelf farm technologies to create productive jobs in countries where the climate and soil are suitable for high-value agriculture. African governments should enable less-skilled farmers to diversify in high-value sectors. Kenya's emergence as a leading global exporter of cut flowers was facilitated by a combination of government policies, foreign investment, private enterprise, and new technologies that helped to preserve fresh flowers for air transport to Europe (Whitaker and Kolavalli 2006). Over time, floriculture, a labor-intensive high-value sector, also emerged in neighboring Uganda, Tanzania, and Ethiopia, and created large numbers of high-productivity rural jobs that paid distinctly higher wages than the informal sector. Uganda's exports of Nile perch to the European Union is another example of a rural industry that benefited from ideal natural conditions, smart policies, and donor support for better technological practices, which helped to improve productivity and create thousands of jobs in fish-filleting plants and in a fishery industry that supported thousands of small fishermen who had earlier depended on meager earnings from fishing in Lake Victoria (Kiggundu 2006). Unfortunately, in the medium term, the scope for technological adaptation to boost productive employment is limited to pockets of nascent high-value sectors. Of course, in the longer term, agricultural scientists may discover new opportunities that will foster a strong agricultural sector in Africa.

A second option is to create large numbers of jobs in the service sectors. At present, service wage jobs in industries such as banking, insurance, and social services are only a slim segment of total employment. This is not surprising, given that the skills requirements for wage jobs in services are generally the most stringent of all sectors, and Africa's current pool of professional skills is small. The exception is ecotourism, which draws uniquely upon Africa's natural beauty with many relatively less-skilled workers to create productive jobs. While there is some scope for expansion, tourism alone cannot create large numbers of new jobs, because most African countries compete for the same set of foreign tourists.

A third option is to turn to industry, but evidence indicates that developing a successful manufacturing sector with a core comprising heavy industries such as machinery is a challenge for even the most advanced economies. Invariably, entry into heavy industry in the near term is constrained by the shortage of STEM PLUS skills that are adaptable to industry-specific requirements.[10] As in the case of primary learning skills that are stymieing digital literacy, the STEM PLUS skills also cannot be acquired in the short term. As Africa cannot afford to postpone job creation, it needs to explore other possibilities that depend on neither these nor digital literacy in the medium term. The lack of options absent digital or STEM skills underscores the urgency of fostering them.

Light Manufacturing Can Create Many Productive Jobs in the Near Term

Light manufacturing[11] combined with agribusiness offers Africa an opportunity to harness its resource wealth and create wage jobs that are more productive and better-paying than informal jobs in agriculture, manufacturing, or services. Africa has a latent comparative advantage in low-tech manufacturing. It has the basic ingredients: a large and growing pool of workers with globally competitive wage levels, ample land that can be developed to accommodate factories, and abundant locally available inputs or raw materials, including agricultural land for agribusiness. (The competitiveness of the apparel and footwear industries does not depend upon locally available inputs.) Other inputs (managerial skills, access to global markets including latching to global supply chains, and knowledge of trends in global fashions and demand) can be imported if Africa opens its door to foreign direct investment and promotes competition in input and output markets. As the sector develops, its spillovers should foster the emergence of domestic entrepreneurial skills and firms. In addition, light industries have significantly larger employment potential than does heavy manufacturing or more sophisticated services, and are not subject to economies of scale, which makes them feasible in small and large countries.

Can Africa Compete in Exporting Light Manufactured Exports?

Ethiopia's recent experience with setting up a light manufacturing industry offers useful pointers for creating large numbers of jobs by making optimal use of domestic resources. Most light manufacturing industries in developing countries are export-oriented, as exports enable a country to overcome the demand constraint imposed by low purchasing power in the domestic market (Harrison and Rodríguez-Clare 2010). A study of light manufacturing sectors in three African countries, Vietnam, and China indicates that a meaningful evaluation of their potential necessitates a country- and industry-specific approach (Dinh et al, 2012; Chandra, Lin, and Wang 2013). Using Ethiopia as the exemplar, the study found that,

Table 10.1 Wages for skilled and unskilled workers in five light manufacturing industries (US$ per month)

Product	China	Vietnam	Ethiopia	Tanzania	Zambia
Skilled					
Polo shirts	311–370	119–181	37–185	107–213	
Dairy milk	177–206		30–63	150–300	106–340
Wood chairs	383–442	181–259	81–119	150–200	200–265
Leather loafers	296–562	119–140	41–96	160–200	
Milled wheat	398–442	181–363	89–141	200–250	320–340
Average range	305–399	154–235	77–131	153–233	284–364
Unskilled					
Polo shirts	237–296	78–130	26–48	93–173	
Dairy milk	118–133	31–78	13–41	50–80	54–181
Wooden chairs	206–251	85–135	37–52	75–125	100–160
Leather loafers	237–488	78–93	16–33	80–140	
Milled wheat	192–236	78–207	26–52	100–133	131–149
Average range	197–278	78–131	35–53	80–130	157–208

Source: Dinh et al. 2012.

to compete globally, the country needed competitively priced domestic inputs. A conducive business climate and availability of land for industrial sites depended directly on the government's commitment to develop the sector. But did Ethiopia have a comparative advantage in low-wage labor? Table 10.1 presents the range of monthly wages per employee in US dollars. The lower figure denotes the average industry wage, while the upper figure is the wage paid by the best-performing firm.

Among Ethiopia, Tanzania, and Zambia, Ethiopia has the lowest wages for skilled and unskilled workers in all five industries, almost a third of Vietnam's wages in three of the five industries—polo shirts, leather loafers, and milled wheat. The data reported in Table 10.1 are for cash wages paid to factory workers. As nonwage costs in Africa are significantly lower than in China and Vietnam, Africa's potential competitive edge in low-wage labor will increase as Chinese wage and nonwage costs rise.

Low wages alone do not guarantee a comparative advantage; labor productivity is equally important. Ethiopia's productivity levels are not uniformly higher than its Asian competitors' in all five industries (table 10.2).

Table 10.2 Productivity levels in five light manufacturing industries

Labor productivity	China	Vietnam	Ethiopia	Tanzania	Zambia
Polo shirts (pieces/employee/day)	18–35	8–14	7–19	5–20	
Dairy milk (liters/employee/day)	23–51	2–4	18–71	10–100	19–179
Wooden chairs (pieces/employee/day)	3–6	1–3	0.2–0.4	0.3–0.7	0.2–0.6
Leather loafers (pieces/employee/day)	3–7	1–6	1–7	4–6	
Milled wheat (tons/employee/day)	0.2–0.4	0.6–8.6	0.6–1.9	1–22	0.62–1.57

Source: Dinh et al. 2012.

Note: The higher end of productivity data shows labor productivity in the best-practice firms.

But, in polo shirts and leather loafers, in which it has a comparative wage advantage, the upper estimates of seven to nineteen shirts and one to seven pieces of footwear per employee per day in the well-managed or best-practice firms indicate that, with competition and professional management, Ethiopia can raise labor productivity to levels that compare favorably with the average firms in China and Vietnam. Tanzania's labor productivity levels in leather footwear also make it competitive with its Asian competitors. However, labor productivity in the three African countries makes them uncompetitive with Asian countries in the wooden chairs industry.

There are several useful takeaways from this study. First, well-managed firms can be a game changer in boosting the competitiveness of light manufacturing industries in Africa. The establishment of the Fujian shoe exports factory, which started production in Ethiopia with 550 employees in 2012, shows that if a country has a comparative advantage in low-wage labor, but has low productivity, then introducing professional management, usually foreign-owned, can leverage world-class organizational standards and technologies to boost productivity and restore the industry's competitiveness to global standards. Second, in industries where labor costs are competitive, lifting of nonlabor constraints by governments can make a significant difference. As an example, labor productivity in polo shirts in Ethiopia's best-managed firm was almost competitive, but poor trade logistics from the factory gate to the port was an obstacle to global competitiveness, which the government could easily resolve. A third take-away is that, although African countries are besieged with innumerable economy-wide resource, capacity, and other constraints (Gelb and Ramachandran 2014), job creation through the scaling-up of light manufacturing does not need to wait until all constraints have been resolved and the perfect investment climate is established. In most developing countries, including African ones such as Lesotho and Ethiopia, smart governments have redressed economy-wide obstacles to light manufacturing by attracting investors to locate in industrial parks where they can provide the necessary services and infrastructure for light industries. This strategy also enables governments to resolve the most binding constraints first, e.g., fixing apparel industry trade logistics to scale up job creation even in the short term. It bears noting that, while industry-specific analysis is necessary to identify the binding constraints, the results apply more broadly to related industries within the same subsector.

Is Light Manufacturing-Led Job Creation Past Its Time?

It is natural for readers to be skeptical about the job creation potential of light manufacturing in Africa. China's experience with this is famous, but also easy to dismiss given its size and government capacity. However, it is more difficult to ignore the success of many other developing countries: Bangladesh has a world-class apparel industry, and there are light manufacturing industries in Sri Lanka, Pakistan, India, and Nepal. Outside Asia, Jordan, Morocco, El Salvador, and Honduras are good examples. Until a few decades ago, most of these were low-income countries and had large, informal agricultural sectors and large pools of less-skilled labor. Their development paths suggest that light manufacturing industries have charted a Flying Geese trajectory in the global economy in the last four to five decades (Chandra, Lin, and Wang 2013). When wages increased in high-income countries, light manufacturing industries moved first to Asia's Tiger Economies, then to other East Asian countries, China, and Vietnam.

Light manufacturing is independent of scale. As long as a country has a low-wage advantage, a conducive investment climate, and industrial land and is open to foreign investors, it can have a thriving light manufacturing sector. As an example, Lesotho, with a population of only two million, exports more apparel per capita ($208) than Bangladesh with its population of 159 million ($135). As Chinese wages rise, light manufacturing is migrating to developing countries in the South. Africa's latent comparative advantage in light manufacturing positions it well to attract these industries and create millions of jobs for its less-skilled workers.

But is reshoring a threat to light manufacturing jobs in Africa? Presently, light-industry reshoring in developed countries is more of a perceived threat than a real constraint to create large-scale employment in Africa. Evidently, robots can cut and sew materials with firm or rigid surfaces such as paper, steel, or wood, but they are unable to apply the same precision to fabrics, especially knits and synthetics, because they shift, move, and wrinkle frequently during the cutting and sewing process. As long as consumers favor variety, designs, and styles over specialization, light industries such as garments are likely to flourish in countries where workers are available in large numbers and wages are low. These forces led light industries to shift from the United States to Asia in the first place. Today, the prevailing wage in the United States for sewing machine operators is $10.84 per hour,[12] compared to $311–370 per month in China, $119–181 per month in Vietnam, $37–185 per month in Ethiopia, and $107–213 per month in Tanzania (Dinh et al. 2012). With the appropriate policy environment, Africa can become the future hub of light manufacturing.

Reshoring of light manufacturing is unlikely to be profitable in the United States given the razor-thin profit margins on Asian T-shirts that sell for as little as $1 or $2 per piece. Eventually, robots will replace humans on the light manufacturing factory floor. If Africa is successful in bridging the digital divide by that time, it should be able to strengthen both its tertiary and vocational education systems, and ensure that subsequent generations of African workers are prepared to compete for jobs similar to those held by their counterparts in other developing countries.

Policies for Addressing Africa's Youth Employment Problem

Giving Light Manufacturing a Chance

Africa will need more than one billion new and better-paying jobs by 2060. Therefore, an ideal strategy should have a longer-term vision that seeks to launch African economies on a path of productive and sustainable job creation to help close its income gap with more prosperous countries. Access to digital technologies and development of STEM PLUS skills should be an integral part of this vision. Above all, a prudent longer-term development strategy should have the flexibility to adjust and respond to ongoing changes in the global economy and create productive jobs that contribute to social and political stability.

In the short term, there is a lot that African governments can do. Light manufacturing supplemented with agribusiness can be a game changer if they have the political will to change the continent's current growth trajectory. Empirical evidence also shows that modern manufacturing has the dynamism to converge with the global frontier even in countries with less-than-ideal investment and governance regimes (Rodrik 2013). There is every reason for Africa to give light manufacturing a serious chance.

Light manufacturing is also a channel to industrialization. It would make optimal use of Africa's human resource wealth—its large and growing pool of relatively less-skilled labor. Africa has a comparative advantage in low-wage labor and will continue to have it in the foreseeable future, especially as Asia's working-age populations shrink. The other domestic inputs essential for light manufacturing are land for industrial sites and a conducive and foreign investor–friendly policy regime that fosters competition in input and output markets. The availability of these local nonlabor inputs hinges on the commitment of African governments. It can also import inputs such as raw materials, managerial and professional skills that connect firms to world markets and contain valuable information about global demand patterns, and financial capital.

The development of light manufacturing in Africa does not have to be postponed until governments have resolved the innumerable economy-wide constraints that stymie the development of agriculture, services, or heavy manufacturing. Typically, light industries thrive in clusters or industrial parks where governments can strategically ensure the availability of basic industrial inputs such as power, industrial water, waste disposal, and connectivity to the port or markets. In some countries, governments also provide rental housing for workers to reduce commuting costs.

It is presumptuous to believe that light manufacturing alone is the panacea for Africa's job creation challenge. Given the size of the youth bulge, no sector alone can satisfy demand. Modern agriculture, services, and capital-intensive manufacturing would each contribute to productive job creation and should be fostered, but their development is invariably constrained by the paucity of STEM PLUS skills that are indispensable for any modern economy. However, Africa does not have to produce all STEM skills. Basic, high-quality primary and secondary education would be sufficient to prepare graduating students to specialize in skills that cater to market demand. There is no shortcut to eliminating Africa's human capital deficit. It will take dedicated resources, commitment, and patience to build its human capital, but when it does, creating large numbers of productive jobs will become a nonissue.

Other Proposals for Job Creation in Africa

The glacial speed of economic transformation in Africa has piqued much interest in the development discourse on possible sources of growth and job creation. The proposed topics range from economic sectors to the types of jobs workers have, sector-neutrality, sector-specificity, and a Flying Geese model. Rodrik (2014) concludes that, while it is difficult to predict the source of Africa's growth, it is clear that it will be different from the growth trajectories charted by East Asia or the developed countries. With the exception of one, all other proposals are sector-specific and converge on various shades of sector-specific industrial policy. The distinction between the positions presented below is the level at which sectors are identified. The unusual pattern of Africa's structural transformation that has led jobs to move from low-productivity agriculture to low-productivity urban services, mostly in the informal sector, led Rodrik (2014) to conclude that neither agriculture nor manufacturing are likely candidates for future sources of growth. In light of the dominance of natural resources and their attendant negative implications, he proposes that African countries leverage a depreciated exchange rate to propel growth. On balance, Rodrik holds that Africa's next model of growth will be different from any seen before.

India's success in fostering a modern services sector driven largely by IT has motivated Ghani, Goswami, and Kharas (2012) to propose that it may be possible for agricultural economies to bypass manufacturing and grow their modern services sectors. While the appearance of services on the list of possible candidates is an encouraging addition, their skill requirements limit their relevance for African countries, which are grossly deficient in technical skills.

Filmer et al. (2014) suggest that the adoption of new farm technologies and investments in human capital, infrastructure, and improving the business climate can help Africa to boost farm productivity and become a pathway to productive work in three sectors: agriculture, nonfarm household enterprises, and modern wage employment. However, while agriculture is critical in propelling productive job creation, it requires a longer-term horizon to implement contentious land reforms, resolve economy-wide infrastructure and business environment–related constraints, and human capital development, which also has a long gestation lag. Attending to agricultural reforms should be a priority for policymakers.

Applying an entirely different lens to study the scope for growth in natural resource–based African economies, Lederman and Maloney (2012) conclude that the products a country exports do not matter as much for growth as how efficiently its firms produce them. The upshot of their hypothesis is that African policymakers need to adopt a sector-neutral approach to removing constraints to growth in firms and farms. At the same time, there is almost universal consensus on Africa's "poor business climate," encompassing costs of power, transport, corruption, regulations, security, contract enforcement, and policy uncertainty, among other impediments (Gelb, Meyer, and Ramachandran 2014). However, Lederman and Maloney's position presents an impossible policy agenda. As the capacity and financial resources of African governments are limited, policies that require resolving economy-wide constraints to job creation are unlikely to succeed in the medium term.

Lin proposes that Africa adopt the Flying Geese model of industrial development, focused on light manufacturing with a difference (Lin and Monga 2010; Lin 2011). To close the income gap with richer countries, African countries need to first pick comparator countries that are 100 to 300 percent more prosperous, then select products they currently export with a comparative advantage. The learning-by-doing that occurs as the country learns to export what its richer comparators export builds superior skills and creates productive jobs. Lin's sector-specific approach contrasts sharply with Lederman and Maloney's sector-neutral one. In practice, it helps to identify labor-intensive industries in which low-income African countries have a latent comparative advantage.

In noting its vision and the channel to create more-productive jobs, ACET, the Africa Center for Economic Transformation (2014), suggests that African countries adopt a sector-specific approach to job creation, because growth does not automatically bring about economic transformation or the formalization of the labor market. A transforming economy would have an increasing share of the labor force in formal employment as the shares of modern agriculture, manufacturing, and high-value services in GDP expand, and as entrants to the labor force become more educated. ACET identifies four pathways to transformation and job creation in Africa: (i) labor-intensive manufacturing; (ii) agroprocessing; (iii) "natural potential" from oil, gas, and minerals—part of the portfolio of assets; and (iv) tourism for leisure and for business.

Policies to Dismantle the Digital Divide

Africa has, unfortunately, missed reaping digital dividends that accelerated progress and even some leapfrogging in many developing countries, but it can no longer afford to let the digital divide persist. As many market failures are constraining the scaling-up of digital access and digital literacy in Africa, its policymakers need to correct both.

Policies to ensure affordable access to the internet for all citizens include promoting market competition, private participation, and independent regulation of the ICT sector. The liberalization of the market for satellite dishes would increase competition and eliminate monopoly status over the international gateway and cable landing stations.

Private internet providers are unlikely to invest in remote areas with low population density, fragile and conflict-affected areas, or small island states because of low returns. As Africa currently has vast rural areas, as well as fragile and small states, private internet providers may charge unaffordable prices or coverage may be spotty. The internet reaches just 1 percent of the rural population in Zambia, and 11 percent in Namibia. Policies for overcoming the digital access divide vary from price controls and regulated prices to public facilities such as telecenters.

The development of digital capabilities to use the internet is also subject to market failure. Education, especially at the foundational stage, is a public good that should be available to all African children at affordable prices. It is efficient for governments to finance basic education and subsidize it at the higher levels (secondary, tertiary) to ensure that students are digitally literate and can use the internet and that workers are prepared for a job. Governments should ensure minimum educational quality standards and partner with the private sector, which is usually more effective in imparting high-quality education and digital skills development. As reforming educational systems and quality requires more than a generation, Africa's work needs to start now. Also, building a continent's human capital foundation cannot be achieved by an individual or agency alone. What is required is a concerted and collective effort on the part of governments, families, individuals, schools, and the private sector to collaborate, design, and cooperate in implementing systemic reforms aimed at turning out students for the digital age.

11

Why and How to Build Universal Social Policy in the South

Juliana Martínez Franzoni and Diego Sánchez-Ancochea

The challenge of securing well-paying formal jobs for the majority of the population—what we (2013) have previously referred to as labor incorporation—is not new across the Global South. Millions of people in this half of the world have wages under the poverty line as part of the informal economy. They coexist with a smaller number of well-paid and protected workers, giving way to a highly unequal income distribution. The process of automatization and robotization discussed elsewhere in this volume further challenges the prospects for good jobs and brings social incorporation—that is, providing people's well-being independent of the cash nexus—to the forefront.

We thank the editor of this book, Eva Paus; participants at the conference "The Future of Jobs: The Dual Challenges of Globalization and Robotization"; and two anonymous referees for valuable comments on earlier drafts. We also appreciate Rocco Zizzamia's careful reading of the previous draft, which allowed us to solve several grammatical and spelling errors.

In recent years, a universal basic income has become a popular response to this need for social incorporation (Van Parijs and Vanderborght 2017). According to venture capitalist Albert Wenger (2015), "we need to move past traditional concepts of work and jobs towards an era of economic freedom enabled by a universal basic income."[1] A universal income would provide cash transfers to those who lack an income of their own because they are too young, too old, sick, or simply unemployed. It would also give income security to the millions of (mostly) women who provide unpaid care. Yet, a basic income should complement rather than replace public social services. It is hard to envision cash transfers high enough to pay for private schooling and hospital fees, early childhood education, and nursing homes for the elderly. Besides, reliance on the private sector for social provision would fuel segmentation and higher inequality.

This chapter evaluates the potential to develop universal social incorporation: that is, to provide similar generous transfers and social services for all. We argue that universal benefits have significant positive effects, contributing to a higher redistribution of income, more support among different segments of the population, and less stigmatization of the poor. Universalism can fuel social cohesion in a world threatened by a sense of injustice and lack of opportunities.

Of course, arguing for universal policy in the South—and even in the North—may sound naïve. Expanding high-quality public health care—let alone new social protection programs such as early childhood education and childcare—in countries with weak institutional and fiscal capacity can be pie in the sky. In the past, more often than not, many programs designed as universal (including primary health care and education) turned into poor services for poor people instead (Arza 2012).

Following our previous work (Martínez Franzoni and Sánchez-Ancochea 2014 and 2016), we argue that building universalism is a long-term, gradual process. To consider this path, we consider the role of "policy architectures" as the blueprint of policy instruments involved in securing entry, funding, benefits, delivery, and outside market options for specific social programs. The architectures help us understand the trajectories of specific policy realms such as health care and pensions.

Based on the experience of countries with robust social policies and those with weak ones, our argument is twofold: first, that to foster universal social policies in the short and long runs, governments must focus on the unification of key components of the architectures; second, that the main constraints to advance in this regard come from the negative incentives created by preexisting policy architectures. Obstacles to secure enough resources are particularly problematic. Expanding the available resources requires linking the demands of the population with tax reforms and to the regulation of private options.

The rest of the chapter is divided into four sections. The first elaborates the reasons, normative and practical, in favor of universal social transfers and services. The second underlines the importance of politics and political requirements, which have so far been insufficiently addressed in the conversation about universalism. The third section explains the role of architectures to expand the chances for universalism by building short- and long-term processes. We argue that the design of the appropriate policy architecture can contribute to creating the political conditions for further social policy expansion. The fourth and final section summarizes our argument and draws out policy implications.

The Importance of Universalism in the South

Most countries in the South have failed to secure adequate commodification of the labor force. Low rates of economic growth, import dependence, the use of inappropriate (capital-intensive) technologies, and the rapid expansion of the population have resulted in an oversupply of workers. The result has been pervasive informality: estimated as percentage of the nonagricultural employment, in sub-Saharan Africa informal employment ranges between 33 percent in South Africa and 82 percent in Mali; in Latin America countries, between 40 percent in Uruguay and 75 percent in Bolivia; and in South and East Asia, between 33 percent in China and 84 percent in India (ILO 2013). One consequence has been growing flows of emigration, which have, in turn, triggered major changes in the organization of families and the participation of women in the labor force. The trends toward mechanization and automatization discussed in other parts of this book may thus only contribute to a situation that was already problematic.

In the context of these dualistic labor markets, social incorporation becomes particularly important to secure people's well-being and reduce inequality. Yet, not all kinds of social incorporation are equally desirable: if benefits set people apart (that is, incorporation is segmented), inequality will remain high and further expansions of social spending difficult. The goal should be to secure universal social incorporation. This takes place when everyone in society has access to similar generous (in level and quality) transfers and services.

Social and Economic Reasons to Promote Universal Social Incorporation

There are several reasons that make universal social incorporation desirable, particularly as compared to measures that target the poor exclusively:

More Effective and Sustainable Redistribution   High-quality social policies for all increase political support for social spending and more generous services, thus creating a redistributive virtuous circle (Huber 2002; Mkandawire 2006b). This happens thanks to what Korpi and Palmer (1998) have called the "paradox of redistribution": since they reach a larger number of beneficiaries—including the better off—universal programs can secure a larger amount of resources for everyone, including the poor. Having the middle class onboard will also increase the chances to pass income-generating tax reforms and to improve the quality of services. By contrast, targeted programs face a higher risk of being discontinued or their coverage and/or level of benefits diminished in times of crisis.

Unfortunately, the evidence on the redistributive impact of nontargeted social policies in the South is both limited and problematic. Data can be unreliable, lack comparability, and miss the benefits received by the top 1 and 5 percent of the population. Most studies also fail to incorporate the value and distribution of social services (Martínez Franzoni and Sánchez-Ancochea 2015). Still, the limited evidence available does point to the large redistributive capacity of massive programs for all. Recent studies by the Inter-American Development Bank (IDB) and the World Bank show that services with the highest coverage and relatively equitable provision—primary education and some health services—have a larger impact on income distribution than targeted but smaller programs (Álvarez et al. 2012; CEPAL 2006; Goñi et al. 2011; Huber and Stephens 2012).

Less Stigmatization   Means-testing creates social divisions between rich and poor and exacerbates the weakness of the latter (Walker 2011). Low-income groups are not only forced to provide detailed information about their living conditions to a myriad of state personnel, but also receive "second-rate" benefits. Across the South, conditional cash transfers (CCTs) are a good example of these problems: CCTs assume that insufficient use of education and health services results from lack of service demand rather than supply—i.e., the poor are not fully aware of how important these services are. In practice, forcing the poor to take their children to school or to medical checkups in exchange for money constitutes a method of social control. It also questions households' capacity to make decisions in light of context-specific circumstances such as the availability and quality of services (Barrientos, Hanlon, and Hume 2010).

Social Cohesion   Universal social programs can create a sense of belonging to the community and become a defining feature of national identity (Béland and Lecours 2008; Neubourg 2009). In the South, social policy has enhanced cohesion and contributed to more inclusive social contracts (ECLAC 2007). Generous services that are truly for all shorten social distance and help different socioeconomic groups become part of a community and realize their shared problems. Social cohesion can contribute to strengthen democracy and trigger other virtuous circles (Andrenacci and Repetto 2006, 100).

More Productive Economies   Even if universalism is desirable for social cohesion and state-building, neoclassical economics often highlights its negative impact on economic growth (Pontusson 2005). The argument is that these policies may be too expensive for countries with low income per capita, weak tax systems, and insufficient levels of social investment. If resources are limited and the primary income distribution unequal, the argument goes, it is best to prioritize the poor, leaving everyone else to rely on markets for their needs. Allegedly, developing "expensive" social programs that cover the whole population with generous benefits is particularly hard under the current economic order.

Few of these antiuniversalist arguments stand up to close scrutiny. Policies that ensure universal outputs are unlikely to be a net cost for countries; quite the contrary, they usually have a positive impact on sustainable economic growth and competitiveness. As Mkandawire (2006a) argues, social policy and economic development are interlinked. Social programs not only compensate for the negative effects of external shocks and economic adjustment, but also contribute to the generation of competitive assets. High-quality social policies can assist in the accumulation of human capital, expand aggregate demand, and improve social capital. Meanwhile, universal basic income programs can provide income security for people to increase risky entrepreneurship projects.

In these ways, universal social transfers and programs can promote higher economic growth and the creation of new competitive advantages, a point that is evident when one considers high growth rates in countries such as Costa Rica and Mauritius, two countries that over the course of the twentieth century also established universal social policy (Martínez Franzoni and Sánchez-Ancochea 2013; Edelman et al. 2007).[2]

Transfers versus Services

All the arguments above apply both to transfers and to services. Universal transfers have received considerable attention in recent times as a way to make up for the difficulties in securing adequate labor incorporation among the "precariat" (Standing 2014) and to compensate (mostly) women for their care work at home. To maximize its distributional impact, the guaranteed income should be funded by higher progressive income taxes, but many other revenue sources are available.

The basic income—which can be partial or full (Howard and Widerquist 2012)—is a measure easy to understand and to implement. It has a broad support basis from acclaimed economists as diverse as Milton Friedman, James Tobin, and John Kenneth Galbraith. It has also attracted politicians from all political persuasions, including some conservatives enthusiastic about measures that can do without larger bureaucracies.

Negative incentives are also low: because basic income is indeed basic, the risk of reducing labor supply is small (e.g., Bosh and Manacorda 2012) while cash transfers can reduce child labor (e.g., Kabeer, Piza, and Taylor 2012) and, potentially, expand wages for labor-intensive, poorly paid activities. Besides, basic income is embraced against state paternalism and on behalf of trusting people's criteria to purchase what they need the most (Barrientos, Hanlon, and Hume 2010).

According to their proponents, the few attempts to adopt the basic income show the potential of this instrument. The best example is the Alaska Permanent Fund Dividend (PFD), which draws from oil revenues to transfer an annual average income of $1,200 to every resident of the state.[3] The PFD has overwhelming cross-class support and has made a significant contribution to poverty reduction and social cohesion (Howard and Widerquist 2012). Alaska has a lower share of households with income under $10,000 than any other US state and, according to some measures, the most equitable distribution of income (Goldsmith 2012).[4] Meanwhile, there is no evidence of a negative effect on the propensity to work.[5]

Policy debates around basic income are also present in South Africa, Namibia, and elsewhere in the South (Zelleke 2012).[6] Proponents there argue that the adoption of the basic income could make a significant contribution to poverty reduction and improved nutrition while minimizing administrative costs and avoiding unnecessary bureaucratic expansions. A basic income—including one below the poverty line—would also reduce vulnerability to negative shocks, even for families above the income poverty line.

And yet, basic income does not entail less of a need for universal public services. Quite to the contrary: in the absence of public services, basic income risks fueling segmentation because people who rely exclusively on this transfer would be able to afford a more limited amount of private services than those with an additional income. Private providers would concentrate their activities in the areas with the largest profits (e.g., cities rather than rural areas; upper-middle- rather than low-income neighborhoods) even if these were not the regions with more needs. Competition between private providers would lead to spending in areas such as marketing, thus reducing the resources available for actual services.

It is thus important to place the adoption of universal basic income programs within the growing discussion of how to expand universal social services in the South. During the past fifteen years, many political parties and a growing number of policy agencies have promoted universalism in services. In Latin America, for instance, Brazil and Uruguay created national health care systems and El Salvador launched a universal system of social protection. Universalism also made inroads into emerging policy issues, as shown by Costa Rica's national care network and Uruguay's national care system.

In recent years, universal services also became a priority in the agenda of international organizations. Two proposals have been particularly influential in different parts of the South: the "social protection floor" and "basic universalism." The basic social protection floor became an ILO policy recommendation in 2012. It asked for the provision of essential health care and basic income security across the life cycle—i.e., for children, adults, and the elderly. Unlike basic universalism, which was basically an inspiring set of ideas following the 2008 global financial crisis, the social protection floor became a policy proposal. By 2012 it had gained the support of the United Nations, the World Bank, the G20, and many international non-governmental organizations (Cimadomore et al. 2013).

Basic universalism is a notion set forth by Latin American scholars under the sponsorship of the IDB in 2006 (Molina 2006). It refers to a set of essential benefits that governments should guarantee to everyone. By gradually expanding key transfers and services, basic universalism seeks to deal incrementally with the tension between social demands, on the one hand, and fiscal constraints, on the other. Benefit expansion in primary education, preventive medicine, and old-age monetary transfers will depend on improvement in the state's fiscal capacity and the emergence of new stakeholders and electoral support for policy expansion (Filgueira et al. 2006). It has also been complemented in the Latin American context by proposals from the Economic Commission of Latin America and the Caribbean (ECLAC) and the World Bank (Barros et al. 2009; ECLAC 2007).

Both of these approaches stress the need for national adaptations to country-specific circumstances; like our analysis, they recognize the importance of combining different policy instruments to achieve universal goals. Both could contribute to consolidate universalism in the South: in particular, the basic social protection floor has the potential to "give way to the global politics of welfare state rebuilding focused on the alliances that need to be constructed between the poor and the non-poor (especially the middle class) to rebuild bonds of solidarity nationally and internationally" (Deacon 2010, 1). This alliance could consider both transfers—creating space for universal basic income—and services. Unfortunately, however, neither the basic universalism nor the social protection floor proposals has paid enough attention to the political requirements behind expansion.

The Central Role of Politics in Building Universalism

Universal income and social transfers and services may be beneficial, but their design, adoption, and effective implementation face significant political, institutional, and financial obstacles, particularly in the South. How can these obstacles be overcome? A small but growing literature focuses on democratic institutions and left-wing parties as key determinants (e.g., Filgueira 2007; Huber and Stephens 2012; Lehouqc 2012; McGuire 2010; Haggard and Rudra 2005; Edelman et al. 2007; Segura-Ubiergo 2008).[7] Electoral competition drives political parties toward higher social spending to increase popular support. For McGuire (2010), elections and a free press have a positive effect on spending in primary health, which is a central dependent variable. In the long run, as shown by Filgueira (2007), democratic regimes gradually develop social coalitions and institutional mechanisms that support large social programs. Social insurance expanded in Argentina and Uruguay under democratic rule during the 1910s and 1920s. Chile's founding push happened under authoritarian rule in the 1920s, but the subsequent expansion took place under democracy.

One of the main contributions of democracy is to open spaces for left-wing parties, which generally favor higher social spending. Huber and Stephens (2012) found that the Latin American countries where left-wing parties prevailed over the previous two decades were more likely to stress spending in health and education—which tend to have broad coverage and more redistributive results—rather than in social insurance and social assistance. In Pribble's (2013) account of universalistic social reforms, having left-wing parties is a necessary yet insufficient condition.

Electoral competition and party ideology clearly influence the level of investment in social policy, becoming preconditions to promote universalism (Martínez Franzoni and Sánchez-Ancochea 2016). Yet, they are by no means enough: there are many instances where progressive governments have lofty ambitions but advance very little or even move in the wrong direction. For example, during most of the twentieth century, vibrant democracies in Chile and Uruguay developed unequal social benefits across occupational groups. In other instances, nominally universal health care and education were, in practice, low-quality services for the poor due to insufficient funding. In the 2000s, after the last wave of democratization, some left-wing administrations have been more willing and capable of delivering redistributive programs than others. As argued by Pribble (2013, 19), some "populist parties of the left/center-left have recently engaged in regressive social policy reforms."

Why do many progressive politicians fail in the promotion of universalism? Part of the problem is that they are often between a rock and a hard place. On the one hand, they want to create ambitious, citizen-based programs funded with general taxes, but lack the resources to do it. On the other hand, they face electoral pressures to expand coverage as quickly as possible and tend to see generosity and quality as features than can follow suit from mere political will and technical design. As a result, they often pay scarce attention to the way programs will evolve over time and to the incentives that can gradually build political coalitions. They should come to terms with the notion that delivering similar high-quality services for all will take a long time and they must identify paths to advance little by little in the right direction.

This lack of attention to long-term political requirements—starting from how initial measures will affect different actors, secure support for additional funding, and forge broad societal coalitions—is evident in recent proposals such as the social protection floor discussed in the previous section. Proponents of this global flagship program mostly neglect the political dynamics and path dependency involved in building it. For instance, the social protection floor is expected to rely on a combination of social assistance and social insurance. However, other than the technical design, the proposal has little to offer regarding the political economy that is required to move forward (Bachelet 2011). Because social insurance and social assistance have distinct constituencies and bureaucratic settings, policy processes that promote cooperation—by, for instance, reaching specific occupations and income brackets through a combination of subsidies and contributions—are crucial. Devoid of this political "backstage" to state-building, social protection floors can easily become an umbrella concept to de facto two-tier systems for the poor and the nonpoor, respectively.

In summary, if countries in the South are going to advance toward universal social incorporation—a fundamental role given the growing lack of good jobs discussed in other contributions—they need to pay more attention to the trajectories of change and the slow creation of the right political and institutional conditions. In the next section, we develop a proposal to do exactly that.

Building Step by Step: The Role of Architectures and Long-Term Processes

How can virtuous paths toward universalism be built? In this section, we address this key question using a series of cases across time, sectors, and countries. We introduce the concept of policy architectures as a useful analytic device to make sense of the combination of policy instruments policymakers have relied upon, and we argue that universalism is best delivered through a combination of policy instruments. The key matter is whether these instruments promote the unification or the fragmentation of policy architectures. Thinking about the right architectures forces us to also think about the ways to create better political conditions for universalism in the long run.

Below, we first define the concept and highlight the need to build unified policy architectures. Second, we explore the challenges to further unification, using examples from countries with diverse commitments to social policy. Lastly, we address resources as a key component of policy architectures that commonly constrain universalism.

Defining Policy Architectures

Given all the constraints previously discussed, promoting universalism in the South will not only require time but demands combining different policy instruments. In the case of health care, policymakers need to use both social insurance and social assistance in creative ways. In the case of basic income, delivering universalism may demand what De Wispelaere and Noguera (2012) refer to as "sequential implementation": combining universal child benefits, a universal basic pension, an antipoverty transfer, and tax credits progressively.[8]

This gradual, step-by-step process requires some guiding principles. Policymakers must understand the end-point and some of the political levers required to get there. To think about these guiding principles, we introduce the concept of policy architectures, which can be defined as the combination of instruments that establish who has access to what benefits, and how. Any policy architecture plays two different roles. First, at any given point in time, different combinations of policy instruments deliver different levels of universalism. Second, dynamically different architectures create distinct opportunities and constraints for subsequent expansion. Later in the chapter, we will discuss some of the architectures that are most likely to trigger constructive political coalitions for universalism.

Policy architectures involve five main components related to who has access to what, when, and how:

Eligibility (Under What Criteria Do People Benefit?) This dimension refers to who is entitled to receive benefits and under what criteria. The three eligibility criteria studied in the literature are citizenship, contributions, and need (Esping-Andersen, 1990). These three criteria can be displayed alone or in different combinations.

Funding (Who Pays and How?) Funding sources may be general revenues (coming from various sources, including commodity rents), earmarked taxes, and/or payroll contributions. The latter may involve different degrees of financial commitment by government, employers, and workers. Any of these funding sources may be complemented by copayments. Funding may be a significant restriction for further expansion but can be overcome, as discussed below.

Benefits (Who Defines Them and How?) States generally stipulate benefits in a statutory fashion. Public agencies can do this in a broad range of ways, from assuming that all benefits are included by default to listing everything included or listing only what is excluded. In some countries, businesses and/or workers also participate in the definition of benefits.

Provision (Who Does It?) Providers can be public or private and, if private, for- or not-for-profit. Each of these arrangements is driven by particular goals that may favor or inhibit universal policy outputs. These outputs also depend on other factors, such as efficiency, that we will not discuss in detail in this book.

Outside Option (How Do Governments Manage Market-Based Providers?) This component refers to the existence of nonpublic alternatives available to those who can afford them. These can trigger exits from state services and transfers (Korpi and Palme 1998). Within the outside option, we do not only consider out-of-pocket-funded private provision, but also the use of public resources for private gains (e.g., doctors' conflicting dual practices).

To promote universalism, policymakers should either design unified policy architectures where everyone has access to the same benefits (even if they do it through different programs) from the very beginning, or gradually unify them over time. Unification is particularly important in the area of benefits and provision; when everyone receives the same services delivered by the same providers, even if funded through different means, they will have more incentives to collaborate with each other and pressure for further expansion. By contrast, a fragmented system (both in services and in transfers such as the basic income) will lead to segmentation and result in different groups pushing different agendas.

Policymakers should pay particular attention to the interactions among components. Regulation of the outside option is a particularly important and understudied matter. Markets have every incentive to fragment further, from picking and choosing specific clients to providing benefits that are more profitable, yet not necessarily the most-needed.

Each policy realm obviously has its own policy architecture. In many countries, fragmentation in one area (e.g., pensions) goes together with some level of unification in others (e.g., health care). This is the case in the North—as shown by Canada and the United States (Béland and Waddan 2013)—and it also happens in the South. The political trajectory in each case will thus be very different and should be considered independently. At the same time, the more countries that can advance toward unification in different policies simultaneously, the stronger the supporting cross-class coalitions will be.

The Challenges to Secure Unification: An Exploration of Cases

This section focuses on three major challenges that policymakers face when trying to unify policy architectures: the existence of unequal benefits from the beginning, a powerful outside option, and the lack of resources. Below, we refer to each of the challenges, drawing on the experience of countries with robust social policies but diverse levels of fragmentation (Mauritius, South Korea, and Uruguay) and of latecomers that have recently witnessed an incipient development of more ambitious social policies (e.g., El Salvador).

When benefits are unequal from the onset, different groups have incentives to expand their own benefits over the long run. Some will be more capable of getting their way, thus reinforcing segmentation over time. In South Korea, for example, during the second half of the twentieth century different occupations created their own health insurance societies. Eligibility, funding, benefits, and provision were all fragmented. Several Latin American countries faced the same problem (Haggard and Kauffman 2008). Uruguay is a good case in point. Since the beginning of the twentieth century, the low-income population relied on public services—formally available to all citizens—based on general taxes, while the middle class had access to mutual aid societies funded through monthly fees and complementary over-the-counter payments. Service delivery was higher-quality (including shorter waiting lists) in the not-for-profit sector than in state-run facilities. The system was therefore fragmented in terms of eligibility, benefits, funding, and providers. The incentives to modify the system were small: the middle class protected their privileged access to high-quality, privately run mutual aid societies, which remained independent from public provision. By 1967, Uruguay had nine autonomous health insurance funds for workers in different manufacturing activities, which spent 3.1 times more resources per person than the public system (Mesa-Lago 1978). Similar problems were evident in neighboring countries: in Chile, social insurance involved more than ten different funds, with entitlements and obligations contained in more than two thousand legal texts (Mesa-Lago 1978; Segura-Ubiergo 2007). The Chilean government undertook legal efforts to unify social insurance, but fragmentation remained due to diverse interests.

A second challenge comes from excessive dependence on the private provision of public services or from allowing a strong independent private sector. In countries with a significant and unregulated outside option, private providers will likely strengthen over time and differences between private and public provision will deepen. Mauritius is an excellent example of this negative trend. It established a citizen-based health care system that granted everyone the same benefits through public facilities in the 1950s. It was funded on general revenues, but resources were scarce and services lacking. The better-off never really joined public services, preferring to use private facilities instead. Physicians complemented their public and private practices, and there were no clear incentives to substantially improve the pool of public resources.

Private doctors and hospitals are not the only outside option; pharmacies and dual practices within the public sector can be as harmful for unification. In El Salvador, for example, pharmacies have traditionally played a central role not only in selling but also in informally prescribing drugs. High prices—significantly higher than in other Latin American countries—fueled incomplete treatments, which in turn made public facilities responsible for treating medical complications. Public costs were high and patients experienced the negative consequences of a simple infection leading to complications.

In Costa Rica, various regulatory changes contributed to the expansion of dual practice (i.e., doctors who work in both the private and public sector), slowly leading to fragmentation. An expanded dual practice has blurred the boundaries between the public and private sectors and contributed to unmet timetables and weakened public performance (Socha 2010). Overpriced medical inputs, purchases of nonessential services, and waiting lists that go well beyond supply shortages are some examples of the conflicts of interest that currently undermine universalism.

The third challenge has to do with insufficient resources, which result in low-quality services and expand the outside option almost by definition. We address this matter in the following section.

How can these challenges be overcome? Solutions are context-specific, geographically and historically. There are no "one size fits all" solutions. In Uruguay, eliminating private providers was almost impossible, so unification had to focus on expanding eligibility and unifying benefits in the private and public sectors. This is precisely what a

2006 reform did through four mechanisms: the creation of a national fund that collects all monthly fees; the allocation to mutual aid societies of a per capita rate that is independent of people's income and instead contingent on their age and risks; the definition of a set of preventive and primary care measures that are enforced across the board; and the possibility that the poor population may choose mutual aid societies as their providers.

In South Korea, the 1997 crisis exposed the shortcomings of relying on a myriad of (relatively small) insurance funds that struggled to contain medical costs. Potential responses to the crisis included expanding payroll contributions, creating government subsidies, or unifying the system. The first one was rather unpopular, particularly because payroll contributions had already increased in previous years and the economy was underperforming. Raising contributions from the self-employed was also hard, as most of these people were poor and adequate information on their income was hard to obtain. Increasing government subsidies was difficult due to fiscal constraints, some of which came from the post-crisis agreement with the International Monetary Fund. The 2000 reform unified almost five hundred insurance funds into a single insurer, the National Health Insurance Corporation. Yet, this did not unify the architecture completely: the existence of powerful private suppliers (paid by procedure) and the reluctance of the government to expand funding maintained limited benefits and high copayments.

In El Salvador, the left-wing party that took office in 2009 decided to regulate pharmaceutical prices—a very popular measure. Subsequent steps involved promoting access to public medical facilities and enforcing formal medical prescriptions in order to encourage a more adequate use of drugs. These changes, which did not focus on health provision directly, encouraged, nevertheless, more unified benefits and strengthened public provision.

What does this tell us about the way progressive policymakers should approach the construction of universalism? It highlights three lessons that are particularly important when introducing new programs (like childcare today in many Latin American countries). First, it is important that benefits be sound: people will go out of their way to avoid insufficient or poor-quality services. Second, eligibility can go from less to more as long as the right incentives are in place. For example, in Costa Rica, social security began with blue-collar workers. Funding became a unifying trigger: it promoted the incorporation of white-collar workers with higher salaries than blue-collar ones. It also promoted the incorporation of dependent family members on an equal footing with fee-contributing workers. So the design of the policy itself triggered the right kind of cross-class coalition to support further expansion. Third, public providers must not be in a conflicting relationship with an outside option.

The Funding Challenge: Gradualism Can Also Help

Financial resources remain one of the most significant constraints to secure universalism (Durán and Pacheco 2012). With some exceptions, such as Argentina and Brazil, most countries in the South have low tax revenues. As a percentage of GDP, tax income is between 10 and 20 percent in the non-OECD countries, compared to an average of 40 percent in OECD ones. Most countries in the South rely largely on regressive taxation and encounter difficulty in expanding the tax base (Besley and Persson 2014). High concentration of income at the top, large informal sectors, and weak state capacity reduce the probability of expanding revenues. Increasing progressive income taxes is particularly difficult; most of the reforms that have been adopted in recent decades have focused on value-added tax and other indirect (regressive) taxes (Schneider 2012).

As a result of the lack of resources, dependence on private spending for public services from old-age pensions to education and health care is much higher—thus reducing the potential for social incorporation.[9] For example, in Chile, private spending amounts to almost half of public spending (4.6 and 10 percent of GDP, respectively) (OECD 2016). A study of health care spending in six Latin American countries reveals that out-of-pocket spending represents between 32 and 60 percent of all health care spending (Debrott Sánchez 2014).

Despite a change of mood during the 2000s (Cummins, Karunanethy, and Ortiz 2015, 1), the fiscal space and its limits are still part of most conversations regarding social policy expansion. Difficulties in expanding the fiscal space often create a chicken and egg problem: low-quality services and weak bureaucracies reduce people's commitment to taxation, which in turn creates problems to fund better services.

Yet, funding shortages are directly linked to the lack of cross-class beneficiaries of state intervention. If large segments of the middle class receive high-quality services, they are more willing to fund social services (Ferreira et al. 2013, Martínez Franzoni and Sánchez-Ancochea, forthcoming). The challenge is to devise the best revenue mechanisms, considering both economic requirements and political expediency. Expanding payroll contributions may be one useful option: it is sometimes easier and more socially legitimate to improve the financial basis of services through social security contributions than through other means (Durán and Pacheco 2012). Moreover, it is possible to combine contributory and noncontributory mechanisms, as shown by social security in Costa Rica and health services in Thailand.

The 2000s created an opportunity to expand revenues from commodities in large parts of the South. In Africa, resource taxes increased from US$45 billion in 2002 to $230 billion in 2008, constituting 40 percent of the tax burden (OECD 2013). In Latin America, tax revenues from mining increased from 4.3 percent in 2002 to a peak of 8 percent in 2008, the most significant share of the celebrated increase in the region's tax burden (CAF 2012; OECD-CEPAL 2016). A few countries used this additional income to fund more ambitious social programs than those then in place. In Bolivia, for example, the universal old-age pension Renta Dignidad was funded in part by a special direct tax on hydrocarbons. Linking revenues and expenditures in this way may reduce macroeconomic flexibility, but can secure the continuity of universal programs in periods of low commodity prices like the ones we are now experiencing.

New income for social spending could also come from official development assistance (ODA) and the elimination of illicit financing flows. The former may be particularly useful for countries with a weaker social incorporation. It may include North-South and South-South aid (e.g., ALBA in Latin America). Of course, aid will do little if (licit and illicit) flows from South to North are not simultaneously reduced.[10] In terms of legal financial flows, according to the United Nations (2015), "net financial flows out of developing economies totaled $970 billion in 2014 . . . poor countries are transferring resources to rich countries, not vice versa" (Cummins, Karunanethy, and Ortiz 2015, 30). The restructuring of total public debt and of debt services can free resources that strengthen social incorporation as it occurred in countries such as Brazil and South Africa (the former) and Brazil, Costa Rica, and Thailand (the second) (Durán and Pacheco 2012). In terms of illegal financial outflows, according to Cummins, Karunanethy, and Ortiz (2015, 30–31) "for every one dollar that developing countries receive in ODA, they are giving back about seven dollars to wealthy countries via illicit outflows."

Some of the sources just discussed call for nationwide strategies; others fall under the realm of social policy itself (Durán and Pacheco 2012). In either case, a key matter is that funding should be seen as part of the process of unification of the architecture and part of the expansion of government supply. In this way, funding can be secured in a piecemeal fashion if beneficiaries tend to be grouped together and to apply all of their resources to the service of a single set of arrangements.

Costa Rica constitutes an excellent example of the type of dynamics we have in mind. In the 1940s, the country started out with health insurance for blue-collar workers. The Costa Rican social insurance (Caja Costarricense del Seguro Social, CCSS) initially contracted out hospital services but immediately built its own. Facilities began to expand, as did the incorporation of family members. The existence of a large segment of social security beneficiaries expanded the demand for resources, which, in turn, resulted in an increase in payroll taxes for other groups. In 1960, for example, the CCSS bureaucrats argued that the financial sustainability of social insurance was at stake due to the combined pressures of growing service demand and government debt (Rosenberg 1983). They demanded the expansion of payroll taxes for high-wage earners, many of whom were previously not incorporated into the system.

This tax increase received ample support from trade unions. Newspapers reported eighteen unions and federations expressing their views to the legislative commission and only one opposing the measure (Martínez Franzoni and Sánchez-Ancochea 2014). Policy legacies partly explain their support, since the program was built from the bottom up: from the outset, Costa Rican workers who were already insured had incentives to support further expansions to higher-income groups who would bring larger tax contributions to the system. At the same time, although high-wage earners were harmed by the reform, the provision of high-quality services made their incorporation into the system attractive.

In the Uruguayan reform, the need to expand coverage and reduce the distance between public and private provision generated pressures to expand revenues and resulted in higher payroll taxes.[11] Something similar happened in Chile, where the expansion of social policy while maintaining fiscal discipline demanded expanded revenues. The creation of a new health program (AUGE) and earlier education reforms relied on value-added taxes (Fairfield 2014; Pribble 2013). Demands for better education in 2011 and 2012 also "dramatically expanded the scope of debate on progressive taxation" (Fairfield 2014, 16). In other scenarios, the start-up of basic services for all can enable the expansion of contributory schemes (Durán and Pacheco 2012).

In addition to increasing the available pull of public resources, governments should regulate the use of private providers, a matter virtually absent in the global conversation about social protection floors. This road may take various forms in different countries and policy sectors, from a larger intervention in private benefits and fees to the standardization of social guarantees between private and public providers and the taxation of private services (through the value-added tax for users and the income tax for owners).

Conclusions and Policy Recommendations

We are living in contradictory times. Declining growth, increased competitive pressures in international markets, more rapid technological change, and more democratic political systems create both growing needs and demands for universal social incorporation in the South. People's vulnerability over their life cycle is such that everyone can understand the importance of social provision and, except for the very wealthy, expect to benefit from it. At the same time, however, countries face mounting financial and political challenges to advance in this direction.

This chapter calls for a gradualist approach to building universalism and highlights the role that policy architectures play in long-term trajectories. We have argued that countries should focus on building unified policy architectures capable of bringing most people under a single roof. To this purpose, the task is to incrementally reduce fragmentation across key components of the policy architecture.

The need to reduce fragmentation may be obvious in well-established policy areas such as health care, but it also extends to emerging policy domains such as early-childhood education and childcare, which are dominated by private services and informal paid work. Because these are labor-intensive services with a large unsatisfied demand, some of these areas of social incorporation are also important to expand labor incorporation. The unification of benefits is also important in any attempt to create a basic universal income, which could be initially built by a combination of programs (e.g., a contributory transfer for formal workers, a noncontributory pension for the elderly, cash transfers for the poor) with a similar transfer amount.

Trajectories are country-specific, but always involve drawing on every instrument available overall and those regarding financial resources—one of the most critical matters—specifically. The range of options goes from contributory-based social insurance and targeted measures to user fees. In most, if not all cases, it is imperative to set in place measures that tame the market, a key driver behind fragmented architectures, while making efforts to unify benefits. A significant challenge is to identify reforms that pay off politically, while avoiding fragmentation of any kind. Doing so is particularly urgent at a time when people feel increasingly vulnerable and when participation in the often informal and poorly paid labor market is unlikely to solve many of their problems.

Of course, reducing fragmentation in the context of stagnant economies and high inequality is not easy. Many countries will struggle to show progress, particularly in the context of growing private sectors. It is to be hoped that the collective search for inclusive solutions to people's well-being will win over furthering exclusion. The main incentive in this search is that almost everyone may face economic uncertainty in the future.

NOTES

1. The Future Isn't What It Used to Be

1. The argument is not dissimilar to Gordon's (2016) that GDP is not a good measure of improved living standards, as it does not include nonprice elements of quality of life that matter to people.

2. The decline was fairly uniform across countries. In the United States, union density fell from 22.1 to 10.8 over this period. But there are important exceptions. In the Nordic countries, Iceland, and Belgium, the unionization rate remained well above 50 percent.

3. Karabarbounis and Neiman (2014) include all countries that had at least fifteen years of data between 1975 and 2012.

4. Song et al. (2015) decompose the growth in inequality in the United States between 1978 and 2012 into growth in equality within firms and growth in inequality across firms.

5. Felipe et al. (2014) argue that the peak manufacturing employment share is an excellent predictor of growth.

6. In 2017, the minimum wage was $7.25 an hour. If it had grown at the same rate as average wages since 1968, it would have been $11.35, or $18.85 if it had grown in sync with productivity (Economic Policy Institute 2016b).

7. Hoy and Sumner (2016) argue that three-quarters of global poverty could be eliminated with taxes on national resources and reallocation of public funding.

2. The Rise of the Robots

1. The text of "The Triple Revolution" and the letters cited are available on the Linus Pauling and the International Peace Movement pages at http://scarc.library.oregonstate.edu/coll/pauling/peace/papers/index.html.

2. Health care and elder care may well be the most promising sectors for future job growth, given the trend toward an aging population. However, there are unlikely to be enough of these jobs, and there are sure to be significant skill and personality mismatches—especially for less-skilled males. For example, is it realistic to assume that a large fraction of the 3.5 million truck drivers in the United States could transition into nursing or elder care jobs if and when they are displaced by the self-driving truck technologies that are already under development?

4. Expanding Job Opportunities through Global Green Growth

1. See Pollin et al. 2014; Pollin, Garrett-Peltier, Heintz, and Chakraborty 2015, Pollin and Chakraborty 2015; and Pollin, Garrett-Peltier, and Chakraborty 2015 in addition to my 2015 book cited above.

2. There have been sharp debates as to the extent of job creation that would have been generated through expanding the Keystone Pipeline. The figures cited here are from the US State Department: https://keystonepipeline-xl.state.gov/documents/organization/221135.pdf.

3. See chapter 6 and appendix 3 of Pollin, Garrett-Peltier, Heintz, and Chakraborty 2015 for a full discussion of the employment-estimating methodology used here. One point to clarify here is that I am not suggesting that spending $1 million on energy efficiency, clean renewable energy, or nonrenewable energy will produce an identical impact on either energy supply (through capacity expansion) or energy demand (through raising efficiency standards). I discuss the distinct effects created by spending a given amount of funds on efficiency, renewables, or nonrenewable energy in Pollin 2015 as well as, in greater depth, Pollin et al. 2014 and Pollin, Garrett-Peltier, Heintz, and Chakraborty 2015.

4. Germany, South Korea, and Spain do all have small oil-refining sectors, even though they are not oil producers. Jobs will be lost in these sectors as clean energy production increasingly supplants imported oil as an energy source. However, these losses should be largely counterbalanced through an increase in bioenergy refining activity—i.e., producing clean-burning ethanol from agricultural wastes and switchgrass.

5. The employment figures for clean energy investments are generated through new investments in these activities. The figures for fossil fuel employment reflect the existing levels of spending in all areas, including operations and maintenance, as well as existing investments.

6. See Pollin, Garrett-Peltier, Heintz, and Chakraborty (2015), 117–21 for a discussion of the Indonesia case as well as, more generally, the relationship between declining fossil fuel export markets for some countries and their growth prospects.

7. Mazzocchi (1993, 41). See also Les Leopold's outstanding biography of Mazzocchi, *The Man Who Hated Work and Loved Labor* (White River Junction, VT: Chelsea Green, 2007) for the historical context on the issues of a Superfund for workers and just transition.

7. Automated but Compensated?

1. For six groups at the two-digit ISCO-88 level, no information on RTI is available. These agricultural, supervisory, and residual occupational groups are also excluded by Goos et al. (2014), Autor et al. (2015), and Autor and Dorn (2013). We also have to exclude individuals in all waves for which information is available only at the one-digit ISCO level. In total, we exclude 12 percent of observations in this way.

2. We use the correspondence table from Ganzeboom, http://www.harryganzeboom.nl/ISCO08/index.htm, which is based on that of the ILO. None of our results change when we exclude 2012, in which the ISCO-08 coding is used, as shown in the sensitivity tests.

3. These include Austria, Belgium, Denmark, Finland, France, Germany, Greece, Ireland, Italy, Luxembourg, the Netherlands, Norway, Portugal, Spain, Sweden, Switzerland, and the UK.

4. See details about the operationalization of respondents' education and income in Thewissen and Rueda (forthcoming).

5. Refusals and "don't know"s are recoded as missing (1.5 percent of the sample).

6. We account for the fact that individuals are nested within countries by applying a multilevel model with random intercepts for countries, and we cluster standard errors at the country level. Our main estimations are based on an ordinary least squares regression; estimations are replicated when using ordered probit instead.

9. Advanced Manufacturing and China's Future for Jobs

1. US Bureau of Labor Statistics, April 2016 (https://www.bls.gov/news.release/archives/empsit_05062016.pdf), and unpublished China data from The Conference Board, International Labor Comparisons program, April 2016.

2. The 2015 UN World Population Prospects report projects continuous growth of China's elderly population while its working population keeps shrinking. While in 2005 ten workers were supporting one retiree, that ratio is projected to decline to four after 2020 (https://esa.un.org/unpd/wpp/publications/files/key_findings_wpp_2015.pdf).

3. US Department of Commerce, Labor Cost database, http://acetool.commerce.gov/labor-costs.

4. See the MIC 2025 website at http://english.cntv.cn/special/madeinchina/index.shtml. For an unofficial translation of the MIC 2025 plan, see http://www.usito.org/content/usito-made-china-2025-unofficial-translation-2015-5-29.

5. Statement by Premier Li Keqiang, quoted on the State Council's website, July 4, 2015, http://english.gov.cn/policies/latest_releases/2015/07/04/content_281475140165588.htm.

6. http://www.usito.org/news/state-council-provides-guidance-internet-plus-action-plan. See also the website of the Internet Plus plan at http://www.gov.cn/zhengce/content/2015-07/04/content_10002.htm.

7. See http://www.gtai.de/GTAI/Navigation/EN/Invest/Industries/Smarter-business/Smart-technologies/cyber-physical-systems,t=agenda-cps,did=626022.html, and http://www.iiconsortium.org/faq.htm.

8. http://www.ifr.org/news/ifr-press-release/statements-of-ceos-on-the-results-of-world-robotics-2015-774/. These data are provided by the Chinese Robot Alliance (CRIA), an important stakeholder in China's MIC 2025 plan.

9. http://www.ifr.org/industrial-robots/statistics/.

10. This, of course, raises the question of what precisely these fifty million needed jobs are. Unfortunately, the State Council website does not provide an answer.

11. See the Xinhua news agency story at http://english.gov.cn/premier/news/2016/03/05/content_281475301612181.htm. It is important to recall that China's official statistics on "newly created urban jobs" do not account for layoffs or other job losses, as explained earlier.

12. Due to the sensitivity of this topic, all interview partners have requested anonymity.

13. Email to the author, dated February 9, 2016, from source C, who requests anonymity.

14. These are value-added figures for service's share in GDP for 2014, as reported in the World Bank database, http://data.worldbank.org/indicator/NV.SRV.TETC.ZS.

10. Light Manufacturing Can Create Good Jobs in Sub-Saharan Africa

1. M-Pesa is the mobile money service launched by Safaricom in 2007 in Kenya. By the end of 2013, seventeen million Kenyans, or more than 66 percent of the adult population, were using their mobile phones, usually the most basic ones, to pay for taxi rides, electricity bills, or daily supermarket purchases (World Bank 2016b).

2. The source of all statistics related to access and use of the internet and access to mobile phones is the World Bank's *World Development Report 2016: Digital Dividends.*

3. The skills subindex is a part of the ITU (2016) ICT Development Index, a composite index combining eleven indicators into one benchmark measure for all countries. The skills subindex measures and monitors ICT capability, or skills to use the internet, and includes three proxy indicators: adult literacy, gross secondary enrollment, and gross tertiary enrollment.

4. The forecast is based on the UN Population Division 2012 medium-variant fertility projections, which assume that the average family size will fall fairly slowly.

5. Poor farmers in India realized large income gains when the Indian Tobacco Company (ITC), a conglomerate, linked them to the internet at the same time that it was benefiting the company. Farmers' distress related to inefficient supply chains in rural agriculture motivated the company to set up small internet kiosks, e-Choupal, in villages in 2000. The Choupal provided farmers access to an efficient and transparent alternative to the traditional *mandi* for marketing their produce; established a direct channel between the farmer and ITC, marginalized the role of middlemen, raised farmers' incomes, and empowered the Indian farmer. ITC extended its e-Choupal framework to deliver core services such as access to health care, education, and information, and even liaised with other consumer goods and finance companies to deliver to rural Indians products and services that had previously commanded huge premiums or were simply unavailable (Farhoomand and Bhatnagar 2008).

6. Fox et al. (2014) used household survey data collected between 2000 and 2010 from forty-seven countries in sub-Saharan Africa to form a baseline.

7. De Vries, Timmer, and De Vries (2015) estimate the share of employment in manufacturing was 8.3 percent in 2010. Manufacturing contributed 10 percent to overall value added in the same year. Their estimates are based on the Groningen dataset, which covers eleven African countries.

8. Using national accounts and sectoral employment data from population censuses of sixteen sub-Saharan African countries, McMillan and Harttgen (2014) decomposed growth in labor productivity during 1995–2009.

9. Africa's share of the global population is projected to rise from 17 percent (one billion) in 2010 to 24 percent (2.2 billion) by 2050 and 35 percent (3.6 billion) by 2100. The forecast is based on the UN's medium-variant fertility projections, which assume that the average family size will fall slowly (UN Population Division 2012).

10. STEM is the acronym for science, technology, engineering, and mathematics. PLUS indicates managerial and professional skills that Africa needs in addition to STEM skills.

11. Light manufacturing industries have low capital intensity and include industries such as footwear, apparel, furniture, agroindustry, and small metal products.

12. 2015 O*NET labor market information from the US Department of Labor, available at https://www.onetonline.org/.

11. Why and How to Build Universal Social Policy in the South

1. See also Schneider (2015), an article claiming that the basic income has become popular in Silicon Valley.

2. Comparisons between Latin America and Nordic countries help explain the importance of the historical link between universalism and economic development. Valenzuela

(2006a and 2006b), for example, shows that Sweden's generous pensions and other social programs introduced early in the twentieth century facilitated female labor market participation, reduced fertility, and increased productivity. Without such a policy, Chile experienced rapid population growth and limited economic expansion.

3. The PFD was not initially developed as a basic income scheme, but as a wealth fund. In 1976, Alaska created the Alaskan Permanent Fund to save a share of its oil revenues for the future. In 1982, the state government decided to distribute a dividend from this wealth fund to every resident as a way to maximize the benefits from oil. See Howard and Widerquist (2012) for a detailed description and evaluation of the Alaskan model of basic income.

4. The PFD's contribution to poverty reduction is limited by the small size and volatility of the transfer. Even in the best year (2008), the dividend amounts to less than 20 percent of the individual poverty line in the United States and 40 percent of the poverty line for a family of four (Zelleke 2012). The fact that this is a resource-based dividend and not a transfer funded through progressive income taxes also reduces its redistributive impact.

5. Other places where minimum basic income is being considered are Switzerland, Finland, and the cities of Utrecht in Holland and Calgary and Edmonton in Canada.

6. In 2004, Brazil became the first country to legally commit to basic income by expanding the conditional cash transfer program Bolsa Familia (Hall 2008).

7. The literature concentrates on social transfers and basic services more than on basic income. In fact, in the latter case, almost all of the research is based on very few successful cases and there is little effort to draw comparative lessons. For a valuable exception, see De Wispelaere and Noguera (2012).

8. See Vanderborght (2004) for a discussion of this approach in Belgium and the Netherlands.

9. The weight of private spending varies across sectors. For health care, for example, in 2000 public and private spending were basically the same: 3.4 and 3.2 percent of GDP, respectively ("Health" 2016).

10. Illegal financial flows involve capital that is illegally earned, transferred, or utilized and include traded goods that are mispriced to avoid higher tariffs, wealth funneled to offshore accounts to evade income taxes, money laundering, and unreported movements of cash.

11. The Uruguayan case also demonstrates the limits of the mechanism we are exploring. During the reform of 2006, the original idea was not to rely on payroll contributions but on a personal income tax that was debated by Congress in parallel to health care reform. Yet, the government avoided bundling both reforms out of fear that failure to change taxes could have a negative effect on the health care agenda.

REFERENCES

Abramovitz, Moses. 1986. "Catching Up, Forging Ahead, and Falling Behind." *The Journal of Economic History* 46, no. 2, no. 1986: 385–406. http://EconPapers.repec.org/RePEc:cup:jechis:v:46:y:1986:i:02:p:385-406_04.

Acemoglu, Daron, and Pascual Restrepo. 2016. "The Race between Machine and Man: Implications of Technology for Growth, Factor Shares and Employment." NBER Working Paper No. 22252. Cambridge, MA: National Bureau of Economic Research. DOI: http://dx.doi.org/10.3386/w22252.

———. 2017. "Robots and Jobs: Evidence from US Labor Markets." NBER Working Paper No. 23285. Cambridge, MA: National Bureau of Economic Research.

Acemoglu, Daron, and James A. Robinson. 2002. "The Politics of the Kuznets Curve." *Review of Development Economics* 6, no. 2: 183–203.

———. 2012. *Why Nations Fail*. Danvers, MA: Crown Business.

African Center for Economic Transformation (ACET). 2014. *Growth with Depth*. African Transformation Report 2014. Accra: African Center for Economic Transformation.

Álvarez, Fernando, Adriana Arreaza, Lucila Berniell, Daniel Ortega, Michael Penfold, and Pablo Sanguinetti. 2012. *Finanzas públicas para el desarrollo: fortaleciendo la conexión entre ingresos y gastos*. Caracas: CAF Development Bank of Latin America.

Andrenacci, Luciano, and Fabián Repetto. 2006. "Un camino para reducir la desigualdad y construir ciudadanía." In *Universalismo básico. Una nueva política social para América Latina*, edited by Carlos Gerardo Molina, 93–114. Washington, DC: Banco Interamericano de Desarrollo/Planeta.

Arias, Elizabeth. 2007. United States Life Tables, 2004. In *National Vital Statistics Report 56*, no. 9. Hyattsville, MD: National Center for Health Statistics. https://www.cdc.gov/nchs/data/nvsr/nvsr56/nvsr56_09.pdf.

Arntz, Melanie, Terry Gregory, and Ulrich Zierahn. 2016. "The Risk of Automation for Jobs in OECD Countries: A Comparative Analysis." OECD Social, Employment and Migration Working Paper No. 189. DOI: http://dx.doi.org/10.1787/5jlz9h56dvq7-en.

Arza, Camila. 2012. "Towards a Rights-Based Policy? The Expansion of Old-Age Pension Coverage in Latin America." Paper presented at the Second Forum of the International Sociological Association, CONICET/FLACSO, Buenos Aires, August 1.

Asis, Maruja M. B. 2006. "The Philippines' Culture of Migration." Migration Policy Institute website. January 1.

Astor, Michael, Mathias Bucksteeg, and Iris Pfeiffer. 2006. *Zukunft Handwerk! Der Beitrag des Handwerks im Innovationsprozess*. Berlin: Studie der Prognos.

Atkinson, Anthony. 1997. "Bringing Income Distribution in from the Cold." *Economic Journal* 107, no. 441: 297–321. DOI: http://dx.doi.org/10.1111/j.0013-0133.1997.159.x.

———. 2015. *Inequality: What Can Be Done?* Cambridge, MA: Harvard University Press.

"Automation and Anxiety." 2016. *The Economist*, June 25. http://www.economist.com/news/special-report/21700758-will-smarter-machines-cause-mass-unemployment-automation-and-anxiety.

Autor, David. 2010. "The Polarization of Job Opportunities in the US Labor Market: Implications for Employment and Earnings." Center for American Progress/The Hamilton Project, April 2010, 8–9. http://economics.mit.edu/files/5554.

Autor, David H., and David Dorn, 2013. "The Growth of Low-Skill Service Jobs and the Polarization of the US Labor Market." *American Economic Review* 103: 1553–97.

Autor, David H., David Dorn, and Gordon H. Hanson. 2015. "Untangling Trade and Technology: Evidence from Local Labour Markets." *Economic Journal* 125: 621–46. DOI: http://dx.doi.org/10.1111/ecoj.12245.

Autor, David, and Michael Handel. 2013. "Putting Tasks to the Test: Human Capital, Job Tasks, and Wages." *Journal of Labor Economics* 31, no. S1 (Part 2, April): S59–96. DOI: http://dx.doi.org/10.1086/669332.

Autor, David H., Frank Levy, and Richard J. Murnane. 2003. "The Skill Content of Recent Technological Change: An Empirical Exploration." *The Quarterly Journal of Economics* 118: 1279–333. DOI: http://dx.doi.org/10.1162/003355303322552801.

Bachelet, Michelle. 2011. *Social Protection Floor: For a Fair and Inclusive Globalization*. Geneva: International Labor Organization.

Balconi, Margherita, Andrea Pozzali, and Riccardo Viale. 2007. "The 'Codification Debate' Revisited: A Conceptual Framework to Analyze the Role of Tacit Knowledge in Economics." *Industrial and Corporate Change* 16, no. 5: 823–49. DOI: https://dx.doi.org/10.1093/icc/dtm025.

Baldwin, Peter. 1990. *The Politics of Social Solidarity: Class Bases of the European Welfare State 1875–1975*. Cambridge, UK: Cambridge University Press.

Banister, Judith. 2013. "China's Manufacturing Employment and Hourly Labor Compensation, 2002–2009." *International Labor Comparisons*, June 7. Washington, DC: US Bureau of Labor Statistics. http://www.bls.gov/fls/china_method.pdf.

Barrientos, Armando, Joseph Hanlon, and David Hume. 2010. *Just Give Money to the Poor: The Development Revolution for the Global South*. London: Kumarian Press.

Barros, Ricardo, Francisco Ferreira, José Molinas Vega, and Jaime Saavedra Chanduvi. 2009. *Measuring Inequality of Opportunities in Latin America and the Caribbean*. Washington, DC: World Bank.

Bartels, Larry. 2008. *Unequal Democracy: The Political Economy of the New Gilded Age*. Princeton, NJ: Princeton University Press.

Barth, Erling, Alex Bryson, James C. Davis, and Richard Freeman. 2016. "It's Where You Work: Increases in the Dispersion of Earnings across Establishments and Individuals in the United States." *Journal of Labor Economics* 34 (Part 2, April: S67–97). DOI: https://dx.doi.org/10.1086/684045.

Baxter, Gordon, John Rooksby, Yuanzhi Wang, and Ali Khajeh-Hosseini. 2012. "The Ironies of Automation: Still Going Strong at 30?" In *Proceedings of the 30th European Conference on Cognitive Ergonomics* (ECCE '12), 65–71. New York: Association for Computing Machinery. DOI: https://dx.doi.org/10.1145/2448136.2448149.

Béland, Daniel, and André Lecours. 2008. *Nationalism and Social Policy: The Politics of Territorial Solidarity*. Oxford, UK: Oxford University Press.

Béland, Daniel, and Alex Waddan. 2013. "Social Policy Universality in Canada and the United States." Paper presented at the conference The Political Economy of Social Policy in North America: Convergence towards Universalism? St Antony's College, Oxford, March 1.

Beramendi, Pablo, and Christopher J. Anderson. 2008. "Income Inequality and Democratic Representation." In *Democracy, Inequality, and Representation: A Comparative Perspective*, edited by Pablo Beramendi and Christopher J. Anderson, 3–24. New York: Russell Sage Foundation.

Besley, Timothy, and Torsten Persson. 2014. "Why Do Developing Countries Tax So Little?" *Journal of Economic Perspectives* 28, no. 4: 99–120.

Betz, Hans-George. 1994. *Radical Right-Wing Populism in Western Europe*. New York: Palgrave Macmillan.

Bhalla, Vibha. 2010. "'We Wanted to End Disparities at Work': Physician Migration, Racialization, and a Struggle for Equality." *Journal of American Ethnic History* 29, no. 3: 40–78.

Bledowski, Kris. 2015. "The Internet of Things: Industrie 4.0 versus the Industrial Internet." MAPI. July 23. https://www.mapi.net/forecasts-data/internet-things-industrie-40-vs-industrial-internet#1.

Bosh, Mariano, and Marco Manacorda. 2012. "Social Policy and Labor Market Outcomes in Latin America and the Caribbean: A Review of Existing Literature." Occasional Paper 32, Centre for Economic Performance, London School of Economics and Political Science. http://cep.lse.ac.uk/pubs/download/occasional/op032.pdf.

Bourgeault, Ivy. 2015. "Double Isolation: Immigrants and Older Adult Care Work in Canada." In *Caring on the Clock: The Complexities and Contradictions of Paid Care Work*, edited by Mignon Duffy, Amy Armenia, and Clare L. Stacey, 117–27. New Brunswick, NJ: Rutgers University Press.

Breman, Jan, and Marcel van der Linden. 2014. "Informalizing the Economy: The Return of the Social Question at the Global Level." *Development and Change* 45, no. 5: 920–40. DOI: http://dx.doi.org/ 10.1111/dech.12115.

Brown, Phillip, and Hugh Lauder. 2013. "Auctioning the Future of Work." *World Policy Journal* 30, no. 20: 16–25. DOI: http://dx.doi.org/10.1177/0740277513494057.

Brynjolfsson, Erik, and Andrew McAfee. 2012. *Race against the Machine: How the Digital Revolution Is Accelerating Innovation, Driving Productivity, and Irreversibly Transforming Employment and the Economy*. Lexington, MA: Digital Frontier Press.

——. 2014. *The Second Machine Age. Work, Progress and Prosperity in a Time of Brilliant Technologies*. New York: W. W. Norton.

Budig, Michelle J., and Joya Misra. 2010. "How Care Work Employment Shapes Earnings in Cross National Perspective." *International Labour Review* 149, no. 4: 441–60. DOI: http://dx.doi.org/ 10.1111/j.1564-913X.2010.00097.x.

Burgoon, Brian. 2014. "Immigration, Integration, and Support for Redistribution in Europe." *World Politics* 66, no. 3: 365–405. DOI: http://dx.doi.org/10.1017/S0043887114000100.

Burgoon, Brian, Ferry Koster, and Marcel van Egmond. 2012. "Support for Redistribution and the Paradox of Immigration." *Journal of European Social Policy* 22, no. 3: 288–304. DOI: http://dx.doi.org/10.1177/0958928712440198.

Cai, Fang. 2013. "Approaching a Neoclassical Scenario: The Labor Market in China after the Lewis Turning Point." *China Finance and Economic Review* 1, no. 1.

Calvino, Flavio, and Maria Virgillito. 2016. "The Innovation-Employment Nexus: A Critical Survey of Theory and Empirics." Working Paper, ISI Growth. http://www.isigrowth.eu/wp-content/uploads/2016/03/working_paper_2016_9.pdf.

Carpenter, Dick M., Lisa Knepper, Angela C. Erickson, and John K. Ross. 2012. *License to Work: A National Study of Burdens from Occupational Licensing*. Arlington, VA: Institute for Justice.

Chan, Jeremy. 2015. "Is China Creating a Workforce with No Soft Skills?" *British Council Voices*, March 2. https://www.britishcouncil.org/voices-magazine/china-creating-workforce-no-soft-skills.

Chandra, Vandana, Justin Yifu Lin, and Yan Wang. 2013. "Leading Dragon Phenomenon: New Opportunities for Catch-Up in Low-Income Countries." *Asian Development Review* 30, no. 1: 52–84. DOI: http://dx.doi.org/10.1162/ADEV_a_00003.

Chang, Ha-Joon. 2010. "Hamlet without the Prince of Denmark: How Development Has Disappeared from Today's 'Development' Discourse." In *Towards New Developmentalism: Market as Means rather than Master*, edited by Shahrukh Rafi Khan and Jens Christiansen. London: Routledge.

Chen, Li-Kai, Mona Mourshed, and Andrew Grant. 2013. "The $250 Billion Question: Can China Close the Skills Gap?" McKinsey & Company white paper, June. http://mckinseyonsociety.com/can-china-close-the-skills-gap/.

"China Unveils Robotics Industry Development Plan." 2016. April 28. http://www. marbridgeconsulting.com/marbridgedaily/2016-04-28/article/92091/china_unveils_ robotics_industry_development_plan.

"China's Tight Talent Market: The Skills Shortage May Hinder Growth Warns Hays." 2016. Hays Specialist Recruitment website, April 14. http://www.hays.cn/en/press-releases/HAYS_248696.

Cimadamore, Alberto D., Gabriele Koehler, and Thomas Pogge, eds. 2013. *Poverty Brief 13: Poverty and the Millennium Development Goals: A Critical Assessment and a Look Forward*. Bergen, Norway: Comparative Research Programme on Poverty (CROP).

Cimoli, Mario, Giovanni Dosi, and Joseph Stiglitz. 2009. *Industrial Policy and Development: The Political Economy of Capabilities Accumulation*. Oxford, UK: Oxford University Press.

Citi GPS. 2016. "Technology at Work v2.0." January 26. https://www.citivelocity.com/ citigps/ReportSeries.action?recordId=49.

Clifford, Stephanie. 2013. "U.S. Textile Plants Return, with Floors Largely Empty of People." *New York Times*, September 19. http://www.nytimes.com/2013/09/20/busi ness/us-textile-factories-return.html.

The Conference Board. 2015. *The Conference Board Productivity Brief 2015: Global Productivity Growth Stuck in the Slow Lane with No Signs of Recovery in Sight*. https://www.conference-board.org/retrievefile.cfm?filename=The-Conference-Board-2015-Productivity-Brief.pdf&type=subsite.

The Conference Board. 2016. The Conference Board International Labor Comparisons. https://www.conference-board.org/ilcprogram/.

Cui, Ernan. 2016a. "Behind the Jobs Target." *Ideas, Gavekal Dragonomics* July 11. http://research.gavekal.com/article/behind-jobs-target.

——. 2016b. "How Good Are Those Service Jobs?" *Ideas, Gavekal Dragonomics*, February 11. http://research.gavekal.com/article/how-good-are-those-service-jobs.

Cummins, Matthew, Kalaivani Karunanethy, and Isabel Ortiz. 2015. "Fiscal Space for Social Protection Options to Expand Social Investments in 187 Countries." ESS Working Paper 48. Geneva: ILO. http://www.ilo.org/wcmsp5/groups/public/---ed_ protect/---soc_sec/documents/publication/wcms_383871.pdf.

Cusack, Thomas, Torben Iversen, and Philipp Rehm. 2006. "Risks at Work: The Demand and Supply Sides of Government Redistribution." *Oxford Review of Economic Policy* 22, no. 3: 365–89. DOI: http://dx.doi.org/10.1093/oxrep/grj022.

Cynamon, Barry Z., and Steven M. Fazzari. 2014. "Inequality, the Great Recession, and Slow Recovery." SSRN, October 24. https://papers.ssrn.com/sol3/papers. cfm?abstract_id=2205524.

Das, Mitali, and Papa M. N'Diaye. 2013. "Chronicle of a Decline Foretold: Has China Reached the Lewis Turning Point?." IMF Working Paper 13/26. Washington, DC: International Monetary Fund. https://www.imf.org/~/media/Websites/IMF/imported-full-text-pdf/external/pubs/ft/wp/2013/_wp1326.ashx.

Daugherty, Paul, Prith Banerjee, Walid Negm, and Allan E. Alter. 2015. "Driving Unconventional Growth through the Industrial Internet of Things." New York: Accenture

Technology. https://www.accenture.com/ph-en/_acnmedia/Accenture/next-gen/reas sembling-industry/pdf/Accenture-Driving-Unconventional-Growth-through-IIoT.pdf.

David, Paul. 1990. "The Dynamo and the Computer. A Historical Perspective on the Modern Productivity Paradox." *American Economic Review* 80, no. 2: 355–61.

Deacon, Bob. 2010. *Poverty Brief 2: From the Global Politics of Poverty Alleviation to the Global Politics of Welfare State Rebuilding.* Bergen, Norway: Comparative Research Programme on Poverty (CROP).

Debrott Sánchez, David. 2014. Consumo efectivo de los hogares en salud: resultado de estudios piloto en seis países de América Latina. Santiago: CEPAL.

De Vries, Gaaitzen, Marcel Timmer, and Klaas De Vries. 2015. "Structural Transformation in Africa: Static Gains, Dynamic Losses." *The Journal of Development Studies* 51, no. 6: 674–88. DOI: http://dx.doi.org/10.1080/00220388.2014.997222.

Dewhurst, Martin, and Paul Willmott. 2014. "Manager and Machine: The New Leadership Equation." *McKinsey Quarterly*, September. http://www.mckinsey.com/global-themes/leadership/manager-and-machine.

De Wispelaere, Jurgen, and José A. Noguera. 2012. "On the Political Feasibility of Universal Basic Income." In *Basic Income Guarantee and Politics: International Experiences and Perspectives on the Viability of Income Guarantees*, edited by Richard Caputo, 17–40. New York: Palgrave Macmillan.

Dinh, Hinh T., Vincent Palmade, Vandana Chandra, and Frances Cossar. 2012. *Light Manufacturing in Africa.* Africa Development Forum. Washington, DC: World Bank.

Domar, Evsey D. 1946. "Capital Expansion, Rate of Growth, and Employment." *Econometrica* 14, no. 2: 137–47.

Dosi, Giovanni. 1982. "Technological Paradigms and Technological Trajectories: A Suggested Interpretation of the Determinants and Directions of Technical Change." *Research Policy* 11, no. 3: 147–62. http://EconPapers.repec.org/RePEc:eee:respol:v: 11:y:1982:i:3:p:147-162.

Duffy, Mignon. 2005. "Reproducing Labor Inequalities: Challenges for Feminists Conceptualizing Care at the Intersections of Gender, Race, and Class." *Gender & Society* 19, no. 1: 66–82.

——. 2007. "Doing the Dirty Work: Gender, Race, and Reproductive Labor in Historical Perspective." *Gender & Society* 21, no. 3: 313–36.

——. 2011. *Making Care Count: A Century of Gender, Race, and Paid Care Work.* New Brunswick, NJ: Rutgers University Press.

Duffy, Mignon, Randy Albelda, and Clare Hammonds. 2013. "Counting Care Work: The Empirical and Policy Applications of Care Theory." *Social Problems* 60, no. 2: 145–67.

Durán, Fabio, and José F. Pacheco. 2012. "Fiscal Space and the Extension of Social Protection: Lessons Learnt from Developing Countries." ESS Working Paper 33. Geneva: ILO. http://www.ilo.org/wcmsp5/groups/public/---ed_protect/---soc_sec/documents/publication/wcms_207665.pdf.

Dwyer, Rachel E. 2013. "The Care Economy?: Gender, Economic Restructuring, and Job Polarization in the U.S. Labor Market." *American Sociological Review* 78, no. 3: 390–416. DOI: http://dx.doi.org/10.1177/0003122413487197.

Dzieza, Josh. 2015. "The Rating Game: How Uber and Its Peers Turned Us into Horrible Bosses." *The Verge*, October 28.

Easterly, William. 2005. "What Did Structural Adjustment Adjust?: The Association of Policies and Growth with Repeated IMF and World Bank Adjustment Loans." *Journal of Development Economics* 76, no. 1: 1–22. DOI: https://dx.doi.org/10.1016/j.jdeveco.2003.11.005.

ECLAC. 2007. *Social Cohesion: Inclusion and a Sense of Belonging in Latin America and the Caribbean*. Santiago: Economic Commission for Latin America and the Caribbean.

Eco, Umberto. 1995. "Ur-Fascism." *New York Review of Books*, June 22. http://www.nybooks.com/articles/1995/06/22/ur-fascism/.

Economic Policy Institute. 2016a. "The Productivity-Pay Gap." http://www.epi.org/productivity-pay-gap/.

——. 2016b. "The Top Charts of 2016." http://www.epi.org/publication/the-top-charts-of-2016-13-charts-that-show-the-difference-between-the-economy-we-have-now-and-the-economy-we-could-have/.

Edelman, Marc, Patrick Heller, Richard Sandbrook, and Judith Teichman. 2007. *Social Democracy in the Global Periphery: Origins and Prospects*. Cambridge, UK: Cambridge University Press.

Ekbia, Hamid, and Bonnie A. Nardi. 2012. "Inverse Instrumentality: How Technologies Objectify Patients and Players." In *Materiality and Organizing: Social Interaction in a Technological World*, edited by Paul M. Leonardi, Bonnie A. Nardi, and Jannis Kallinikos, 157–76. Oxford, UK: Oxford University Press.

——. 2014. "Heteromation and Its (Dis)contents: The Invisible Division of Labour between Humans and Machines." *First Monday* 19, no. 6, June. DOI: http://dx.doi.org/10.5210/fm.v19i6.5331.

England, Paula, Michelle Budig, and Nancy Folbre. 2002. "Wages of Virtue: The Relative Pay of Care Work." *Social Problems* 49, no. 4: 455–73.

Erikson, Robert, and John Goldthorpe. 1992. *The Constant Flux: A Study of Class Mobility in Industrial Societies*. Oxford, UK: Oxford University Press.

Ernst, Dieter. 2009. *A New Geography of Knowledge in the Electronics Industry?: Asia's Role in Global Innovation Networks*. East-West Center Policy Studies, No. 54. http://www.eastwestcenter.org/publications/new-geography-knowledge-electronics-industry-asias-role-global-innovation-networks.

——. 2011a. "China's Innovation Policy Is a Wake-Up Call for America." Asia Pacific Issues 100, May. East-West Center. http://papers.ssrn.com/sol3/papers.cfm?abstract_id=2770063.

——. 2011b. *Indigenous Innovation and Globalization: The Challenge for China's Standardization Strategy*. La Jolla, CA: UC Institute on Global Conflict and Cooperation; Honolulu: East-West Center. http://www.eastwestcenter.org/publications/indigenous-innovation-and-globalization-challenge-chinas-standardization-strategy.

——. 2015. *From Catching Up to Forging Ahead: China's Policies for Semiconductors*. East-West Center Special Study, September. http://www.eastwestcenter.org/system/tdf/private/ernst-semiconductors2015_0.pdf?file=1&type=node&id=35320.

Esping-Andersen, Gosta. 1990. *The Three Worlds of Welfare Capitalism*. Princeton, NJ: Princeton University Press.

Fairfield, Tasha. 2014. "The Political Economy of Progressive Tax Reform in Chile." *Woodrow Wilson Center Update on the Americas*, March.

———. 2015. *Private Wealth and Public Revenue in Latin America. Business Power and Tax Politics.* Cambridge, UK: Cambridge University Press.

Farhoomand, Ali, and Saurabh Bhatnagar. 2008. "ITC e-Choupal: Corporate Social Responsibility in Rural India." Harvard Business Review case study.

Farrell, Diana, and Andrew Grant. 2005. "Addressing China's Looming Talent Shortage." McKinsey Global Institute (MGI). http://www.mckinsey.com/global-themes/china/addressing-chinas-looming-talent-shortage.

Federal Reserve Economic Data (FRED). Federal Reserve Bank of St. Louis. https://fred.stlouisfed.org/.

Felipe, Jesus, Aahish Mehta, and Changyong Rhee. 2014. "Manufacturing Matters . . . But It's Jobs That Count." ADB Economics Working Paper 420. Manila: Asian Development Bank. https://www.adb.org/sites/default/files/publication/149984/ewp-420.pdf.

Feng, Shuaizhang, Yingyao Hu, and Robert Moffitt. 2015. "Long Run Trends in Unemployment and Labor Force Participation in China." NBER Working Paper 21460. Cambridge, MA: National Bureau of Economic Research. http://www.nber.org/papers/w21460.

Ferreira, Francisco, Luis F. López-Calva, Maria Ana Lugo, Julian Messina, Jamele Rigolini, and Renos Vakis. 2013. *Economic Mobility and the Rise of the Latin American Middle-Class.* Washington, DC: World Bank.

Filgueira, Fernando. 2007. "The Latin American Social States: Critical Juncture and Critical Choices." In *Democracy and Social Policy*, edited by Yusuf Bangura, 136–63. New York: Palgrave/UNRISD.

Filgueira, Fernando, Carlos Molina, Jorge Papadópulos, and Federico Tobar. 2006. "Universalismo Básico: Una Alternativa Posible Y Necesaria Para Mejorar Las Condiciones De Vida." In *Universalismo Básico. Una Nueva Política Social Para América Latina*, edited by Carlos Gerardo Molina, 19–58. Washington, DC: Inter-American Development Bank.

Filmer, Deon, and Louise Fox, with Karen Brooks, Aparajita Goyal, Taye Mengistae, Patrick Premand, Dena Ringold, Siddharth Sharma, and Sergiy Zorya. 2014. *Youth Employment in Sub-Saharan Africa.* Washington, DC: World Bank.

Folbre, Nancy. 2006. "Nursebots to the Rescue? Immigration, Automation, and Care." *Globalizations* 3, no. 3: 349–60. DOI: http://dx.doi.org/10.1080/14747730600870217.

———. 2012. *For Love and Money: Care Provision in the United States.* New York: Russell Sage Foundation.

Ford, Martin. 2009. *The Lights in the Tunnel: Automation, Accelerating Technology and the Economy of the Future.* Sunnyvale, CA: Acculant.

———. 2015. *Rise of the Robots: Technology and the Threat of a Jobless Future.* New York: Basic Books.

Freeman, Chris, and Carlota Perez. 1988. "Structural Crises of Adjustment, Business Cycles and Investment Behaviour." In *Technical Change and Economic Theory*, edited by Giovanni Dosi, 38–66. London: Francis Pinter.

Freeman, Richard. 2006. "The Challenge of the Growing Globalization of Labor Markets to Economic and Social Policy." In *Global Capitalism Unbound. Winners and Losers from Offshore Outsourcing*, edited by Eva Paus, 23–39. New York: Palgrave Macmillan.

——. 2016a. "A Tale of Two Clones." *Third Way*, Sept 27. http://www.thirdway.org/report/a-tale-of-two-clones.

——. 2016b. "Who Owns the Robots Rules the World: The Deeper Threat of Robotization." *Harvard Magazine*, May–June. http://harvardmagazine.com/2016/05/who-owns-the-robots-rules-the-world.

Frey, Carl Benedikt. 2014. "Creative Destruction at Work." *Project Syndicate*, July 15. https://www.project-syndicate.org/commentary/carl-b--frey-assesses-how-technological-change-is-transforming-the-structure-of-employment.

Frey, Carl Benedikt, and Michael Osborne. 2013. "The Future of Employment: How Susceptible Are Jobs to Computerisation?" Oxford Martin School, Programme on the Impacts of Future Technology, September 17. http://www.oxfordmartin.ox.ac.uk/downloads/academic/future-of-employment.pdf.

——. 2017. "The Future of Employment: How Susceptible Are Jobs to Computerisation?" *Technological Forecasting and Social Change* 114: 254–80. http://dx.doi.org/10.1016/j.techfore.2016.08.019.

Fromm, Eric. 1949. *Escape from Freedom*. New York: Henry Holt.

——. 1976. *To Have or to Be?: A New Blueprint for Mankind*. New York: Harper and Row.

Fukuyama, Francis. 1992. *The End of History and the Last Man*. New York: Avon.

"The Future of Agriculture." 2016. *The Economist*, June 9. http://www.economist.com/technology-quarterly/2016-06-09/factory-fresh.

"The Gap Widens Again." 2012. *The Economist*, March 10. http://www.economist.com/node/21549944.

Gardels, Nathan. 2017. "Weekend Roundup: A Tale of Two Globalizations." *HuffPost/The WorldPost*, June 10. http://www.huffingtonpost.com/entry/weekend-roundup-173_us_593aacd6e4b0240268788e70.

Garling, Caleb. 2014. "Hunting Task Wabbits." Medium.com, December 2.

Gelb, Alan, Christian J. Meyer, and Vijaya Ramachandran. 2014. "Development as Diffusion: Manufacturing Productivity and Africa's Missing Middle." Working Paper 357. Washington, DC: Center for Global Development.

Gerencer, Tom. 2015. "The Net Worth of Congress." *MoneyNation*, November 12. http://moneynation.com/the-net-worth-of-congress/.

Ghani, Ejaz, Arti Grover Goswami, and Homi Kharas. 2012. "Service with a Smile." Economic Premise 96. Washington, DC: World Bank.

Gilens, Martin, and Benjamin I. Page. 2014. "Testing Theories of American Politics: Elites, Interest Groups, and Average Citizens." *American Political Science Review* 12, no. 3: 564–81. DOI: https://dx.doi.org/10.1017/S1537592714001595.

Glaser, April. 2017. "Six Jobs Are Eliminated for Every Robot Introduced into the Economy, a New Study Says." Recode, March 28. https://www.recode.net/2017/3/28/15094424/jobs-eliminated-new-robots-workforce-industrial.

Glenn, Evelyn Nakano. 2010. *Forced to Care: Coercion and Caregiving in America*. Cambridge, MA: Harvard University Press.

Goldin, Claudia, and Lawrence F. Katz. 2008. *The Race between Education and Technology: The Evolution of U.S. Educational Wage Differentials, 1890 to 2005*. Cambridge, MA: Harvard University Press.

Goldsmith, Scott. 2012. "The Economic and Social Impacts of the Permanent Fund Dividend on Alaska." In *Alaska's Permanent Fund Dividend: Examining Its Suitability as a Model*, edited by Michael W. Howard and Karl Widerquist, 49–63. New York: Palgrave Macmillan.

Goñi, Edwin, Humberto López, and Luis Servén. 2011. "Fiscal Redistribution and Income Inequality in Latin America." *World Development* 39, no. 9: 1558–69.

Goos, Maarten, and Alan Manning. 2007. "Lousy and Lovely Jobs: The Rising Polarization of Work in Britain." *Review of Economics and Statistics* 89, no. 1: 118–33. DOI: http://dx.doi.org/10.1162/rest.89.1.118.

Goos, Maarten, Alan Manning, and Anna Salomons. 2014. "Explaining Job Polarization: Routine-Biased Technological Change and Offshoring." *American Economic Review* 104: 2509–26. DOI: http://dx.doi.org/10.1257/aer.104.8.2509.

Gordon, Robert. 2016. *The Rise and Fall of American Growth*. Princeton, NJ: Princeton University Press.

Graetz, Georg, and Guy Michaels. 2015. "Robots at Work." Discussion paper 1335, LSE Centre for Economic Performance. http://cep.lse.ac.uk/pubs/download/dp 1335.pdf.

Gramsci, Antonio. 1971. *Selections from the Prison Notebooks of Antonio Gramsci*. Edited and translated by Quinton Hoare and Geoffrey Nowell Smith. New York: International Publishers. https://archive.org/stream/AntonioGramsciSelectionsFrom-ThePrisonNotebooks/Antonio-Gramsci-Selections-from-the-Prison-Notebooks_djvu.txt.

Hacker, Jacob, and Paul Pierson. 2011. *Winner-Take-All Politics*. New York: Simon and Schuster.

Haggard, Stephan, and Robert Kaufman. 2008. *Development, Democracy, and Welfare States: Latin America, East Asia, and Eastern Europe*. Princeton, NJ: Princeton University Press.

Haggard, Stephan, and Nita Rudra. 2005. "Globalization, Democracy, and Effective Welfare Spending in the Developing World." *Comparative Political Studies* 38, no. 9: 1015–49.

Hall, Anthony. 2008. "Brazil's Bolsa Familia: A Double-Edged Sword?" *Development and Change* 39, no. 5: 799–822.

Hall, Jonathan V., and Alan B. Krueger. 2015. "An Analysis of the Labor Market for Uber's Driver-Partners in the United States." Working Paper 587. Princeton University, Industrial Relations Section.

Hangler, Frank, and Gili Vidan. 2014. "Global Mobile Broadband Prices ($/GB, USD PPP, 2014 Data)." http://hangler.net/mobile-broadband/. Adapted from Google's International Broadband Pricing Survey.

Harris, Seth D., and Alan B. Krueger. 2015. "A Proposal for Modernizing Labor Laws for Twenty-First-Century Work: The 'Independent Worker.'" The Hamilton Project Discussion Paper 2015–10. Washington DC: Brookings Institute.

Harrison, Ann, and Andres Rodríguez-Clare. 2010. "Trade, Foreign Investment, and Industrial Policy for Developing Countries." In *Handbook of Development Economics* Vol. 5, edited by Dani Rodrik and Mark Rosenzweig, 4039–214. Amsterdam: North-Holland.

Harrison, J. D. 2013. "Who Actually Creates Jobs: Start-Ups, Small Businesses, or Big Corporations?" *Washington Post*, April 25. https://www.washingtonpost.com/business/on-small-business/who-actually-creates-jobs-start-ups-small-businesses-or-big-corporations/2013/04/24/d373ef08-ac2b-11e2-a8b9-2a63d75b5459_story.html.

Häusermann, Silja, Thomas Kurer, and Hanna Schwander. 2015. "High-Skilled Outsiders? Labor Market Vulnerability, Education and Welfare State Preferences." *Socio-Economic Review* 13, no. 2: 235–58. DOI: https://dx.doi.org/10.1093/ser/mwu026.

"Health Expenditure—Total (% of GDP) in Latin America and Caribbean." 2016. Trading Economics Indicators. http://www.tradingeconomics.com/latin-america-and-caribbean/health-expenditure-total-percent-of-gdp-wb-data.html.

Heng, Stefan, and Jan Trenczek. 2015. "Industry 4.0: China Seizes an Outstanding Opportunity in the 'Year of Innovation.'" Deutsche Bank website, June 18.

Hochschild, Arlie Russell. 2002. "Love and Gold." In *Global Woman: Nannies, Maids and Sex Workers in the New Economy*, edited by Barbara Ehrenreich and Arlie Russell Hochschild, 15–31. New York: Henry Holt.

Holz, Carsten A. 2015. "China's Investment Rate: Implications and Data Reliability." MPRA Paper 68120. https://mpra.ub.uni-muenchen.de/68120/.

Hondagneu-Sotelo, Pierrette. 2007. *Doméstica: Immigrant Workers Cleaning and Caring in the Shadows of Affluence*. Berkeley: University of California Press.

"Hours and Earnings in Private Nonagricultural Industries, 1966–2012." 2013. *Economic Report of the President*, Table B-47. Washington, DC: Executive Office of the President, Council of Economic Advisers.

Howard, Michael W., and Karl Widerquist, eds. 2012. *Alaska's Permanent Fund Dividend: Examining Its Suitability as a Model*. New York: Palgrave Macmillan.

Hoy, Chris, and Andy Sumner. 2016. "Global Poverty and Inequality: Is There a New Capacity for Redistribution in Developing Countries?" *Journal of Globalization and Development* 7, no. 1: 117–57.

Huber, Evelyne. 2002. *Models of Capitalism. Lessons for Latin America*. University Park: Pennsylvania State University Press.

Huber, Evelyne, and John D. Stephens. 2012. *Democracy and the Left: Social Policy and Inequality in Latin America*. Chicago: University of Chicago Press.

Hullinger, Jessica. 2016. "16 Things You Might Not Know about Uber and Its Drivers." *mentalfloss.com*, January 19.

Huws, Ursula, and Simon Joyce. 2016. "Size of the UK's 'Gig Economy' Revealed for the First Time." Crowd Working Survey, University of Hertfordshire. February.

Industrial Research Institute (IRI). 2016. Global R&D Funding Forecast, Winter. https://www.iriweb.org/sites/default/files/2016GlobalR%26DFundingForecast_2.pdf.

International Labour Organization. 1990. *International Standard Classification of Occupations: ISCO-88*. Geneva: ILO.

——. 2013a. *Global Wage Report, 2012/13*. Geneva: ILO.

——. 2013b. *Women and Men in the Informal Economy: A Statistical Picture*. Geneva: ILO/WIEGO.

International Labour Organization and Organisation for Economic Co-operation and Development (ILO/OECD). 2015. "The Labour Share in G-20 Economies."

Geneva: ILO/OECD. https://www.oecd.org/g20/topics/employment-and-social-policy/
The-Labour-Share-in-G20-Economies.pdf.

International Telecommunication Union. 2016. *Measuring the Information Society Report*. Geneva: ITU.

Intuit. 2008. "The New Artisan Economy." The Intuit Future of Small Business Series SR-1037C. http://http-download.intuit.com/http.intuit/CMO/intuit/futureofsmall business/SR-1037C_intuit_future_sm_bus.pdf.

Iversen, Torben, and Thomas R. Cusack. 2000. "The Causes of Welfare State Expansion: Deindustrialization or Globalization?" *World Politics* 52: 313–49. DOI: https://dx.doi.org/10.1017/S0043887100016567.

Iversen, Torben, and David Soskice. 2001. "An Asset Theory of Social Policy Preferences." *American Political Science Review* 95, no. 4: 875–93.

——. 2009. "Distribution and Redistribution: The Shadow of the Nineteenth Century." *World Politics* 61, no. 3: 438–86. DOI: https://dx.doi.org/10.1017/S0043887 10900015X.

Jackman, Sophie. 2015. "Crowdsourcing May Hold Key to Unlocking Japan's Working Potential." *Japan News*. January 2.

Jacobson, Margaret, and Filippo Occhino. 2012. "Behind the Decline in Labor's Share of Income." Federal Reserve Bank of Cleveland website. February 3.

Kabeer, Naila, Caio Piza, and Linnet Taylor. 2012. "What Are the Economic Impacts of Conditional Cash Transfer Programmes?: A Systematic Review of the Evidence." Technical report. London: EPPI-Centre, Social Science Research Unit, Institute of Education, University of London.

Karabarbounis, Loukas and Brent Neiman. 2013. "The Global Decline of the Labor Share." NBER Working Paper 19136. Cambridge, MA: National Bureau of Economic Research.

——. 2014. "The Global Decline in the Labor Share." *Quarterly Journal of Economics* 129, no. 1: 61–103.

Karsten, Jack, and Darrell M. West. 2015. "New Skills Needed for New Manufacturing Technology." Brookings Institution website, July 15. https://www.brookings.edu/blog/techtank/2015/07/15/new-skills-needed-for-new-manufacturing-technology/.

Katz, Lawrence. 2014. "Get a Liberal Arts B.A., Not a Business B.A., for the Coming Artisan Economy." PBS.org, July 15. http://www.pbs.org/newshour/making-sense/get-a-liberal-arts-b-a-not-a-business-b-a-for-the-coming-artisan-economy/.

Katz, Lawrence F., and Alan B. Krueger. 2016. "The Rise and Nature of Alternative Work Arrangements in the United States, 1995–2015." NBER Working Paper 22667. Cambridge, MA: National Bureau of Economic Research.

Keisner, C. Andrew, Julio Raffo, and Sacha Wunsch-Vincent. 2015. "Breakthrough Technologies—Robotics, Innovation and Intellectual Property." WIPO Economic Research Working Paper 30, November. Geneva: World Intellectual Property Organization. http://www.wipo.int/publications/en/details.jsp?id=4001.

Kenworthy, Lane. 2011. *Progress for the Poor*. Oxford, UK: Oxford University Press.

Keynes, John Maynard. 1930. "Economic Possibilities for Our Grandchildren." In *Essays in Persuasion*. 1963, 358–73. New York: W. W. Norton. http://www.econ.yale.edu/smith/econ116a/keynes1.pdf.

Kiggundu, Rose. 2006. "Technological Change in Uganda's Fishery Exports." In *Technology, Adaptation and Exports: How Some Developing Countries Got It Right*, edited by Vandana Chandra, 301–34. Washington, DC: World Bank.

Kitschelt, Herbert, and Philipp Rehm. 2014. "Occupations as a Site of Political Preference Formation." *Comparative Political Studies* 47, no. 12: 1670–1706. DOI: https://dx.doi.org/10.1177/0010414013516066.

Kittur, Aniket, Jeffrey V. Nickerson, Michael S. Bernstein, Elizabeth M. Gerber, Aaron Shaw, John Zimmerman, Matthew Lease, and John J. Horton. 2013. "The Future of Crowd Work." *Proceedings of the 2013 Conference on Computer Supported Cooperative Work*, 1301–18. New York: ACM.

Klorer, Elena, and Mattias Stepan. 2015. "Off Target: China's Vocational Education and Training System Threatens the Country's Rise to Industrial Superpower Status." *MERICS China Monitor* 24, October 2. Mercator Institute for China Studies. https://www.merics.org/fileadmin/templates/download/china-monitor/China_Monitor_No_24_EN.pdf.

Kofman, Michael, and Andrei Sushentsov. 2016. "What Makes a Great Power War Possible." *Russia in Global Affairs*, June 17. http://eng.globalaffairs.ru/number/What-Makes-A-Great-Power-War-Possible-18241.

Korpi, Walter, and Joachim Palme. 1998. "The Paradox of Redistribution and Strategies of Equality: Welfare State Institutions, Inequality, and Poverty in the Western Countries." *American Sociological Review* 63, no. 5: 661–87.

Krugman, Paul. 2013. "Sympathy for the Luddites." *New York Times*, June 13. http://www.nytimes.com/2013/06/14/opinion/krugman-sympathy-for-the-luddites.html.

Lall, Sanjaya. 1992. "Technological Capabilities and Industrialization." *World Development* 20, no. 2, 165–86. http://EconPapers.repec.org/RePEc:eee:wdevel:v:20:y:1992:i:2:p:165-186.

Lall, Sanjaya, Manuel Albaladejo, and Jinkang Zhang. 2004. "Mapping Fragmentation: Electronics and Automobiles in East Asia and Latin America." *Oxford Development Studies* 32, no. 3: 407–32. DOI: http://dx.doi.org/10.1080/1360081042000260601.

LaPlante, Rochelle, and Six Silberman. 2015. "Design Notes for a Future Crowd Work Market." *medium.com*. February 13.

Lawrence, Jennifer. 2015. "What Scarce Labor Means for Talent Development in China." US-China Business Council, June 1. https://www.chinabusinessreview.com/what-scarce-labor-means-for-talent-recruitment-in-china-best-practices/.

Lawrence, Robert Z., and Lawrence Edwards. 2013. "US Employment Deindustrialization: Insights from History and the International Experience." Policy Brief PB 13–27. October. Washington, DC: Peterson Institute for International Economics.

Lederman, Daniel, and William Francis Maloney. 2012. *Does What You Export Matter?: In Search of Empirical Guidance for Industrial Policies*. Washington, DC: World Bank.

Lee, Xin En. 2014. "Unemployment in China: Degree to Nowhere?" CKGSB Knowledge website, July 21. http://knowledge.ckgsb.edu.cn/2014/07/21/employment/unemployment-in-china-degree-to-nowhere/.

Lehoucq, Fabrice. 2012. *The Politics of Modern Central America: Civil War, Democratization and Underdevelopment*. Cambridge, UK: Cambridge University Press.

Levine, Steve. 2017. "No One Is Prepared to Stop the Robot Onslaught. So What Will We Do When It Arrives?" *Quartz*, April 14. https://qz.com/940977/no-one-is-prepared-to-stop-the-robot-onslaught-so-what-will-we-do-when-it-arrives/.

Levy, Steven. 2012. "Can an Algorithm Write a Better News Story Than a Human Reporter?" *Wired*, April 24. http://www.wired.com/2012/04/can-an-algorithm-write-a-better-news-story-than-a-human-reporter/all/.

Lewis, Sinclair. 1935. *It Can't Happen Here*. New York: Doubleday, Doran.

Lichbach, Mark. 1989. "An Evaluation of 'Does Economic Inequality Breed Political Conflict?' Studies." *World Politics* 41: 431–70. DOI: http://dx.doi.org/10.2307/2010526.

Lightman, Naomi. 2016. "Discounted Labour? Disaggregating Care Work in Comparative Perspective." *International Labour Review* (forthcoming). DOI: http://dx.doi.org/10.1111/ilr.12001.

Lin, Justin Yifu. 2011. "New Structural Economics: A Framework for Rethinking Development." *The World Bank Research Observer* 26, no. 2: 193–221. DOI: http://dx.doi.org/10.1093/wbro/lkr007.

Lin, Justin Yifu, and Célestin Monga. 2010. "Growth Identification and Facilitation: The Role of the State in the Dynamics of Structural Change." Policy Research Working Paper Series 5313. Washington, DC: World Bank. DOI: http://dx.doi.org/10.1596/1813-9450-5313.

List, Friedrich. 1841. *Das nationale System der politischen Oekonomie*. Stuttgart: J. G. Cotta'schen.

"Made to Measure." 2015. *The Economist*, May 30. http://www.economist.com/news/technology-quarterly/21651925-robotic-sewing-machine-could-throw-garment-workers-low-cost-countries-out.

Malerba, Franco, and Luigi Orsenigo. 1996. "The Dynamics and Evolution of Industries." *Industrial and Corporate Change* 5, no. 1: 51–87. DOI: https://dx.doi.org/10.1093/icc/5.1.51.

Maney, Kevin. 2016. "How Artificial Intelligence and Robots Will Radically Transform the Economy." *Newsweek*, November 30.

Manyika, James, Susan Lund, Jacques Bughin, Kelsey Robinson, Jan Mischke, and Deepa Mahajan. 2016. "Independent Work: Choice, Necessity, and the Gig Economy." McKinsey Global Institute, October.

Manyika, James, Susan Lund, Kelsey Robinson, Jan Mischke, Hohn Valentino, and Richard Dobbs. 2015. "Connecting Talent with Opportunity in the Digital Age." McKinsey Global Institute, June. http://www.mckinsey.com/global-themes/employment-and-growth/connecting-talent-with-opportunity-in-the-digital-age.

Markoff, John. 2012. "Skilled Work, without the Worker." *New York Times*, August 18. http://www.nytimes.com/2012/08/19/business/new-wave-of-adept-robots-is-changing-global-industry.html.

Marsili, Orietta, and Bart Verspagen. 2001. "Technological Regimes and Innovation: Looking for Regularities in Dutch Manufacturing." Paper presented at Artigo apresentado em Nelson and Winter Conference, Aalborg, Denmark, June 12. https://www.researchgate.net/publication/228591437_Technological_regimes_and_innovation_looking_for_regularities_in_Dutch_manufacturing.

Martínez-Franzoni, Juliana, and Diego Sánchez-Ancochea. 2013. *Good Jobs and Social Services*. New York: Palgrave Macmillan.

——. 2014. "The Double Challenge of Market and Social Incorporation: Progress and Bottlenecks in Latin America." *Development Policy Review* 32, no. 3: 275–98. DOI: http://dx.doi.org/10.1111/dpr.12055.

——. 2015. "Public Social Services and Income Inequality." In *Labour Markets, Institutions and Inequality: Building Just Societies in the 21st Century*, edited by Janine Berg, 287–312. Cheltenham: Edward Elgar.

——. 2016. *The Quest for Universal Social Policy in the South: Actors, Ideas and Architectures*. Cambridge, UK: Cambridge University Press.

——. Forthcoming. "Achieving Universalism in Developing Countries." Background paper for the 2016 Human Development Report.

Marvit, Moshe Z. 2014. "How Crowdworkers Became the Ghosts in the Digital Machine." *The Nation*. February 5.

Mayer, Jane. 2016. *Dark Money: The Hidden History of the Billionaires behind the Rise of the Radical Right*. New York: Doubleday.

Mazzocchi, Tony. 1993. "A Superfund for Workers." *Earth Island Journal* 9, no. 1: 40–41.

Mazzucato, Mariana, and Carlota Perez. 2014. "Innovation as Growth Policy: The Challenge for Europe." University of Sussex, Science Policy Research Unit Working Paper Series 2014–13. DOI: http://dx.doi.org/10.2139/ssrn.2742164.

McCaig, Brian, and Nina Pavcnik. 2013. "Moving Out of Agriculture: Structural Change in Vietnam." NBER Working Paper Series 19616. Cambridge, MA: National Bureau of Economic Research. DOI: http://dx.doi.org/10.3386/w19616.

McCloskey, Deirdre. 2010. *Bourgeois Dignity and Liberty: Why Economics Can't Explain the Modern World*. Chicago: University of Chicago Press.

McDonald, Mark P. 2013. "Platforms Are the New Foundation of Corporate IT." *Harvard Business Review*, August 1. https://hbr.org/2013/08/from-infrastructure-to-platfor.

McGuire, James. 2010. *Wealth, Health and Democracy in East Asia and Latin America*. Cambridge, UK: Cambridge University Press.

McMillan, Margaret S., and Kenneth Harttgen. 2014. "What Is Driving the African Growth Miracle?" NBER Working Paper 20077. Cambridge, MA: National Bureau of Economic Research.

McMillan, Margaret, Dani Rodrik, and Íñigo Verduzco-Gallo. 2014. "Globalization, Structural Change, and Productivity Growth, with an Update on Africa." *World Development* 63: 11–32.

McNamara, Keith, and Jean Batalova. 2015. "Filipino Immigrants in the United States." Migration Policy Institute website, July 21.

Meltzer, Allan H., and Scott F. Richard. 1981. "A Rational Theory of the Size of Government." *Journal of Political Economy* 89: 914–27.

Mesa-Lago, Carmelo. 1978. *Social Security in Latin America: Pressure Groups, Stratification, and Inequality*. Pittsburgh: University of Pittsburgh Press.

Michaels, Guy, Ashwini Natraj, and John Van Reenen. 2014. "Has ICT Polarized Skill Demand?: Evidence from Eleven Countries over Twenty-Five Years." *Review of Economics and Statistics* 96: 60–77. DOI: http://dx.doi.org/10.1162/REST_a_00366.

Middlehurst, Charlotte. 2015. "Robotics Revolution Rocks Chinese Textile Workers." *Al Jazeera America*, June 16. http://www.aljazeera.com/indepth/features/2015/06/robotics-revolution-rocks-chinese-textile-workers-150614073735531.html.

Milanovic., Branko. 2011. *The Have and the Have Nots: A Brief and Idiosyncratic History of Global Inequality.* New York: Basic Books.

——. 2016. *Global Inequality: A New Approach for the Age of Globalization.* Cambridge, MA: Harvard University Press.

Mishel, Lawrence. 2015. "Uber Is Not the Future of Work." *The Atlantic.* November 15.

Mishel, Lawrence, and Josh Bivens. 2017. "The Zombie Robot Argument Lurches On." Economic Policy Institute website, May 24. http://www.epi.org/publication/the-zombie-robot-argument-lurches-on-there-is-no-evidence-that-automation-leads-to-joblessness-or-inequality/.

Mkandawire, Thandika. 2006a. *Social Policy in a Development Context.* Geneva: United Nations Research Institute for Social Development (UNRISD).

——. 2006b. *Targeting and Universalism in Poverty Reduction.* Geneva: United Nations Research Institute for Social Development (UNRISD).

Moene, Karl Ove, and Michael Wallerstein. 2001. "Inequality, Social Insurance, and Redistribution." *American Political Science Review* 95, no. 4: 859–74.

Mokyr, Joel. 2002. *The Gifts of Athena: Historical Origins of the Knowledge Economy.* Princeton, NJ: Princeton University Press.

Molina, Carlos Gerardo. 2006. *Universalismo básico: una nueva política social para América Latina.* México, DF: Editorial Planeta Mexicana.

National Academy of Engineering. 2012. *Making Value: Integrating Manufacturing, Design, and Innovation to Thrive in the Changing Global Economy.* Washington, DC: The National Academies Press.

National Development and Reform Commission (NDRC), People's Republic of China. 2016. "The 13th Five-Year Plan for Economic and Social Development of the People's Republic of China (2016–2020)." http://en.ndrc.gov.cn/newsrelease/201612/P020161207645765233498.pdf.

Neubourg, Chris de. 2009. "Social Protection and Nation-Building: An Essay on Why and How Universalist Social Policy Contributes to Stable Nation-States." In *Building Decent Societies: Rethinking the Role of Social Security in State Building*, edited by Peter Townsend, 63–120. Geneva: ILO/Palgrave Macmillan.

Nübler, Irmgard. 2013. "Education Structures and Industrial Development: Lessons for Education Policies in African Countries." Paper presented at the UNU-WIDER Conference on Learning to Compete. Industrial Development and Policy in Africa UNU-WIDER Development Conference, June 24–25, Helsinki, Finland, 2013. https://www.wider.unu.edu/sites/default/files/Events/PDF/Nubler.pdf.

——. 2014. "A Theory of Capabilities for Productive Transformation: Learning to Catch Up." In *Transforming Economies: Making Industrial Policy Work for Growth, Jobs and Development*, edited by José M. Salazar-Xirinachs, Irmgard Nübler, and Richard Kozul-Wright, 113–49. Geneva: ILO.

——. 2016. "New Technologies: A Job-Less Future or a Golden Age of Job Creation?" Working paper 13, Research Department International Labour Organization. http://www.ilo.org/wcmsp5/groups/public/---dgreports/---inst/documents/publication/wcms_544189.pdf.

Nunn, Ryan, 2016. *Occupational Licensing and American Workers.* The Hamilton Project. Washington, DC: Brookings Institute.

O'Connor, Sarah. 2015. "Recovery Prompts Rise in Precarious Job Contracts." *Financial Times*, Aug 5.

Oesch, Daniel. 2006. "Coming to Grips with a Changing Class Structure: An Analysis of Employment Stratification in Britain, Germany, Sweden and Switzerland." *International Sociology* 21, no. 2: 263–88. DOI: https://dx.doi.org/10.1177/02685809 06061379.

———. 2013. *Occupational Change in Europe: How Technology and Education Transform the Job Structure*. Oxford, UK: Oxford University Press.

Organisation for Economic Co-operation and Development (OECD). 2013. *African Economic Outlook 2013: Structural Transformation and Natural Resources*. Paris: OECD.

———. 2016. "Social Expenditure—Aggregated Data." http://stats.oecd.org/Index.aspx? datasetcode=SOCX_AGG.

———. 2017a. "Hours Worked." DOI: http://dx.doi.org/10.1787/47be1c78-en.

———. 2017b. "Trade Union Density." https://stats.oecd.org/Index.aspx?DataSetCode= UN_DEN.

Organization for Economic Cooperation and Development and Economic Commission for Latin America and the Caribbean. 2016. *Revenue Statistics in Latin America and the Caribbean 2016*. Paris: OECD-CEPAL.

O'Rourke, Kevin, and Jeffrey G. Williamson. 1999. *Globalization and History: The Evolution of a Nineteenth-Century Atlantic Economy*. Cambridge, MA: MIT Press.

Ostry, Jonathan D., Prakash Loungani, and Davide Furceri. 2016. "Neoliberalism: Oversold?" *Finance & Development* 53, no. 2 (June): 38–41. http://www.imf.org/ external/pubs/ft/fandd/2016/06/ostry.htm.

Parreñas, Rhacel Salazar. 2001. *Servants of Globalization: Women, Migration, and Domestic Work*. Stanford, CA: Stanford University Press.

Paus, Eva. 2017. "Escaping the Middle Income Trap: Innovate or Perish." Working Paper 685. Tokyo: Asian Development Bank Institute. https://www.adb.org/publications/ escaping-middle-income-trap-innovate-or-perish.

Perez, Carlota. 1983. "Structural Change and Assimilation of New Technologies in the Economic and Social Systems." *Futures* 15, no. 4: 357–75.

———. 2002. *Technological Revolutions and Financial Capital: The Dynamics of Bubbles and Golden Ages*. London: Edward Elgar.

———. 2013. "Financial Bubbles, Crises and the Role of Government in Unleashing Golden Ages." Discussion Paper, FINNOV. No. 2.12. http://policydialogue.org/files/ events/FINNOV_DP212_Perez.pdf.

Pew Research Center. 2015. "The American Middle Class Is Losing Ground." December 9. http://www.pewsocialtrends.org/2015/12/09/the-american-middle-class-is-losing-ground/.

———. 2016. "Campaign Exposes Fissures over Issues, Values, and How Life Has Changed in the U.S." March 31. http://www.people-press.org/2016/03/31/campaign-exposes-fissures-over-issues-values-and-how-life-has-changed-in-the-u-s/.

Pierce, Justin R., and Peter K. Schott. 2012. "The Surprisingly Swift Decline of U.S. Manufacturing Employment." NBER Working Paper 18655, revised January 2014. Cambridge, MA: National Bureau of Economic Research. http://www.nber.org/ papers/w18655.pdf.

Pierson, Christopher, and Francis Castles. 2006. *The Welfare State Reader*. Cambridge, UK: Polity.

Piketty, Thomas. 2014. *Capital in the Twenty-First Century*. Translated by Arthur Goldhammer. Cambridge, MA: Belknap Press.

Polanyi, Karl. 1944. *The Great Transformation: The Political and Economic Origins of Our Time*. Foreword by Robert M. MacIver. Boston, MA: Beacon Press.

Polanyi, Michael. 1958. *Personal Knowledge*. London, Routledge.

"The Politics of Anger." 2016. *The Economist*, July 2. http://www.economist.com/news/leaders/21701478-triumph-brexit-campaign-warning-liberal-international-order-politics.

Pollin, Robert. 2015. *Greening the Global Economy*. Cambridge, MA: MIT Press.

Pollin, Robert, and Shouvik Chakraborty. 2015. "An Egalitarian Green Growth Program for India." Political Economy Research Institute (PERI) Working Paper 389. Amherst, MA: University of Massachusetts Amherst.

Pollin, Robert, Heidi Garrett-Peltier, and Shouvik Chakraborty. 2015. "A Clean Energy Investment Program for Spain." Political Economy Research Institute (PERI) Working Paper 390. Amherst, MA: University of Massachusetts Amherst.

Pollin, Robert, Heidi Garrett-Peltier, James Heintz, and Shouvik Chakraborty. 2015. "Global Green Growth: Clean Energy Industrial Investments and Expanding Job Opportunities." New York: United Nations Industrial Development Organization (UNIDO) and Global Green Growth Institute (GGGI).

Pollin, Robert, Heidi Garrett-Peltier, James Heintz, and Bracken Hendricks. 2014. *Green Growth: A U.S. Program for Controlling Climate Change and Expanding Job Opportunities*. Washington, DC: Center for American Progress.

Pontusson, Jonas. 2005. "Varieties and Commonalities of Capitalism." In *Varieties of Capitalism, Varieties of Approaches*, edited by David Coates, 163–88. New York: Palgrave Macmillan.

Posner, Stefan. 2011. "Leisure Time and Technology." *European History Online*, September 26. http://ieg-ego.eu/en/threads/crossroads/technified-environments/stefan-poser-leisure-time-and-technology.

Prestowitz, Clyde. 2016. "Free Trade Is Dead." *Washington Monthly* June/July/August 2016. http://washingtonmonthly.com/magazine/junejulyaugust-2016/free-trade-is-dead/.

Pribble, Jennifer. 2013. *Welfare and Party Politics in Latin America*. Cambridge, UK: Cambridge University Press.

Pritchett, Lant. 1997. "Divergence, Big Time." *Journal of Economic Perspectives* 11, no. 3: 3–17.

Rehm, Philipp. 2009. "Risks and Redistribution: An Individual-Level Analysis." *Comparative Political Studies* 42, no. 7: 855–81. DOI: https://dx.doi.org/10.1177/0010414008330595.

Renner, Michael, Sean Sweeney, and Jill Kubit. 2008. *Green Jobs: Toward Decent Work in a Sustainable, Low-Carbon World*. Nairobi: United Nations Environmental Programme.

Ricardo, David. 1817. *On the Principles of Political Economy and Taxation*. London: John Murray.

"Rise of the Artisan Entrepreneur." 2014. *Relevant Magazine* 71 (September/October): 46. http://www.relevantmagazine.com/life/maker/rise-artisan-entrepreneur.

Rodrik, Dani. 2011. *The Globalization Paradox: Democracy and the Future of the World Economy.* New York: W. W. Norton.

——. 2013. "Unconditional Convergence in Manufacturing." *Quarterly Journal of Economics* 128, no. 1: 165–204.

——. 2014. "An African Growth Miracle?" The Ninth Annual Richard H. Sabot Lecture. Washington, DC: Center for Global Development. https://www.cgdev.org/publication/african-growth-miracle-ninth-annual-sabot-lecture.

——. 2015. "Premature Deindustrialization." John F. Kennedy School of Government, Harvard University. http://drodrik.scholar.harvard.edu/files/dani-rodrik/files/premature_deindustrialization_revised2.pdf.

Romer, Paul M. 1990. "Endogenous Technological Change." *Journal of Political Economy* 98: S71–102. DOI: http://dx.doi.org/10.1086/261725.

Rosenberg, Mark. 1983. *Las luchas por el seguro social en Costa Rica.* San José: Editorial Costa Rica.

Rosenberg, Nathan. 1993. *Exploring the Black Box: Technology, Economics and History.* Cambridge, UK: Cambridge University Press.

Rosenstone, Steven, and John M. Hansen. 1993. *Mobilization, Participation and Democracy in America.* New York: Macmillan.

Rosin, Hanna. 2010. "The End of Men." *The Atlantic*, July/August: 56–73.

Rueda, David, 2014. "Food Comes First, Then Morals: Redistribution Preferences, Altruism and Group Heterogeneity in Western Europe." Competitive Advantage in the Global Economy (CAGE) Working Paper 200.

Rueda, David, Daniel Segmueller, and Timon Idema. 2014. "The Effects of Income Expectations on Redistribution Preferences in Western Europe." Presented at the Annual Meeting of the American Political Science Association (APSA).

Saez, Emmanuel. 2013. "Striking It Richer: The Evolution of Top Incomes in the United States." University of California, Berkeley. http://elsa.berkeley.edu/~saez/saez-UStopincomes-2012.pdf.

Sanguinetti, Pablo, Lucila Berniell, Fernando Álvarez, Daniel Ortega, Adriana Arreaza, and Michael Penfold. 2012. *RED 2012: Public Finance for Development: Strengthening the Connection between Income and Expenditure.* Caracas: CAF Development Bank of Latin America. http://scioteca.caf.com/handle/123456789/600.

Sassen, Saskia. 2002. "Global Cities and Survival Circuits." In *Global Woman: Nannies, Maids and Sex Workers in the New Economy,* edited by Barbara Ehrenreich and Arlie Russell Hochschild, 254–74. New York: Henry Holt.

Schneider, Aaron. 2012. *State-Building and Tax Regimes in Central America.* Cambridge, UK: Cambridge University Press.

Schneider, Nathan. 2015. "Why the Tech Elite Is Getting behind Universal Basic Income." VICE, January 6. http://www.vice.com/read/something-for-everyone-0000546-v22n1.

Schumpeter, Joseph. 1911. *The Theory of Economic Development: An Inquiry into Profits, Capital, Credit, Interest, and the Business Cycle.* Piscataway, NJ: Transaction.

——. 2008 (1942). *Capitalism, Socialism, and Democracy.* New York: HarperPerennial Modern Thought.

Schwab, Klaus. 2016. "The Fourth Industrial Revolution: What It Means, How to Respond." *World Economic Forum*, January 16. https://www.weforum.org/agenda/2016/01/the-fourth-industrial-revolution-what-it-means-and-how-to-respond/.

Schwartz, Nelson D. 2014. "The Middle Class Is Steadily Eroding. Just Ask the Business World." *New York Times*, February 2. http://www.nytimes.com/2014/02/03/business/the-middle-class-is-steadily-eroding-just-ask-the-business-world.html.

Segura-Ubiergo, Alex. 2007. *The Political Economy of the Welfare State in Latin America*. Cambridge, UK: Cambridge University Press.

Sennett, Richard. 2008. *The Craftsman*. New Haven, CT: Yale University Press.

Shao Yongyu. 2015. "Strategic Vision and Outlook of 'Made in China 2025.'" *Mizuho China Monthly*. Part 1, July. https://www.mizuhobank.com/service/global/cndb/economics/monthly/pdf/R512-0070-XF-0105.pdf. Part 2, September. https://www.mizuhobank.com/service/global/cndb/economics/monthly/pdf/R512-0072-XF-0102.pdf.

Shipp, Stephanie, et al. 2012. "Report on Emerging Global Trends in Advanced Manufacturing." IDA Paper P-4603. Washington, DC: Institute for Defense Analyses–Science Technology Policy Institute (IDA-STPI). https://www.ida.org/idamedia/Corporate/Files/Publications/STPIPubs/ida-p-4603.ashx.

Sinn, Hans-Werner. 1995. "A Theory of the Welfare State." *Scandinavian Journal of Economics* 97, no. 4: 495–526. DOI: http://dx.doi.org/10.2307/3440540.

Slothower, Chuck. 2015. "U.S. Economy Points toward Portland." *Durango Herald*, April 8. http://www.durangoherald.com/article/20150408/NEWS01/150409653/Portland-professor:-Artisan-economy-expanding.

Smith, Adam. 1790 (1759). *The Theory of Moral Sentiments*, Sixth Edition. London: A. Millar. Accessed at: http://www.econlib.org/library/Smith/smMS1.html.

Socha, Karolina. 2010. "Physician Dual Practice and the Public Health Care Provision." Health Economics Working Paper 2010:4. The Research Unit of Health Economics, University of South Denmark. http://www.sdu.dk/-/media/files/om_sdu/centre/cohere/working+papers/20104.pdf.

Solow, Robert. 1987. "We'd Better Watch Out." *New York Review of Books*, July 12.

Solt, Frederick. 2014. "The Standardized World Income Inequality Database." Working paper SWIID version 5.0 2014.

Sommeiller, Estelle, Mark Price, and Ellis Wazeter. 2016. "Income Inequality in the U.S. by State, Metropolitan Area, and Country." Washington, DC: Economic Policy Institute, June 16. http://www.epi.org/publication/income-inequality-in-the-us/.

Song, Jae, David J. Price, Fatih Guvenen, Nicholas Bloom, and Till von Wachter. 2015. "Firming Up Inequality." NBER Working Paper 21199. Cambridge, MA: National Bureau of Economic Research. https://www.nber.org/papers/w21199.pdf.

Spitz-Oener, Alexandra. 2006. "Technical Change, Job Tasks, and Rising Educational Demands: Looking outside the Wage Structure." *Journal of Labor Economics* 24: 235–70. DOI: http://dx.doi.org/10.1086/499972.

Standing, Guy. 2009. *Work after Globalization: Building Occupational Citizenship*. Cheltenham, UK: Edward Elgar.

——. 2011. *The Precariat: The New Dangerous Class*. London: Bloomsbury.

——. 2014. *A Precariat Charter: From Denizens to Citizens*. London: Bloomsbury Academic.

——. 2016. *The Corruption of Capitalism: Why Rentiers Thrive and Work Does Not Pay*. London: Biteback.

——. 2017. *Basic Income*. New Haven, CT: Yale University Press.

State Council of the People's Republic of China. 2017. "How Mass Entrepreneurship and Innovation Shaped 2016." January 27. http://english.gov.cn/premier/news/2017/01/27/content_281475552844391.htm.

Stern, Andy, with Lee Kravits. 2016. *Raising the Floor: How a Universal Basic Income Can Renew Our Economy and Rebuild the American Dream*. New York: Perseus Books.

Stone, Katherine V. W. 2017. "Unions in the Precarious Economy: How Collective Bargaining Can Help Gig and On-Demand Workers." *American Prospect*, February 21: 97–100.

Streitfeld, David. 2014. "Airbnb Listings Mostly Illegal, New York State Contends." *New York Times*, October 15.

Strietska-Ilina, Olga, Christine Hofmann, Mercedes Durán Haro, and Shinyoung Jeon. 2011. *Skills for Green Jobs: A Global View*. Geneva: ILO.

"Study on Monitoring Chinese Industry 4.0 Technology and Patents—Results Published." 2015. Fraunhofer Institute of Industrial Engineering. June 24. http://www.iao.fraunhofer.de/lang-en/technology-innovation-management/iao-news/1230-top-50-chinese-industry-4-0-patents.html.

Susskind, Richard, and Daniel Susskind. 2015. *The Future of Professions: How Technology Will Transform the Work of Human Experts*. Oxford, UK: Oxford University Press.

Sutton, John, and Nebil Kellow. 2010. *An Enterprise Map of Ethiopia*. London: International Growth Center.

Thewissen, Stefan, and David Rueda. Forthcoming. "Automation and the Welfare State. Technological Change as a Determinant of Redistribution Preferences." Comparative Political Studies.

Thewissen, Stefan, and Olaf van Vliet. Forthcoming. "Competing with the Dragon: Employment and Wage Effects of Chinese Trade Competition in 17 Sectors across 18 OECD Countries." Political Science Research and Methods.

Thomas, Robert. Alex Kass. and Ladan Davarzani. 2014. "From Looking Digital to Being Digital: The Impact of Technology on the Future of Work." New York: Accenture Technology. https://www.accenture.com/t20150523T023643__w__/us-en/_acnmedia/Accenture/Conversion-Assets/DotCom/Documents/Global/PDF/Dual-pub_11/Accenture-Impact-of-Technology-April-2014.pdf.

Thompson, Derek. 2015. "A World without Work." *The Atlantic*, July-August. https://www.theatlantic.com/magazine/archive/2015/07/world-without-work/395294/.

Timmer, Marcel P., Erik Dietzenbacher, Bart Los, Robert Stehrer, and Gaaitzen de Vries. 2015. "An Illustrated User Guide to the World Input–Output Database: The Case of Global Automotive Production." *Review of International Economics* 23: 575–605.

Timmer, Marcel P., Bart Los, and Gaaitzen de Vries. 2014. "Incomes and Jobs in Global Production of Manufactures." Paper presented at the Third World KLEMS Conference, Tokyo, Japan, May 19–20. http://www.worldklems.net/conferences/worldklems2014/worldklems2014_De_Vries.pdf.

Timmer, Marcel P., Bart Los, Robert Stehrer, and Gaaitzen de Vries. 2013. "Fragmentation, Incomes and Jobs: An Analysis of European Competitiveness." European Central Bank Working Paper 1615. https://www.ecb.europa.eu/pub/pdf/scpwps/ecbwp1615.pdf?5a69eadb888a7325159cf5e3dd42af82.

Tung, Irene, Janneth Lathrop, and Paul Sonn. 2015. "The Growing Movement for $15." National Employment Law Project. http://www.nelp.org/content/uploads/Growing-Movement-for-15-Dollars.pdf.

UNESCO Institute for Statistics. 2013. *EdStats 2013*. Paris: United Nations Educational, Scientific and Cultural Organization.

United Nations Development Programme. 2015. *Human Development Report: Work for Human Development*. Edited by Selim Jahan. New York: UNDP.

United Nations Industrial Development Organization (UNIDO). 2005. *Industrial Development Report: Capability Building for Catching Up: Historical, Empirical and Policy Dimensions*. Vienna: UNIDO.

United Nations, Population Division. 2013. *World Population Prospects: 2012 Revision, Methodology of the United Nations Population Estimates and Projections*. New York: United Nations.

Upwork and Freelancers Union. 2016. "Freelancing in America 2016." Mountain View, CA: Upwork. https://www.upwork.com/i/freelancing-in-america/2016/.

US Bureau of Labor Statistics. 2011. "The Compensation-Productivity Gap." *TED: The Economics Daily*, February 24. http://www.bls.gov/opub/ted/2011/ted_20110224.htm.

——. 2015. "2015 Wage Data and 2014–2024 Employment Projections." Washington, DC: US Department of Labor.

——. 2016. "Fastest-Growing Occupations." In *Occupational Outlook Handbook*. http://www.bls.gov/ooh/fastest-growing.htm.

——. 2017. "Economic News Release. Job Opening and Labor Turnover Summary." May 9. https://www.bls.gov/news.release/jolts.nr0.htm.

"US Companies Increasingly Turning to Temporary Workers to Fill Positions." 2013. Associated Press, July 8.

Valenzuela, Samuel. 2006a. "Demografía familiar y desarrollo. Chile y Suecia desde 1914." In *El eslabón perdido. Familia, modernización y bienestar en Chile*, edited by Samuel Valenzuela, Eugenio Tironi, and Timothy Scully, 97–136. Santiago de Chile: Taurus.

——. 2006b. "Diseños dispares, resultados diferentes y convergencias tardías. Las instituciones de bienestar social en Chile y Suecia." In *El eslabón perdido. Familia, modernización y bienestar en Chile*, edited by Samuel Valenzuela, Eugenio Tironi, and Timothy Scully, 359–430. Santiago de Chile: Taurus.

Vanderborght, Yannick. 2004. "Universal Basic Income in Belgium and the Netherlands: Implementation through the Back Door." EUI Working paper SPS 2004/4, Department of Political and Social Sciences, European University Institute, Florence. http://cadmus.eui.eu/bitstream/handle/1814/1875/sps2004-04.pdf.

Van Parijs, Phillipe, and Yannick Vanderborght. 2017. *Basic Income: A Radical Proposal for a Free Society and a Sane Economy*. Cambridge, MA: Harvard University Press.

Van Zandweghe, Willem. 2012. "Interpreting the Recent Decline in Labor Force Participation." Federal Reserve Bank of Kansas City Economic Review. QI: 5–34.

Verba, Sidney, Norman Nie, and Jae-on Kim. 1978. *Participation and Political Equality*. New York: Cambridge University Press.

Vivarelli, Marco. 2007. Innovation and Employment: A Survey. IZA Discussion Papers 2621. Institute for the Study of Labor (IZA). http://EconPapers.repec.org/RePEc:iza:izadps:dp2621.

Wadhwa, Tarun. 2015. "On-Demand Economy Goes White Collar: The Rise of the Lawyer-Entrepreneur." *Forbes*, October 26.

Walker, Carol. 2011. "For Universalism and against the Means Test." In *Fighting Poverty, Inequality and Injustice: A Manifesto Inspired by Peter Townsend*, edited by Alan Walker, Adrian Sinfield, and Carol Walker, 133–52. Bristol, UK: Policy Press.

Walter, Stefanie. 2010. "Globalization and the Welfare State: Testing the Micro-Foundations of the Compensation Hypothesis." *International Studies Quarterly* 54, no. 2: 403–26. DOI: http://dx.doi.org/10.1111/j.1468-2478.2010.00593.x.

——. 2014. "Globalization and the Demand-Side of Politics: How Globalization Shapes Individual Labor Market Risk Perceptions and Policy Preferences." Working Paper.

Wang Wei. 2013. "Features, Restrictions, and Policy Recommendations in the Service Sector of the People's Republic of China." In *Developing the Service Sector as an Engine of Growth for Asia*, edited by Donghyun Park and Marcus Noland, 232–59. Manila: Asian Development Bank.

Wang, Yuqian, and Coco Feng. 2016. "Manufacturing Rebounds after 16 Months of Contraction, with Caixin China Purchasing Managers' Index (PMI) at 50.6." http://www.chinaeconomicreview.com/caxin-pmi-china-manufacturing-rebounds-after-16-month-contraction.

Waters, Richard. 2017. "Technology and Society." *Financial Times*, February 25–26: 9.

Wenger, Albert. 2015. "Debating the Gig Economy: Going past Industrial Thinking." *Continuations*, July 14. http://continuations.com/post/124069363855/debating-the-gig-economy-going-past-industrial.

Whitaker, Meri, and Shashi Kolavalli. 2006. "Floriculture in Kenya." In *Technology, Adaptation and Exports: How Some Developing Countries Got It Right*, edited by Vandana Chandra, 335–67. Washington, DC: World Bank.

Womack, James, Daniel Jones, and Daniel Roos. 1990. *The Machine That Changed the World*. New York: Free Press.

World Bank. 2012. *World Development Report 2013: Jobs*. Washington, DC: World Bank. DOI: http://dx.doi.org/10.1596/978-0-8213-9575-2.

——. 2016a. "Migration Overview." http://www.worldbank.org/en/topic/migrationremittancesdiasporaissues/overview.

——. 2016b. *World Development Report 2016: Digital Dividends*. Washington, DC: World Bank. http://www.worldbank.org/en/publication/wdr2016.

Wren, Anne. 2013. "Introduction: The Political Economy of Post-Industrial Societies." In *The Political Economy of the Service Transition*, edited by Anne Wren, 1–70. Oxford, UK: Oxford University Press.

Wren, Anne, and Philipp Rehm. 2014. "The End of the Consensus?: Labour Market Developments and the Politics of Retrenchment." *Socio-Economic Review* 12, no. 2: 409–35. DOI: https://dx.doi.org/10.1093/ser/mwu012.

Yeates, Nicola. 2010. "The Globalization of Nurse Migration: Policy Issues and Responses." *International Labour Review* 149, no. 4: 423–40. DOI: http://dx.doi.org/10.1111/j.1564-913X.2010.00096.x.

Yu Xie and Xiang Zhou. 2014. "Income Inequality in Today's China." *Proceedings of the U.S. National Academy of Sciences* 111, no. 19: 6928–33.

Zelleke, Almaz. 2012. "Basic Income and the Alaska Model: Limits of the Resource Dividend Model for the Implementation of an Unconditional Basic Income." In *Alaska's Permanent Fund Dividend: Examining Its Suitability as a Model*, edited by Michael W. Howard and Karl Widerquist, 141–56. New York: Palgrave Macmillan.

Zika, Gerd, and Tobias Maier. 2015. *Qualifikation und Beruf in Deutschlands Regionen bis 2030. Konzepte, Methoden und Ergebnisse der BIBB-IAB-Projektionen*. Gütersloh: Bertelsmann. DOI: http://dx.doi.org/10.3278/300875w.

Zimmerman, Mary K. 2015. "Paying Family Caregivers: Parental Leave and Gender Equality in Sweden." In *Caring on the Clock: The Complexities and Contradictions of Paid Care Work*, edited by Mignon Duffy, Amy Armenia, and Clare L. Stacey, 213–24. New Brunswick, NJ: Rutgers University Press.

Zimmerman, Mary K., Jacquelyn S. Litt, and Christine E. Bose. 2006. *Global Dimensions of Gender and Carework*. Stanford, CA: Stanford University Press.

Zwolinski, Matt. 2014. "The Pragmatic Libertarian Case for a Basic Income Guarantee." *Cato Unbound*, August 4. https://www.cato-unbound.org/2014/08/04/matt-zwolinski/pragmatic-libertarian-case-basic-income-guarantee.

CONTRIBUTORS

Vandana Chandra is a senior economist in the Africa's Finance and Private Sector and DEC Operations and Strategy Departments at the World Bank.

Mignon Duffy is associate professor and chair of the Department of Sociology and associate director of the Center for Women and Work at the University of Massachusetts–Lowell.

Dieter Ernst is a senior fellow at the East-West Center in Honolulu and the Centre for International Governance Innovation in Waterloo, Canada.

Vinnie Ferraro is the Ruth Lawson Professor of International Politics (emeritus) at Mount Holyoke College, Massachusetts.

Martin Ford is a software entrepreneur and author.

Juliana Martínez Franzoni is a professor at the Institute of Social Science Research at the University of Costa Rica.

Irmgard Nübler   is a senior economist and coordinator of the Technology and Jobs Program in the Research Department of the International Labor Organization.

Eva Paus   is the Carol Hoffmann Collins Director of the McCulloch Center for Global Initiatives and professor of economics at Mount Holyoke College, Massachusetts.

Robert Pollin   is the codirector of the Political Economy Research Institute and Distinguished Professor of Economics at the University of Massachusetts, Amherst.

David Rueda   is professor of comparative politics in the Department of Politics and International Relations at Oxford University.

Diego Sánchez-Ancochea   is the director of the Latin American Centre and associate professor in the political economy of Latin America at Oxford University.

Guy Standing   is professorial research associate at SOAS University of London.

Stefan Thewissen   is a postdoctoral researcher affiliated with the Institute for New Economic Thinking at the Oxford Martin School, the Department of Social Policy and Intervention, and Nuffield College at Oxford University.

INDEX

See also basic income; redistribution; regulation; universal social policy
Putin, Vladimir, 167
putting-out system, 118

racial dynamics in care sector, 104–5
racial identity, 166
ratings, of taskers, 121–22
R&D, 52
Reagan, Ronald, 30
recessions, 34. *See also* Great Recession (2007–2009)
redistribution, 12, 24, 134–55; automation of routine occupations and, 12, 13, 139–54; basic income and, 231 (*see also* basic income); income inequality and, 149–52; material self-interest and, 138–39; politics of, 136–39; tax increases and, 174–76; technological change and, 135–36, 145–49, 152–55; universal social incorporation and, 233; of work, 21–22
regulation, 162; of globalization, 19–20; of labor brokers, 12, 20, 128–32
Rehm, Philipp, 148
renewable energy. *See* clean energy economy
Renta Dignidad, 247
Republic of Korea. *See* South Korea
reshoring, 209, 224
Restrepo, Pascual, 7
retail jobs, 36
retrofits, clean energy, 81, 84, 87
Ricardo, David, 197
right-wing politics, 12, 13, 24, 156–57, 170–72, 174
Robinson, James A., 65
robotization, 1, 4, 7–9, 18, 28–29, 35–38, 41–43, 46–47, 76, 93, 165; China, 41–42, 182–83, 194–95; cross-country studies on, 60–63; in light manufacturing, 224; market value of labor and, 163; mobile robots, 54, 57; right-wing politics and, 156

Rodrik, Dani, 19, 42, 158, 183, 184, 205, 226
Rohingya, 170
Roosevelt, Franklin, 45, 175
routine tasks, automated, 8, 13, 29, 33, 49, 134–36, 139–54
RTI index (routine task intensity), 141–52
Rueda, David, 13, 145, 147–49, 165
Russia, 167, 170, 173, 207
Rwanda, 217

Saez, Emmanuel, 30
safety net, 160. *See also* universal social policy
Salomons, Anna, 141–42
Sánchez-Ancochea, Diego, 17–18, 175
Sanders, Bernie, 167
Sassen, Saskia, 103, 105
Schott, Peter K., 168
Schumpeter, Joseph, 5, 65
Schwab, Klaus, 1, 2
Scotland, 171
self-driving cars. *See* driverless vehicles
self-employment, 12, 53, 73, 89, 120, 245
Senegal, 212
Sennett, Richard, 56
services, demand for, 20–21
services sector, 204, 208, 217, 226
sharing economy, 116–17, 130, 132
Sharing Economy UK, 130
Singapore, 192, 210
skills: automation and, 37; clean energy sector, 90–91; craft sector, 55–57; differentials, 11; high-skill jobs, 33, 37, 38, 54–55, 164; low-skill jobs, 33, 38, 61; middle-skill jobs, 33, 62; training in, 128. *See also* STEM PLUS skills
smart machines, 54
Smith, Adam, 161
social assistance, 240
social capabilities: concept of, 65–67; for innovations and job creation, 64–73
social cohesion, 234

Lightning Source UK Ltd.
Milton Keynes UK
UKHW01n0610110518
322453UK00009B/187/P